A MODERN HISTORY OF SOVIET GEORGIA

Also by David Marshall Lang

Lives and Legends of the Georgian Saints

The Wisdom of Balahvar: A Christian Legend of the Buddha

The First Russian Radical: Alexander Radishchev 1749–1802
(Published by George Allen & Unwin)

The Last Years of the Georgian Monarchy, 1658–1832
(Published by Columbia University Press)

A MODERN HISTORY OF
SOVIET GEORGIA

DAVID MARSHALL LANG, M.A., D.Lit.

Reader in Caucasian Studies in the
University of London

GROVE PRESS, INC.   NEW YORK

TO THE GEORGIAN PEOPLE
AND THE NEW GEORGIA

CONTENTS

CONTENTS

LIST OF ILLUSTRATIONS

PREFACE

THE WORLD today is witnessing a resurgence of nationalism among the peoples of Asia and Africa. Western Colonialism is everywhere in flight. Self-determination for all is the order of the day, even when the granting of independence brings with it an intensification of economic problems and social contradictions. In the Soviet Union alone, the advocates of self-determination are silent, or else devote their energies to encouraging the aspirations of peoples outside the frontiers of the USSR. There may therefore be some degree of topicality in offering to the Western reader an outline of the modern history of one of the smaller peoples now embraced within the Soviet Union, in tracing the rise and fall of Tsarist autocratic rule over Georgia and Caucasia, and in showing how this led to Georgia's present membership of the family of Soviet nations, of which she is now a leading representative.

Some of my Soviet friends have expressed misgivings at my attempt to write an objective history of the Georgian Soviet Socialist Republic, on the grounds that this may revive painful memories best wrapped in oblivion. It is true that our generation stands too close to the cataclysmic events which attended the birth of Russia's social and industrial revolution, and that books written today will have to be radically revised in the broader perspective enjoyed by historians of a future age. None the less, I think that some useful purpose may be served by putting down on paper some salient facts of recent Georgian history while eyewitnesses and protagonists are alive to be consulted, and impressions from visits to Soviet Georgia in 1960 and 1962 remain fresh. At the same time, I hope that this book may arouse interest in a fascinating and congenial people whom the accidents of history have too often cut off from the Western civilization with which they have so many

xiii

affinities, and to which they are in a position to make so worthwhile a contribution.

When this book was virtually completed, the generosity of the School of Oriental and African Studies, University of London, and the co-operation of the Soviet authorities enabled me to pay a second visit to Georgia, extending throughout the month of January 1962. Most of my time was spent in the capital, Tbilisi, but I also managed to visit the great industrial centre of Rustavi, Stalin's birthplace at Gori, Tskhinvali (formerly Stalinir), capital of South Ossetia, the resort of Sukhumi and other interesting places in Abkhazia, and the Black Sea port of Batumi. No attempt was made to restrict my movements either in Moscow or within Georgia itself: it was possible to walk about the streets and call at the offices and houses of friends and acquaintances without let or hindrance, while visits to collective farms, tea plantations, wine factories, schools and other institutions were often of an unrehearsed and decidedly impromptu nature. It was encouraging in Tbilisi to find great new residential suburbs practically complete and to visit the fine 'Palace of Sport'. The Georgian stage and cinema are filled with vitality and creative originality. Important industrial developments are afoot, such as the building of a new nylon factory, construction of a pipeline to bring natural gas from North Caucasia, and an irrigation scheme for Kakheti. There exists an irresistible urge towards a higher standard of living, while Party control over Press and publication is exercised now with more restraint than was the case a few years ago. My visit left me optimistic about the evolution of Soviet society generally and of Georgia in particular. The next few years—international tensions apart—should bring both the Georgians and the Russians many more of those material advantages and personal freedoms which we in the West tend rather complacently to take for granted.

D. M. LANG

School of Oriental and African Studies,
London, W.C.1.
11 February 1962

CHAPTER I

THE LAND AND THE PEOPLE

Geographical position of Caucasia — Ethnic variety — By rail to Tbilisi — Origins of Georgian Christianity — Tbilisi old and new — Industry and agriculture — National characteristics of the Georgians — Literature and the arts

Geographical position of Caucasia

THE SOVIET UNION, like the Russian empire before it, is a multiracial, multinational and multilingual confederation of peoples of diverse ethnic origins, many of whom have no direct affinity with the Russians and other Slavonic peoples. No better example of this rich diversity exists than Caucasia, where at least fifty tribes and nations live today, each with its distinctive language or dialect, its history and its traditions. Of these Caucasian peoples, the Georgians are the most numerous, and culturally and economically among the most important. They have a civilization stretching back over more than three thousand years, an extensive literary and artistic heritage, and a rapidly developing industrial and agricultural economy. As the native country of Stalin, Georgia is assured of a place in the modern political history of the world.

Caucasia lies between two continents, at the junction of historical trade routes, which gives to it a strategic and economic role transcending its physical borders. The Caucasus range is situated between two seas, which receive the waters of the biggest river arteries in Europe. From the Sea of Azov and the Black Sea in the west, to the Caspian in the east, this imposing range of mountains stretches for some seven hundred miles, its line broken by narrow passes and defiles and by lofty peaks. It dominates a vast natural region, the centre of which forms an isthmus linking Europe with Asia, and connecting the Volga basin and the black earth lands of the Ukraine with Turkey and Persia. Soviet Central Asia and Transcaucasia together form the southernmost region of the USSR.

Climatically and geographically, the Caucasus is a land of extreme and abrupt contrasts. In western Caucasia, snow-capped mountains and alpine pasture lands overlook the waters of the Black Sea, whose shores are skirted by a sub-tropical zone of plantations and luxuriant vegetation. In the Rioni delta of Western Georgia, the draining of swamps has been an essential preliminary to any form of settled life; in Eastern Georgia, there are arid stretches of steppe land which have to be irrigated to yield up their wealth. Much of Georgia, however, consists of pleasant valleys and uplands planted with corn, vineyards and orchards. The main Caucasus range separates Georgia and Transcaucasia from European Russia and the North Caucasian steppe. Georgia's southern boundary is provided by a system of mountains and upland plains extending downwards from the Surami range and dividing into two arms, pointing towards Turkey and Persia respect-ively. This is the Little Caucasus, which runs to the south of the Rioni and Kura basins, and merges into the Armenian plateau and the Taurus mountains.

The Caucasus has from prehistoric times been a meeting point for the civilizations of East and West and a market place for the exchange of the products of Europe and Asia. Across the Black Sea, the Caucasus is linked with the Mediterranean world, the cultures of Greece and Rome. Its Caspian littoral gives on to Iran and Central Asia, through which ran the trade routes to Turkestan, India and China. The wealth of Colchis, today a part of the Georgian SSR, once fired the imagination of Jason and the Argonauts, who are said to have sailed there in quest of the Golden Fleece. The Meshech and Tubal of the Prophet Ezekiel were ancient tribes of metal-workers, related to the ancestors of the Georgians of today. It was to the peak of Kazbek, in the Central Caucasus, that the gods of the Greek pantheon chained Prometheus, who conferred on mankind the divine secret of fire. The Scythians and Cimmerians, warlike nomads of the Eurasian steppe, passed through the Caucasus as they rode against the empires of antiquity which ruled over Asia Minor and Mesopotamia. Nearer to our own day, Russia

2

in her drive to the warm seas has found the Caucasus a natural stepping-stone towards those coveted outlets, the Bosphorus and the Persian Gulf.

Ethnic variety

The ethnological face of Caucasia, with its numerous races and tribes, came into being over many centuries. Like a lofty fortress, the Caucasus provided a natural refuge for all manner of peoples drifting southwards from the Eurasian plain or northwards from Asia Minor and the Iranian plateau. In its upland fastnesses, the remnants of a nation could live on undisturbed over the ages, oblivious of events taking place in the world beneath. Immigrant tribes in many cases became blended with local, aboriginal inhabitants in such remote antiquity that racial origins are tangled and obscure. The Caucasus was situated at the focal point of important Neolithic and Bronze cultures. The great empires of the ancient world extended their sway into the Caucasian isthmus. Among the greatest of these were the Sumerians, the Hittites, the Babylonians and the Assyrians. The kingdom of Urartu, a formidable rival of Assyria, included within its borders many of the peoples of Transcaucasia. From the west came the impact of the civilizations of Troy and of the Aegean world. In Classical times, Greece and Rome vied with Persia under the Achaemenids and later the Parthians for supremacy over the area. In this way, Caucasia became a living museum of ancient races and the repository of a deep stratification of various cultures and creeds.

Although the peoples of the Caucasus speak many languages and profess a variety of different religions, the region possesses a characteristic atmosphere and way of living which permeates every racial group and walk of life. There is a distinctive Caucasian code of honour, of chivalry, of personal pride, of hospitality. The cult of woman and the family occupies a central place in the outlook of all Caucasians. Ethnic conservatism is even today wedded among the Caucasian peoples to strong individualism and hostility to all forms of regimentation. This deep-rooted individualism has in fact proved a major obstacle to the creation at any period of a pan-Caucasian state or federation capable of holding its own in face of the great powers by which the Caucasian isthmus has always been ringed about.

Within the Soviet system, Caucasia is divided into a number of political and administrative units. In the south, Georgia, Armenia and Azerbaijan form three Soviet Socialist Republics. In the north-west corner of Georgia, on the Black Sea coast, live the Abkhaz, who have their own Autonomous SSR, as do the Muslim Atcharans or Ajars whose capital is Batumi. The Adyghe peoples—Circassians and Kabardians—live in north-west Caucasia; the Kabardian ASSR and the Cherkess and Adyghe Autonomous Districts are affiliated to the Russian Federative SSR. Towards the centre of the Caucasus range and to the north of it is the home of the Ossetes and of the Balkar, the Karachay, the Chechens and the Ingush. The Ossetes are reckoned to be descended from the once mighty Alans and speak a language belonging to the Iranian family. The Balkar, Karachay, Chechens and Ingush were deported on Stalin's orders to Siberia and Central Asia in 1943–44, as punishment for alleged collaboration with the German invaders during World War II. Most of the survivors have now been permitted to return. The eastern region of Caucasia is called Daghestan— 'the land of mountains'. The Daghestanis with their diverse ethnic origins form a bewildering medley of tribal groupings, among which we may name the Avar, the Lak, the Dargwa, the Lezghians, the Agul and the Tabasaran. There is an Autonomous SSR of Daghestan, with its capital at Makhach-Kala.

The two main religious faiths of the Caucasus are Christianity and Islam. The Georgians and the Armenians are Christians, though they differ extensively on points of doctrine. The Georgians form an autonomous or 'autocephalous' Church within the Greek Orthodox communion. The Armenians have their own ritual and body of dogma; their national Church is called the Gregorian, after Saint Gregory the Illuminator, who brought Christianity to Armenia about the year A.D. 300, in the reign of Diocletian. There also exist communities of Armenian and Georgian Catholics, mainly outside the Soviet Union. Among the Azerbaijanis and other peoples of Turkish and Tatar origins, throughout Daghestan, and in Circassia, Islam is strong. It is also practised among the Atcharans or Ajars, the Muslim Georgian people living around

Batumi, and by the Laz, whose country is now part of Turkey's Black Sea littoral. While the Atcharans and Laz retain close affinities with the Christian Georgians, they have been much influenced by Turkish customs since they came under Ottoman dominion in the sixteenth century. The Abkhaz and Circassians were once predominantly Christian, though retaining many pagan cults; they too absorbed Islam from the Turks. There are a number of Jewish communities in various parts of Caucasia, including several colonies of Georgian-speaking Jews, and the 'Mountain Jews' or Judeo-Tats.

The present-day Soviet republic of Georgia lies between the two systems of the Caucasian mountains—the Great Caucasus in the north and the Little Caucasus to the south. In the west, Georgia extends to the Black Sea, between the River Pso in the north and the village of Sarp, a short distance south-west of Batumi, in the south. The eastern tip of Georgia is formed by the junction of the rivers Alazani and Iori. Beyond Georgia's eastern frontier is the Soviet republic of Azerbaijan. The Armenian SSR lies to the south. To the south-west Georgia has a common frontier with Turkey. Within these boundaries, Georgia occupies an area of about 70,000 square kilometres, of which total 8,600 square kilometres are taken up by the Abkhazian ASSR, 2,800 by the Ajarian ASSR, and 3,800 by the South Ossetian Autonomous District. A recent official estimate (1959) sets Georgia's total population at 4,044,000 made up of an urban population of 1,698,480 and a rural one of 2,345,520. Whereas the Georgians themselves comprise the majority of the inhabitants, a substantial proportion is also made up of Russians, Armenians, Turks, Ossetes, Abkhaz, Jews, Kurds, Persians and Greeks. There were formerly several large colonies of Germans, now virtually all dispersed. The Georgians call their homeland *Sakartvelo*, the land of the *Kartvel-ebi* or Georgians; both these names are linked with that of Kartli, the principal province of central Georgia, in which Tbilisi (Tiflis) is situated. The European name—'Georgian', 'Georgia' (Russian: *Gruzin*, *Gruziya*)—has a different origin, being connected with Arabic and Persian *Gurji*, *Gurjistan*. The Islamic names are to be compared with Syriac *Gurzan*, Middle Iranian *Wyrshn* and Armenian *Vir-k*, the equivalent of the *Iveroi* or 'Iberians' familiar to the ancient geographers. In spite of popular belief, the country's name has nothing to do with that of its patron, Saint George, whose cult Georgia shares with England.

The territory of the modern Georgian Soviet Socialist Republic does not entirely coincide with the areas contained within the country's historical boundaries, which in mediaeval times embraced considerably larger areas. Among such regions, situated today outside Georgia's borders, are the Zakatali district in the east, part of Borchalo in the south, and Artvin, Ardahan, Artanuji and Olti in the south-west. These last four districts, wrested by Russia from the Ottoman Empire in the war of 1877–78, were ceded back to Turkey by the Bolsheviks at the Treaty of Kars in March 1921. The middle basin of the Chorokhi, the Klarjeti-Tortum-Ispir area, and Lazistan along the Black Sea coast, are all inhabited by peoples of Georgian stock, and have now been for some four centuries under Turkish rule.

The mediaeval Georgian kingdom was composed of a number of principalities, duchies and tribal areas, which tended at times of national weakness to break away and form minor independent states on their own. There has always been a basic division between Western and Eastern Georgia, marked by the Surami range, beyond which, looking from the capital city of Tbilisi, lay Imereti—'the land on the far side'—as Western Georgia is commonly called. Imereti was reckoned to comprise the Colchis of the ancients, including the low-lying, densely vegetated land of Mingrelia on the Black Sea coast; Guria, between the Rioni and Cholok rivers; Atchara around Batumi; and mountainous Svaneti, land of the Svans, once a nation of warriors ruled by their own king and council of elders and capable of launching into battle an army many thousands strong. The main cities of Western Georgia are Kutaisi, Akhaltsikhe, Makharadze (formerly Ozurgeti), Zugdidi, and the ports of Batumi, Poti and Sukhumi. Eastern Georgia with its more temperate, continental climate includes the former kingdom of Kartli, with the metropolis of Tbilisi, and the towns of Gori, Mtskheta and Rustavi. Kakheti, the easternmost region of Georgia, is a fertile wine-growing and silk-raising district, which once had its own kings with their capital at Telavi. On Eastern Georgia's northern borders are

Tusheti, Pshaveti and Khevsureti, inhabited by fierce mountain clans famed for their allegiance to the Georgian kings of old. The Georgian provinces of the south-west, notably Meskheti or Samtskhe, land of the Meskhians, and Tao-Klarjeti, the latter now within Turkey, played a vital part in the evolution of Georgia's national language and civilization.

By rail to Tbilisi

The traveller who lands at Batumi and proceeds by train to the Georgian capital of Tbilisi traverses in a span of two hundred and eighteen miles almost every conceivable variety of scenery and vegetation. Situated at the foot of a semi-circular range of cliffs rising steeply from the sea, Batumi has a high rainfall and humid climate which favours the growth of lush sub-tropical plants and trees. The lowlands of the adjoining Ajarian ASSR (Atchara) are rich alluvial flats, enriched by streams heavy with fertile loam. For some miles after leaving Batumi station, the railway runs through forests of magnolia and blue hydrangea, and there are many flourishing plantations of tea and citrus fruits. At Samtredia Junction the Batumi line joins the main line from Sukhumi, Sochi, Tuapse and the North-west Caucasus. Further up the main line, there is a branch down to the Black Sea port of Poti. Before the war of 1877–78 and the Russian acquisition of Batumi, Poti was the terminus of the Transcaucasian railway; it was then little more than a swamp with a few huts built on piles, amidst which frogs kept up a cheerful chorus of croaks, and was noted for its pestiferous, malarial climate. Today, Poti is a modern port, with extensive harbour installations.

After leaving Samtredia Junction, the train continues eastwards through pleasant, undulating country. The traveller is now in the heartland of the former West Georgian kingdom of Imereti. This is the country of which the eighteenth-century Georgian historian and geographer Vakhushti wrote:

'This land is very wooded and its open spaces, apart from stretches of cultivated ground, are of small extent. In some places the grape and other fruits grow in the woods. The air is excellent and mild, though owing to the woods it is very hot in summer, as the air can scarcely circulate; however, it is bearable except in certain spots. It is warm in winter, so that the running waters and muddy places do not freeze hard enough for beasts and men to pass over. However, snow lies in great drifts, sometimes a fathom or more deep. . . . Seen from a lofty hill top, Imereti appears as one vast expanse of woodland, without any trace of habitation.'

Vakhushti goes on to say that grain would grow plentifully in Imereti, as would rice and cotton. However, the natives seldom took the trouble to plant such crops, and contented themselves with millet, from which the people made their staple diet, a paste called *ghomi*. A labouring man equipped with mattock and hoe could easily produce enough to support his family and pay taxes to boot. Cheap silken fabric and coarse cotton cloth were produced. Apples, peaches and chestnuts grew wild, as well as melons; in the fields and woods, lilies and roses grew in sweet-scented abundance.

'All sorts of animals are found in this country, with the exception of the camel, though not in such quantities as in other parts of Georgia. There are sheep, with and without the fat tail, always with two and sometimes three or four lambs; they are not kept in regular flocks. Oxen and buffaloes are kept in herds, horses by the stud. . . . As for birds—sparrows, nightingales and pigeons are so numerous that a man with a snare can catch five hundred of them on a single trip. . . . The bees yield plenteous supplies of honey and wax; this honey is excellent and in some places it comes in honeycombs, white and firm as sugar. While there are a lot of reptiles and serpents, the snakes are not dangerous.'

Vakhushti found the men of Imereti handsomer and more dignified than those of other parts of Georgia, the women more beautiful. The peasants' sons were just like young aristocrats.

'They are clean and well turned out. They keep their horses, weapons and armour in good condition. They are agile and athletic, sweet of tongue, nimble and ardent, valiant and strong in the fray, but prone to lose heart rapidly therein, as they do in other branches of activity. They are prodigal and no misers, living from one day to the next without bothering about the morrow; fond of singing and music and skilled calligraphers; many of them possess fine voices and various other natural talents. In religion and language they are one with the Kartlians, but more vivacious in their manner of speech.'[1]

The coming of the Russians, the building of roads and railways, the digging of mines, and the introduction and development of collective and state farms have greatly changed the face of Imereti over the last century and a half. Yet the landscape described by Vakhushti, the fauna and flora he enumerates, and many of the characteristics of the people, are immediately recognizable at the present day.

From Rioni Junction, about twenty miles east of Samtredia, a branch line runs north to the chief city of Western Georgia, Kutaisi. Famed as the residence of the legendary King Aietes of Colchis, father of the sorceress Medea, Kutaisi is mentioned as an important town by the classical geographers, and was for centuries the capital of the mediaeval kings of Imereti. The town is situated on the banks of the fast-running Rioni, in a wide green valley surrounded by wooded hills. It is today an industrial and administrative centre of some 120,000 inhabitants, with theatres, cinemas, botanical gardens and a Museum of History and Ethnography. Five miles from Kutaisi is the monastery of Gelati, to which in mediaeval times was attached an academy renowned as a centre of learning. At the terminus of the Kutaisi branch line, some thirty miles further to the north-east of the city, are the Tqibuli coal-mines, and a short distance further on over the mountains, the immensely rich Chiatura manganese mines.

The Ossetian Military Road runs northwards from Kutaisi towards the Mamison Pass, passing through the picturesque, thickly settled Rioni valley. Collective farms and the fences of small peasant holdings stretch in an unbroken line on both sides of the road, with cornfields, and grape-vines climbing exuberantly over the trees. The houses of the Imeretian peasant farmers are board huts on piles, with covered galleries running round them. At Alpani, thirty miles from Kutaisi, a secondary road branches off to the left towards Tsageri, the main centre of Lechkhumi, whence one can proceed into the mountain fastnesses of Lower and Upper Svaneti.

Svaneti is a country of outstanding beauty, covered in tall grass and brightly coloured flowers, birch groves and clusters of rhododendrons. The traveller has a close-up view of the glaciers and peaks of the main Caucasus range rearing up behind the dark slate cliffs of the Svaneti range and surmounted by the snow-capped summits of Tetnuld (15,920 feet)

9

and the still more impressive peak of Shkhara (17,040 feet). The Svans were cut off for centuries from the main stream of Georgian civilization. Half-Christian and half-pagan, they retained many of the ancient beliefs of the Georgian race and preserved in ruined shrines priceless manuscripts and relics long given up as lost to the world. Until modern times the Svans and their neighbours lived by hunting, subsistence farming, and raiding the villages of rival clans. They lived in tower-dwellings from which they kept a constant lookout for the foe's approach. A British sportsman of the last century, who went to the Caucasus in 1882 to shoot bears, chamois and mountain sheep, depicted the Svans as a people with 'no games, no mental culture, to all intent and purpose no religion, no houses better than dens; they don't work much when they can, and there are at least nine months of the year when they cannot work if they would'. Filling up their time by indiscriminate love-making and the prosecution of the blood feuds resulting therefrom, the Svans were too idle even to clear away the mountains of refuse which accumulated in front of their hovels. 'Mercifully for these filthy householders, the snow that buries their villages for nine months in the year carries away most of the refuse which they neglect to remove, purifying and saving them from the results of their disorderly sloth.'[2]

Whatever one may think of the impact of Russian ways upon the Caucasian peoples generally, there is no doubt that recent improvements in Svaneti have been highly beneficial. Mestia, the administrative, political and cultural centre of Upper Svaneti, is today the seat of a local Party executive committee, and has a hospital, a school for peasant youth, and a co-operative society. Mestia serves in summer as a supply base for the ascent of Elbruz (18,465 feet) and Ushba (15,410 feet), which are favourite goals of Soviet and foreign climbers. The town is now connected by road with Zugdidi in Mingrelia and by light aeroplane with the Georgian capital, Tbilisi.

Reverting to the Batumi-Tbilisi itinerary, one now picks up the train at Rioni Junction and continues over the Surami range into Eastern Georgia. The original railway track was hastily run up in a hazardous fashion, winding up hillsides and climbing over mountains, through tunnels and over viaducts at very steep gradients. It was not unprecedented in the last century to pass an engine which had come off the rails and capsized, 'apparently enjoying repose after the fatigue of ascending such unheard-of gradients'.[3] The system is operated nowadays by modern electric locomotives and such mishaps are rare. After crossing the Surami pass at a height of 3,000 feet, the line descends into the valley of the River Kura or Mtkvari. Soon the train stops at Gori, birthplace of Stalin, a town of some 35,000 inhabitants overlooked by the ruins of an old citadel.

Gori is the centre of a prosperous agricultural district, noted for its peaches, apricots and apples, with a fruit-raising station and canning factories. The climate is already different from that of Western Georgia—drier and less humid, though hot in summer. From Gori the line continues south-eastwards, and passes through the ancient capital of Georgia, Mtskheta, situated at the confluence of the Aragvi and the Kura. The Georgian military highroad runs northwards from Mtskheta over the Daryal Pass to Dzaujikau (formerly Vladikavkaz, later Orjonikidze) and then onwards into European Russia. This former metropolis is now merely a large village of mud-brick and wooden houses interspersed with trees and muddy lanes. In the middle stands the patriarchal cathedral of the Living Pillar (*Sveti Tskhoveli*), founded by Saint Nino, razed to the ground by Tamerlane, and reconstructed in the fifteenth century. The cathedral is surrounded by a stone fortification wall with embrasures and towers, and contains before the altar the tombs of many of Georgia's kings, queens and princes of the blood.

Origins of Georgian Christianity

Saint Nino, to whom is attributed the conversion of the Georgians to Christianity, is traditionally portrayed as a holy captive woman living about the year A.D. 330, in the time of Constantine the Great. She possessed a miraculous gift of healing and cured a little child of some grave disease. The Georgian queen, Nana, also experienced Nino's wondrous powers, and was converted to Christianity. The king, Mirian by name, was also converted following an eclipse of the sun which enveloped him and his followers in pitch darkness until he bethought himself of Nino's God and resolved to pray to Him for deliverance. The Georgian people followed their monarch and declared themselves Christians. They all set to work to build a church at Mtskheta. The construction proceeded according to plan until they came to erect the main pillar, which no force of men or machinery could raise above a slanting angle.

'But when at nightfall everyone went away, and both the toilers and their toil fell into repose, the captive woman remained alone on the spot and passed the whole night in prayer. And behold, when the king with all his people arrived full of anxiety in the morning, he saw the column, which so many machines and so many men could not shift, standing upright and freely suspended above its pedestal—not set upon it, but hanging in the air about a foot above. As soon as the whole people witnessed this, they glorified God and began to declare this to be a proof of the king's faith and the religion of the captive woman. And behold, while they were all paralysed with amazement, the pillar slowly descended on to its base before their eyes, without anyone touching it, and settled in perfect balance. The rest of the columns were erected with such ease that the remainder were all set in place that same day.'

Pious Georgian chroniclers later embroidered on the original simple account of Saint Nino's life. Among the episodes added were the bringing of Our Lord's tunic from Jerusalem to Mtskheta by Elioz the Jew, the destruction of the pagan idols by a hailstorm sent from heaven, the fashioning of crosses from the wood of a miracle-working tree, and the appearance of a fiery cross over Nino's church, the saint's mission to Kakheti, and her death at Bodbe.[4]

From the time of Saint Nino onwards, the Georgian Church grew and prospered, in spite of persecution by Persian, Arab and Turkish invaders. The Georgians won the right to elect their own Catholicos-Patriarch, who resided at Mtskheta. The Georgian Orthodox Church has played an outstanding role in the country's history and national consciousness. We read in the Passion of Saint Abo, put to death by the Saracens in A.D. 786: 'Georgia is called Mother of the Saints; some of these have been inhabitants of this land, while others came among us from time to time from foreign parts to testify to the revelation of Our Lord Jesus Christ.' The biographer of Saint Gregory of Khandzta wrote in the tenth century: 'Georgia is reckoned to consist of those spacious lands in which church services are celebrated and all prayers said in the Georgian tongue. Only the *Kyrie eleison*, which means "Lord, have mercy", or "Lord be merciful to us", is pronounced in Greek'. Colonies of Georgian monks settled at the monastery of Saint Savva near Jerusalem and at the Holy Sepulchre itself, near Antioch in Syria, on Mount Sinai and Mount Athos. Priceless collections of ancient Georgian manuscripts testify to the scholarly zeal of those pious fathers. A Latin Patriarch of Jerusalem, Jacques de Vitry, describes the Georgian knights and pilgrims who used to visit the Holy City at the time of the Crusades 'with banners displayed, without paying tribute to anyone'.—'These men . . . especially revere and worship Saint George, whom they make their patron and standard-bearer in their fight with the infidels.' Among the titles adopted by mediaeval Georgian rulers were those of 'Slave of the Messiah' (King David the Builder), 'Sword of the Messiah' (Kings Giorgi III and IV) and 'Champion of the Messiah' (Queens Tamar and Rusudan).

Yet Georgian Christianity has never been exclusive or intolerant; it has not been a persecuting faith. Narrow fanaticism is alien to this easy-going people, who found it no strain to tolerate in their midst Muslims, Jews, Catholics and members of other persuasions. Several stories are told illustrating the kindness of the Georgian kings to their Muslim subjects. When King David the Builder (1089–1125) recaptured the city of Tbilisi, he 'guaranteed to the Muslims everything they wished, according to the pact which is valid even today', and stipulated that pigs should not be brought over to the Muslim quarter of the town. Likewise, King Dimitri of Georgia visited the Tbilisi cathedral mosque on a Friday, sat on a platform opposite the preacher and remained in his place throughout the service; on his way out, he granted the mosque two hundred gold dinars.[5] Since the Russian revolution, the Georgian Church has undergone eclipse, although the Patriarchate continues to exist. The principal churches and cathedrals, though classed as historical monuments, are in a sadly decayed structural condition.

Tbilisi old and new

The capital of the Georgian kingdom of Iberia was transferred about the sixth century A.D. from Mtskheta to the new
town of Tbilisi, some twenty miles further down the River
Kura to the south-east. Following the Arab conquest of
Georgia, Tbilisi was ruled by Muslim *amirs* or governors and
was an important commercial centre of the Arab caliphate,
celebrated for its natural hot springs and healing waters.
Possession of the city was disputed during the Middle Ages
between the Georgian kings and various Mongol, Persian and
Turkish conquerors. Under the Safavi shahs, Tbilisi was one
of the chief towns of the Persian empire, with its bustling
markets and caravanserais, its churches and royal palaces, and
its citadel, now in ruins and surrounded by a botanical garden,
from which one can look down over a vast expanse of housetops and spires, through the midst of which the muddy Kura
winds. Tbilisi was virtually razed to the ground by Agha
Muhammad Khan of Persia in 1795. After the Russian
annexation in 1801, the city became the centre of the viceroyalty of the Caucasus. Public buildings in the Russian style
sprang up, together with an extensive European quarter
intersected by wide streets and boulevards. Long and narrow,
the city stretches today for eight miles along the river banks,
and numbers 800,000 inhabitants. The old part of the town
lies at the south-eastern end, where the hills converge and
form a ravine through which the river fights its way with swift
eddies and much noise. A rocky spur here is surmounted by
the remains of the old castle, with its ancient and now dilapidated church. The Metekhi prison stood on this site in
Tsarist times, in which many prominent revolutionaries were
confined at one time or another. The Bolshevik secret police or
Cheka also made intensive use of these premises, which have
now been razed to the ground. Opposite the castle, on the right
bank of the Kura, are the Tatar and Persian quarters, with their
mosque, close to which is a large Armenian church. Also
overlooking the city is the holy mountain of Saint David,
reached by a winding road, a funicular railway and an over-
head cable car. There is a park with an excellent restaurant
on the summit, in addition to the Georgian state television

studios. Halfway up the mountain is the Georgian national shrine or pantheon, with a chapel and a graveyard in which many leading Georgian writers of modern times lie buried.

Tbilisi has played a dominant part in the history of trade, industry and municipal institutions in Georgia. The old Tbilisi craft and merchant guilds had a very long tradition, and worked for the most part on the 'closed-shop' principle. As early as about A.D. 540, when the former capital of Mtskheta had not yet lost its erstwhile importance, we read of a corporation of Persian shoemakers plying their trade there and holding an annual festival with special rites. When one of their number turned Christian and refused to join in, the cobbler's union denounced him as a renegade and forced the authorities to arrest him. There existed in mediaeval Tbilisi guilds of armourers, tailors, blacksmiths, butchers, bakers, barbers, wine-merchants and others. The members were divided into three ranks, master craftsmen, journeymen, and apprentices. The guild councils were drawn from among the principal master craftsmen, each guild having its high master and two assistants, and its own banner, rules and customs. The master craftsmen were known as *qarachokhelis* or 'black coats', after the official garb they wore. They were noted for their formal and dignified bearing. The trade guilds and merchants had their own tribunal for settling disputes. Sundry privileges granted by Georgian kings of olden times were confirmed and extended by the Russian viceroys. In sharp contrast to these solid burghers were the *kintos* or petty traders of the Tbilisi street markets. They hawked fruit, vegetables and fish, and sold them from trays which they carried on their heads. The *kinto* is renowned as a cynic and a scoffer, a real Cockney of the Caucasus, with a raucous voice and a grotesque, earthy sense of humour.

The growth of modern industry and other changes brought about by the Tsarist and Soviet régimes have greatly altered the face of Tbilisi. Today, it has a fine university, an Academy of Sciences, museums and theatres. Tree-lined boulevards, modern schools and blocks of flats, a large railway station and marshalling yard, and numerous factories form a striking contrast to the old Asiatic city, much of which continues to exist side by side with the new. Forty years ago, Sir Harry Luke, then British Chief Commissioner to Transcaucasia, could encounter in the main avenue of Tbilisi representatives of the mountain Khevsurs, who live not far from the Daryal pass. The armour and chain mail which they wore sometimes misled travellers into deeming them descendants of Crusading knights of old.

'Be this as it might, one was afforded a very distinct glimpse into the past when one saw these stalwarts, armed *cap-à-pie* and complete with boss and spear, taking the air on the Golovinski among a fashionably dressed assembly. And when one encountered, as I did one morning when walking back to the Mission after visiting the President, one of these braves balancing the spear in one hand with a volume of Karl Marx's *Kapital* under the other arm, one felt that in the matter of contrasts life could have nothing more wonderful to offer.'[6]

Today such charming survivals of bygone ages are rarer. The impact of European ways is spreading apace. The smartly dressed young ladies whom one sees hurrying to work down the Rustaveli Avenue present a refreshing contrast to the shapeless and baggy matrons of Moscow. In the bazaar quarter and down the back streets, however, glimpses of old Tbilisi may still be snatched. Though organized today into collective craft associations, the metal workers and cobblers carry on their trades as before or gather in lively discussion at tea and coffee houses, while Armenian stall holders argue over prices and clansmen from the hills swagger by in their *cherkesskas*, their ornamental cartridge belts and high boots.

Industry and agriculture

From Tbilisi, one may motor rapidly down to the great metallurgical combine at Rustavi, which has done so much over the last dozen years to transform the economic life of Georgia. Alternatively, one may take the dusty road which leads over a dry upland plateau into the easternmost Georgian province of Kakheti, or else take the little train which meanders slowly down the Telavi branch line. It was in 1920, when Georgia was an independent republic, that the French authoress Odette Keun visited this part of Georgia.

16

'It was early summer when I saw Kakhetia lying under a languid, lowering sky, a flat land of vivid green fields and sombre green woods, with ravines and broken ground where the soil showed hard and yellow, and steep, narrow cuttings that crossed its ample spaces. . . . The first impression was one of whiteness—the delicate whiteness of new silver—made by the vast dry beds of the rivers. The rushing water that flowed in narrow threads between the great smooth stones was milk-white, and the orange blouse of a passing peasant would break suddenly into this monochrome paleness like the sound of a horn quickly silenced. . . . Buffaloes, hiding their heavy bodies in the yellow lakes, raised their coal-black heads to the surface and stood motionless—they might have been the monstrous, black, aquatic flora of some unexplored land—and when, their rest over, they emerged shining in their heavy beatitude, they had the air of unknown creatures massively sculptured in livid and varnished clay. . . . Legions of little pigs with blunt noses and naked haunches obscenely pink, ran about like animated brushes, squealing out their discoveries and their discomforts to an indifferent world.'

The men impressed Odette Keun by their quick and muscular carriage; their faces were tanned to the colour of leather, like sails burned through by the sun and hot winds. 'The type is lean and hardy and, with their black hair cut straight across the forehead, their bushy beards and the little felt caps that encircle the crown of their heads, they remind one of jovial clerics.' Their wit, she sensed, was sharp and teasing, and there was a stinging quality about the banter they exchanged with one another.[7]

Kakheti today is a prosperous land of vineyards operated on the collective and state farm systems. The capital, Telavi, is a charming place, approached by a stony road through wine-growing centres such as Gurjaani and Tsinandali, trademarks now well known in countries abroad. At Telavi, one can look out from the eighteenth-century palace and chapel of King Erekle II, now converted into a regional museum, over the great green plain of Kakheti to the mountains of Daghestan, or walk down the road to an immense tree under which Georgian writers and poets of half a century ago used to assemble and talk. The world-wide export of Kakhetian wine, combined with sericulture, tobacco and fruit growing, and other rural industries seem to assure the people of growing prosperity.

17

National characteristics of the Georgians

Like most Caucasian peoples, the Georgians do not fit into any of the main ethnic categories of Europe and Asia. Their language is neither Indo-European, Turkic nor Semitic. The present-day Georgian or 'Kartvelian' nation no doubt results from a fusion of aboriginal, autochthonous inhabitants with immigrants who infiltrated into Transcaucasia from the direction of Asia Minor in remote antiquity. The principal geographical regions of Georgia are distinguished from one another by distinct linguistic or dialectal differences. Standard literary Georgian corresponds more or less to the idiom of Kartli, around Tbilisi. Svanian and Mingrelo-Laz, on the other hand, are separate languages within the South Caucasian or Ibero-Caucasian group, and not mere dialects of Georgian. Such regions as Guria, Ratcha, Khevsureti and Pshaveti have well-defined dialects, which provide much interesting material for the linguist.

Generalizations about national characteristics are sometimes dangerous. In the eighteenth century, Prince Vakhushti had this to say about his fellow-countrymen.

'In outward appearance, the men and women are comely and handsome, black of eye, brow and hair; their complexion is white and rosy, less frequently swarthy or sallow. . . . They are slim of waist, the girls particularly, and seldom stout; they are brave and hard-working, with great powers of endurance, bold cavaliers and eager for a fray, nimble and quick off the mark. . . . They are doughty warriors, lovers of arms, haughty, audacious; and so avid of personal glory that they will sacrifice their fatherland or their sovereign for the sake of their own advancement; they are hospitable to guests and strangers, and cheerful of disposition; if two or three are assembled together, they are never at a loss for amusement; they are generous and prodigal of their own goods and of other people's, and never think of amassing possessions; they are intelligent, quick-witted, self-centred and lovers of learning. . . . They lend loyal support to one another and will remember and repay a good turn but will exact retribution for an insult. They change rapidly from a good mood to a bad one; are headstrong, ambitious, and apt both to flatter and to take offence. . . .'[8]

Georgian women share with those of Circassia a high reputation for grace and beauty, and in olden times were often

18

carried off to grace the harems of the Ottoman Sultans and the Shahs of Persia. The Georgians are not an inhibited race, though they preserve a rigid code of sexual morality. They produce excellent wine and are lavish with hospitality. A French traveller entering Georgia from Turkey in 1701 expressed himself delighted with his reception at the hands of the honest country folk, who 'come and present you with all manner of provisions, bread, wine, fowls, hogs, lambs, sheep'. He contrasted the Georgians' smiling and courteous manners with the 'serious fellows that survey you gravely from head to foot' in Turkey.[9] In modern times, scores of travellers have expressed their pleasure at the delights of Georgian picnics and banquets, where the shashlik is roasted over a coal fire, and toast upon toast proposed by the eloquent *tamada* or master of the feast.

The Georgians have always been renowned as men-at-arms. In Roman times, Pompey found the Iberians hard to vanquish; their king, Artag, and his spirited followers, defeated in pitched battle, climbed up trees and shot at the Roman legions until the forests themselves were chopped or burnt down. Another Georgian king, Farsman II, visited Rome with a suite of knights and delighted the Emperor Hadrian with a display of equestrian exercises. The mediaeval Arabic writer al-'Umari, who served the Mamluk Sultan of Egypt, described Georgia as 'an extensive land and an important kingdom', whose warriors were 'the kernel of the religion of the Cross and a people of courage and valour'. The Grand Vizier of Persia regarded the Georgian king as 'his most particular associate and his truest friend'. 'He called upon him on any important occasion and asked his help in difficulties, and counted him a support for his army and a remover of any unpleasantness.' The same author also gives the opening formula deemed appropriate for use in official despatches from the Egyptian Sultan to the King of Georgia:

'May God make permanent the felicity of the exalted presence, the presence of the great monarch, the hero, the bold, the lion, the illustrious, the attacker, the dauntless, the enthroned, the crowned, a scholar in his community, just to his subjects, the successor of the Greek kings, Sultan of the Georgians, treasure of the kingdom of the seas and gulfs, protector of the homeland of the knights, the heir of his fathers in thrones and crowns, bulwark of the lands of Asia Minor and Iran, offspring of the Hellenes, the quintessence of the kings of the Syrians, the successor of the sons of thrones and crowns, the strengthener of Christianity, supporter of the religion of Jesus, the anointed leader of the Christian heroes, who glorifies Jerusalem by sincere purpose, the pillar of the sons of baptism, the helper of the Bab who is the Pope of Rome, the lover of the Muslims, the best of close companions, and the friend of Kings and Sultans.'[10]

It would of course be wrong to idealize the Georgian character.

Every medal has its reverse. In many Georgians, quick wit is matched by a quick temper, and a proneness to harbour rancour. The bravery associated with heroes like Prince Bagration, an outstanding general of the Napoleonic wars, is matched by the cruelty and vindictiveness found in such individuals as Stalin and Beria. One may also cite in this context the ill-famed trio, Gvishiani, Goglidze and Kobulov, assistants of the NKVD chief Ivan Serov; these three were shot after the fall of Beria in 1953.

Literature and the arts

The Georgians are justly proud of their long tradition of achievement in literature and the fine arts. Before the introduction of Christianity, they wrote in the Greek and Iranian languages, using the Greek alphabet and also a variety of the Aramaic script. An original and distinctive Georgian alphabet came into being in the fifth century A.D. This existed at first only in the angular ecclesiastical or *khutsuri* form, but by the eleventh century, a cursive, rounded form of writing had evolved, the modern *mkhedruli* or knightly (i.e. layman's) script. Georgian literature began in the fifth century with lives of saints and translations of the Holy Scriptures. Historical chronicles followed, collected together during the Middle Ages under the general title of *Kartlis tskhovreba*, or *The Life of Georgia*. At first, the Church exercised complete control over literature. As the country came into closer contact with the literature of Muslim Persia, writers turned to composing odes, romances and epic poems, of which the most famous is Shota Rustaveli's *The Man in the Panther's Skin*, said to have been composed during the reign of Queen Tamar (1184-1213). Since that time Georgian writers have shown themselves prolific as lyric poets, collectors of fables and folklore, compilers of dictionaries and astronomical and geographical treatises. Georgian novelists and essayists have in modern times attained a high standard of originality.

The history of Georgian art stretches back into remote antiquity. B. A. Kuftin's excavations in Trialeti, for example, resulted in the discovery of precious objects dating from the second millennium before Christ, including a superb gold cup adorned with filigree work and set with gems. Engraved seals of Classical inspiration and silver ware of Sassanian style have been found in ancient sites explored recently, notably in the vicinity of the ancient Iberian capital of Mtskheta-Armazi. With the introduction of Christianity, church architecture and sculpture made rapid strides. Georgian and Armenian architecture played a role in the evolution of Byzantine and even of the Romanesque building style. Georgian mediaeval churches are characterized by their elegant geometrical proportions and drum-shaped tower crowned with a pointed cone. Repoussé work in gold and silver, enamel ware, icons, wood carving and fresco painting are other branches of the fine arts in which the Georgians excelled. During the seventeenth century, Georgia came under the artistic sway of Safavi Iran, as is shown by many beautiful miniatures executed in that period. Modern Georgian art shows traces of the influence of Russian academicism, and lately, of Soviet realism. There have also been some talented and highly original 'primitive' artists, such as Niko Pirosmani, and painters of individual genius, like Lado Gudiashvili (b. 1896).

The theatrical arts—drama, ballet, opera—are cultivated in Georgia with outstanding success. When the Georgian State Dance Company performed at the Albert Hall in London in November 1959, the British Press and public were full of praise for 'these men with fire in their feet' and responded enthusiastically to 'the charm of the company's tall, dark-eyed women'. 'Every one of these Caucasian beauties, doe-eyed and petal-cheeked, behaved as though they loved dancing only slightly less than they admired the decorous chivalry of their nimble-footed galants.'[11] The Georgian film industry, though cramped by directives from Moscow, has made its own contribution to cinematic art. Mikheil Chiaureli, producer of *The Fall of Berlin*, had earlier made his name as the creator of films about heroic figures in Georgian history, such as Giorgi Saakadze, Grand Constable of Georgia in the seventeenth century, and Arsena of Marabda, a kind of Georgian Robin Hood of the Tsarist period. A film of A. Matchavariani's ballet on the theme of Othello was shown in London in 1961. Now that the barriers of the Stalin era are breaking down, bodies like the Georgian Society for Friendship and Cultural Relations with Foreign Countries (GODIKS) are able to broaden their activities, to the advantage both of Georgia and of the outside world. A new generation of students, artists and intellectuals is emerging in present-day Georgia, loyal Soviet citizens, and filled at the same time with a zest for knowledge that augurs well for the future of their country.

CHAPTER II

RISE AND FALL
OF THE GEORGIAN KINGS

From tribe to monarchy — The coming of the Romans — Christianity and the growth of feudalism — The rise of the Bagratid dynasty — The Mongol yoke — Ottoman Turkey and Safavi Persia — Rapprochement with Russia — Collapse of the monarchy — The Russians take over

From tribe to monarchy

THE INSTITUTION of monarchy in Georgia stretches back into remote antiquity. In the age of myth and legend, Jason and his Argonauts are said to have found Colchis, the present-day Mingrelia and Imereti, ruled by King Aietes, father of the sorceress Medea; through her magic lore, the Greeks gained possession of the Golden Fleece. Legends such as this combine with the findings of archaeology to imply the existence in Western Georgia from time immemorial of petty monarchies, governed in a simple patriarchal fashion.

The other main region of Georgia known to the ancients— Caucasian Iberia—lay to the east of Colchis, across the Surami range; Iberia included the modern Kartli and Kakheti, together with Samtskhe and other regions to the south-west. In Iberia was situated the ancient capital city of Mtskheta-Armazi, a short distance up the River Kura from the modern metropolis of Tbilisi. Armazis-tsikhe, the Greek Harmozika, signifies 'castle of Armazi', and took its name from the local embodiment of the Zoroastrian deity Ahura-Mazda. Thanks to its strategic position at the confluence of the rivers Kura and Aragvi, Mtskheta-Armazi became the chief city in the land. The Georgian chronicle tells us that the chiefs and patriarchs of the tribes vied for control of it: 'He who possessed

Mtskheta stood above all the others, for the city of Mtskheta was greater than the other towns, and it was called the Mother-city.'

During the last five centuries before the Christian era, general progress in agriculture and trade, in metal-working and in building techniques, led to the emergence in Iberia of a relatively advanced social order. Towns and villages sprang up. Wide differences in wealth and status declared themselves and became perpetuated from one generation to another. Besides the kings themselves, there were provincial magnates and tribal chiefs, men of substance and power. This is demonstrated by such finds as the Akhalgori hoard, discovered in the river Ksani valley, and dating from some four hundred years before Christ. The articles of great magnificence, fashioned in gold, silver and bronze, which make up this hoard, were consigned to the earth along with the body of a prominent local grandee.

The coming of the Romans

The campaigns of Pompey brought the Georgians into the Roman sphere of influence. The Romans, according to the geographer Strabo, found Iberia a rich, thickly populated land, divided into two climatic and economic zones—the mountainous uplands and the low-lying river valleys. The highlanders, who composed the majority of the population, made their living by rearing sheep, horses and cattle, and formed the backbone of the Iberian armed forces. The lowlanders engaged in agriculture and in tending orchards and vineyards. The towns were walled and contained markets and public buildings with roofs, all constructed on approved architectural principles.

According to Strabo, Iberian society was divided into four main classes. The first was made up of the royal family, the senior member of which occupied the throne, while the second in rank administered justice and commanded the army. The next class was that of the priests, who also served as diplomats and councillors of state. The third category was that of the free farmers, herdsmen and warriors. The fourth was made up of the lower orders of the common people, comprising, so it seems, serf labourers on the royal estates, domestic slaves, prisoners of war and so forth. Strabo tells us nothing about the aristocracy, the knights and the high officers of state, of whose existence contemporary inscriptions provide definite evidence. Nor has he anything to say about a Georgian merchant and artisan class, perhaps because this was composed of Jews, Syrians, Persians, Greeks and other foreigners.

The presence of Roman garrisons and officials had far-reaching effects on Georgia's social and economic life. The Georgians became acquainted with manners and customs, products and techniques, of which they had previously no conception. The building of roads gave the country access to markets in Asia Minor and other parts of the Roman Empire. The kings of Iberia became 'friends and allies of the Roman people'. As shown by an inscription of Vespasian discovered near Mtskheta, the Romans sent engineers there to build fortifications against the Parthians, Scythians and other common enemies. Colchis to the west was reduced to an even more subservient position. Roman legionaries were stationed in the main ports and strategic points around the Black Sea coast.

At the same time, the Iberians retained their traditional cultural links with Iran, then ruled by the Parthian dynasty of the Arsacids, sworn foes of the Romans. Symptomatic of the mingled Iranian and Greco-Roman influences on the life and habits of the Georgian upper classes are the names borne by the Iberian kings and higher dignitaries during this period. Alongside Iranian names like Parnavaz, Farasmanes (Farsman), Ksefarnug and Asparukh, we encounter an impeccable Roman name like Publicius Agrippa, and even hybrid forms such as Flavius Dades.

Under the later Roman emperors, Roman power in the east fell into decay. With the rise of the Sassanids in Iran during the third century A.D., Iranian political supremacy over Eastern Georgia became marked. With this went an increased attachment to the Zoroastrian religion. As evidence of this, one may cite two interesting Sassanian silver dishes discovered in Georgia at Armazi and Bori respectively: each portrays the sacrificial figure of a horse standing before the ritual fire altar.

Christianity and the growth of feudalism

A new phase in Georgian history opened with the country's conversion to Christianity by Saint Nino about the year 330, during the reign of Constantine the Great. The adoption of the Christian faith had momentous consequences for the entire nation, which became an outer bulwark of Christendom in the pagan Orient. Christianity imparted to the people a unity which transcended the political vicissitudes arising from the struggle of the great powers for mastery of the Near East—a struggle in the course of which Georgia was repeatedly invaded and partitioned by Persians and Greeks, by Arabs, Turks and Mongols.

Modern historians of the Marxist school connect the adoption of Christianity with the decline of a slave-owning economy in Georgia, and the coming into existence of a society based on feudal principles. There remains, however, some doubt as to the dominant role of slave labour in the ancient Iberian and Colchian economies. Unlike the Egyptians, Babylonians, Persians or even the neighbouring Armenians, the Georgians of antiquity never succeeded in overrunning large tracts of territory whose inhabitants could be led away wholesale into slavery. Nor do we have the impression of an urban society on the scale of Athens or Rome, where every citizen of substance was attended by scores of slaves, and entrepreneurs made a handsome living by leasing out thousands of slave labourers to mine operators and industrial contractors. That there were rich and poor, high and low, in ancient Georgia is shown beyond doubt by the archaeological evidence. That prisoners of war were used as forced labourers, that domestic slavery existed in the households of the great, is hardly open to question. But it is highly probable that the bulk of the people were free husbandmen and herdsmen, some with their own clan organization, or else vassals or serfs of the king or leading nobles. It has yet to be proved that chattel slaves were a dominant factor in the economy and the social order.

It would seem more logical to regard the emergence of a feudal monarchy in Georgia as the natural outcome of the patriarchal rule of the ancient Georgian *mamasakhlisni*, or 'fathers of the house', as the tribal chiefs of old were called. We have already spoken of the struggle between these heads of tribes for possession of the city of Mtskheta, control of which conferred supremacy on its owner. The Georgian chronicle speaks of the ruler of Mtskheta appointing nine dukes or *eristavs* ('heads of the people'), who were simultaneously civil governors and military heads of their respective provinces. These *eristavs* were an agency whereby the kings could keep in order the old territorial nobility of the *mtavars* or hereditary princes. The latter, naturally enough, did their best to resist any undue extension of the royal prerogative. Beneath the great nobles and the viceroys of the king came the class of the gentry and the knights, vassals of the princes or of the king himself. The knights in turn had suzerainty over their peasants, whom they would lead into battle when the summons came. This, in broad outline, is the social structure of which a fifth-century writer gives us a glimpse when he speaks of 'the grandees and noble ladies, the gentry and common folk of the land of Georgia'.[12]

Historians have been struck by the resemblance between the social and political structure which prevailed in Georgia virtually up to the Russian occupation in 1801, and the feudal institutions of mediaeval Europe. It has even been conjectured that Georgia's feudal system might owe something to the influence of the Crusaders. But it is clear that the roots of Georgian feudalism can be traced back to a far earlier epoch. Analogies should rather be sought in Byzantium and in Sassanian Iran. Under the Sassanian kings, the royal power rested on a delicate balance between feudal allegiances and bureaucratic absolutism. Under the supreme authority of the Iranian king of kings was a motley assemblage of vassal kings, provincial satraps and chiefs of clans, some hereditary dynasts, and others viceroys appointed by the king. Beneath these were ranged the nobles and knights, some vassals of the great princes, others of the sovereign himself. At the lower end of the scale came the peasants, who followed their lords into battle and formed the rank and file of the Persian army.[13] While the Georgian monarchy was on a far smaller scale and possessed individual features of its own, there are manifest similarities between the structure of the two states, which existed for centuries side by side.

During the later Sassanian period, the Iberian monarchy was weakened both by civil strife and by the struggle between Byzantium and Iran for dominion over the Caucasus. This decline had become so marked by the time of the Persian king, Khusrau I (531–79), that the Persians were able to abolish the monarchy and assert direct control over Georgia's internal affairs. For the next three centuries, hereditary magnates ruled over each province under the supervision of governors appointed by the Great Kings of Iran and the Byzantine emperors, and later, after about A.D. 650, by the Arab caliphs.

The rise of the Bagratid dynasty

While the Georgian monarchy was in abeyance, a new and virile ruling family was rising to prominence in the marchlands of Georgia and Armenia. This was the clan of the Bagratids, who were to unify Georgia under a single crown and reign there for a thousand years. Although the Bagratids claimed for prestige purposes to be descended from David and Solomon of Israel, they were in reality princes of Speri (Ispir), in the Upper Chorokhi valley north of Erzurum, and had a castle at the modern Bayburt. The family first attained the highest dignities of state in the Armenian kingdom, and then spread into Georgia. Towards the end of the eighth century, Ashot the Great settled at Artanuji in Tao, south-western Georgia, receiving from the Byzantine emperor the title of *Kuropalates* or 'Guardian of the Palace'. As time went on, Ashot profited by the relative weakness of the emperors at Constantinople and the Arab caliphs of Baghdad, and set himself up as hereditary prince in Iberia.

From then on, the unification of the Georgian lands proceeded apace. In 1008, Bagrat III became king of a united Eastern and Western Georgia, having inherited Iberia from his father, and Abasgia (as Western Georgia was then called) through his mother. Excluded from his dominions was the capital city of Tbilisi, still ruled by independent Muslim *amirs*, the Ja'farids. Tbilisi fell at last to King David the Builder (1089–1125), who was aided by the arrival of the Crusaders in the Near East, and the consequent demoralization of the Saracens. David won victories over the Seljuk Turks and annexed large tracts of the former Armenian kingdom. In this way there was erected the imposing structure of the Georgian monarchy, a veritable Caucasian empire, exercising suzerainty over the Muslim kingdom of Shirvan on the Caspian Sea and

later, over the Christian realm of Trebizond on the Black Sea—
an empire renowned for its political and military might, its
cultural efflorescence and its economic prosperity.

The zenith of Georgia's power and prestige was reached
under Queen Tamar (1184–1213). This was Georgia's heroic
age. The Georgian realm was a political organism of considerable complexity. The monarch ruled by the doctrine of
divine right. The existence of strong feudal institutions
prevented the royal power from degenerating into sheer
despotism. Indeed, there was a movement at the outset of
Tamar's reign to limit the royal prerogative by setting up a
kind of House of Lords with authority equal to that of the
sovereign. Unlike the efforts of the English barons under
Tamar's contemporary, King John, this Georgian constitutional movement came to naught. Nevertheless, the power of
the great nobles and ecclesiastics who sat upon the royal
council of state had always to be reckoned with, as had that of
the provincial tribal chieftains.

The central administration was headed by five *vazirs*
or ministers: the High Chancellor (an office long associated
with the dignity of Archbishop of Tchqondidi), the War
Minister, the Lord Chamberlain, the Chancellor of the Ex-
chequer and the *Atabag* or High Constable, each with a staff
of subordinate officials. The *eristavs* or dukes who ruled the
provinces were nominally viceroys, removable at will by the
sovereign. In practice, once a province had been governed
for generations by the same princely family, it was hard for the
monarch to dislodge such vassals without provoking open strife.

The rulers of mediaeval Georgia, who were proud to style
themselves 'Servants of the Messiah', were very conscious of
their role as bulwarks of Christendom against the infidel
nations. The Orthodox Church of Georgia bulked large in the
country's life, and battling bishops led their troops into the
fray alongside the armies of the king. The Church had wide
powers of jurisdiction over morals and private conduct, a
monopoly in the field of education, as well as enormous
economic privileges, grants of land, and valuable immunities
and benefactions. The kings themselves submitted philosophic-
ally to ecclesiastical censure when they happened to overstep
the bounds of decorum: thus, Ashot the Great was once

soundly castigated for his moral lapses by a mother superior. 'In spirit he rejoiced because wisdom had conquered pernicious weakness; in a pure heart he revered the blessed ones who had bestowed on his soul the crown of eternal salvation.'[14] By a rational division of authority between Church and State, the Georgian kings avoided both the Byzantine and Muscovite system of Caesaro-papism, and the unresolved conflicts which often wrought havoc in Western Christendom, leading on occasion to such tragedies as the murder of Thomas à Becket in Canterbury Cathedral.

It was in Tamar's time that the Georgian feudal system reached its apogee. Fiefs and arrière fiefs, allodium and immunity, vassalage, investiture and homage—all these familiar terms of Western feudalism had their equivalents in the social system of mediaeval Georgia. The nation could be divided into the categories of *patroni*, or lord, and *qma*, which meant either vassal or serf according to context and social position. The term *patroni* was employed to denote both protector and master. A nobleman, logically enough, would normally be a *patroni* in regard to his peasants, and a *qma*, or vassal, in the eyes of his suzerain prince or king.

This hierarchical division of Georgian society is strikingly exemplified in the official table of *wergild* or blood money rates, drawn up at the beginning of the eighteenth century by King Vakhtang VI. Though compiled relatively late, this table includes data handed down from earlier periods.

At the top of the scale are the king and the Catholicos-Patriarch of Georgia. Both of them are accorded equivalent status as heads of the temporal and spiritual orders of the nation respectively. No sum of blood money is prescribed to be exacted from a man slaying either of them, for such a crime was punished as high treason, by execution. The princes and dukes were divided into three classes. The highest class, the *didebulni* or grandees, were equated with archbishops of the rank of Metropolitan. If slain by an individual of equal rank, the blood money payable in respect of a prince or archbishop of the first class amounted to 1,536 tomans, equivalent in King Vakhtang's time to 15,360 silver rubles. The lesser nobility or squirearchy (*aznaurni*) were likewise divided into three categories. The highest of these was assessed at 192 tomans, also the blood money of an abbot. The lowest grade mentioned in Vakhtang's table is that of peasant or small tradesman, for whom the *wergild* payable was 12 tomans.

These figures represent the amount of indemnity payable by an assassin to the relatives of his victim, in cases where an individual was slain by another of his own social standing. But if a peasant or squire killed someone of a higher grade, then he would have to pay at least one and a half times the basic rate, and probably suffer some other form of punishment in addition. In cases of wounding, abduction of a wife, and other forms of insult or injury, full *wergild* or a fixed portion of it would be payable by way of compensation to the injured party.

Another remarkable feature of Georgian judicial procedure was the system of ordeals. These no doubt derived from those practised in ancient Iran; they also have features in common with the ordeals so familiar in Western Christendom. In Georgia, the presumed guilt or innocence of an accused party was established by single combat; by the ordeals of boiling water and red-hot iron; by solemn oath on an icon; and by an odd ceremony known as saddling oneself with sin, in which the accused took the plaintiff upon his back and declared: 'May God hold me responsible for thy sins at the Last Judgement, and may I be judged in thy place, if this deed has really been committed by me.'[15] These ordeals continued in use right up to the eighteenth century.

The Mongol yoke

The invasions of Transcaucasia by the Mongols from A.D. 1220 onwards brought the Golden Age of Georgia to an abrupt end. The country was reduced to vassalage under the Mongol Il-khans of the line of Hulagu Khan. In the fourteenth century, there were signs of a national revival. The onslaughts of Tamerlane created great havoc in Georgia's economic and cultural life, from which the kingdom never fully recovered. The countryside was strewn with the ruins of churches, castles and towns, the people fled to the hills, and once busy roads were overgrown with grass and bushes.

The last king of united Georgia was Alexander I (1412–43), under whose sons the realm split up into squabbling princedoms. The disintegration of the monarchy was further aggravated by the fall of Constantinople to the Ottoman Turks in 1453, and the resulting isolation of Georgia from Western Christendom. The Black Sea became a Turkish lake, and the land routes from the Caucasus to the Mediterranean and the West through Anatolia and Syria were all in enemy hands.

The Bagratid royal family was now divided into three branches. The senior line ruled at Tbilisi over the kingdom of Kartli; a second ruled over Western Georgia or Imereti—'the land on the far side'; a third possessed Kakheti, Georgia's most easterly province. Five princely families took advantage of this break-down of the central monarchy to set themselves up as independent dynasts on their own. These were the Jaqelis of Samtskhe in the south-west; the Dadianis of Mingrelia, which comprised a large part of ancient Colchis; the Gurielis in Guria, on the Black Sea immediately south of Mingrelia; the Sharvashidzes in Abkhazia, on Georgia's north-western Black Sea fringe; and the Gelovanis in highland Svaneti among the peaks of the Caucasus range.

Ottoman Turkey and Safavi Persia

This political fragmentation rendered Georgia powerless to resist the designs of Ottoman Turkey and Safavi Persia, who now vied for control over Caucasia. In 1510 the Turks invaded Imereti and sacked the capital, Kutaisi. Not long afterwards, Shah Ismail Safavi of Iran invaded Kartli—a foretaste of many onslaughts which the land was to suffer at the hands of this dynasty of Persian rulers.

From the north, the Grand Princes of Muscovy had already begun their drive towards the Caspian Sea and the North Caucasian steppe. In 1492, King Alexander of Kakheti sent an embassy of friendship to Ivan III of Moscow. After Kazan and Astrakhan had fallen to Ivan the Terrible in 1552 and 1556 respectively, the Tsar sent King Levan of Kakheti a Cossack bodyguard and took him under Russian protection. Threats and protests from the Shah of Persia soon led to the Cossacks being withdrawn. However, the Grebensky and Terek Cossack settlements in the North Caucasian steppe became an important factor in Caucasian politics. In 1594, Tsar Fedor Ivanovich sent an army to seize the strategic fortress of Tarku in Daghestan, capital of the dynasty of the Shamkhals. This, and subsequent expeditions, ended in disaster for the Russians. However, a further Russian advance into Caucasia was only a matter of time and opportunity.

During the closing decades of the sixteenth century, a period of anarchy in Persia enabled the Ottoman Turks to overrun the whole of Transcaucasia and Persian Azerbaijan. Their triumph was short-lived. The Safavi dynasty in Persia soon rose to new heights of power under the brilliant and ruthless Shah 'Abbas I (1587–1629). The expulsion of the Turks from Eastern Georgia by Shah 'Abbas was followed by a reign of terror instituted by the Shah with a view to eliminating the more vigorous Georgian princes, and turning the land into a Persian province. Many thousands of the Christian population were deported to distant regions of Iran, where their descendants live to this day. The Dowager Queen of Kakheti, Ketevan, was given the choice of abandoning the Christian faith and entering the Shah's harem, or of a cruel martyrdom. She chose the latter fate, and is numbered among the saints of the Georgian Church.

It was only with the arrival in Tbilisi of Khusrau-Mirza, an illegitimate, renegade scion of the Bagratid royal line, that the country's wounds began to heal. King Rostom, as Khusrau was styled within Georgia, was an elderly politician with an excellent knowledge of diplomacy and considerable influence at the Persian court. Himself a Muslim, Rostom took to wife the daughter of a leading Georgian aristocrat, and was married according to both Christian and Muslim rites. The patriotic extremists, of course, regarded Rostom as a traitor and resented his introduction of Persian ways—'luxury and high living, dissipation and unchastity, dishonesty, love of pleasure, baths and unseemly attire, lute and flute players', the historian Prince Vakhushti disapprovingly termed them. However, Rostom pursued undeterred his policy of conciliation. 'Everywhere', as the French traveller Chardin records, 'he re-established peace and order, and governed with much clemency and justice.'[16]

While the Persians were establishing their rule over Eastern Georgia, the Turks dominated Imereti and the minor principalities of Western Georgia. Without actually annexing these regions, they maintained a loose suzerainty over them. From time to time, they would stage an invasion to dethrone some disobedient prince and remind the people of the nearness of Ottoman power. Otherwise they left the people of Imereti, Mingrelia and Guria very much to their own devices, apart from levying a frequent tribute of male and female Georgian slaves, who were highly prized in Turkey. Being mostly engaged in civil wars among themselves, these minor kings and princes of Western Georgia presented little danger to Turkey's eastern frontiers.

Rapprochement *with Russia*

During the reign of King Rostom (1632–58) and his immediate successors, the Russian court avoided becoming embroiled in military intervention in the Caucasus. At the Kremlin, Tsar Alexis had plenty to occupy him in the way of tumult, religious schism, and wars with his European neighbours. Russia was also loth to relinquish the flourishing trade which she carried on with Persia via the Caspian Sea. This did not mean that Russia lost interest in Georgian affairs. Peaceful penetration was intense. The Dadian or reigning prince of Mingrelia and the King of Imereti, both within the Turkish zone of influence, were taken under nominal Russian suzerainty. Several embassies were exchanged with King Teimuraz I of Kakheti, son of the martyred Queen Ketevan, who visited Moscow to appeal for Russian aid against the Persians. Community of faith led the Russians, as the great Orthodox power in the East, to lend a sympathetic ear to the pleas of the Georgians, while the latter, like the Balkan Slavs, looked confidently to Christian Muscovy as a certain deliverer from the Muslim yoke.

The consequences of this touching but misguided confidence were seen most clearly during the reign of King Vakhtang VI of Kartli, who governed at Tbilisi as regent from 1703 until 1711, and then as king, with interruptions, until 1723. Vakhtang was one of the most gifted monarchs Georgia has produced; as patron of the arts and sciences, he may be compared with the Renaissance princes of Italy. He codified the laws, set up a commission to edit the national chronicles, installed a printing press at Tbilisi, built palaces, restored churches, dug canals for irrigation purposes, and generally improved Georgia's economic and social position. In 1721, the Caucasus was suddenly affected by an international crisis. The Afghans of Qandahar had revolted against the King of Persia, Shah Sultan Husayn, and marched on Isfahan from the east. From the north, Peter the Great of Russia cast covetous eyes on Persia's Caspian provinces and sent messengers to Tbilisi to rally the Georgians to his banner. King Vakhtang VI, whom the Shah had coerced into abjuring Christianity and embracing Islam, responded with alacrity to the Tsar's overtures. When the Shah sent to him for military help, Vakhtang refused, with the result that Isfahan fell to the Afghans in 1722 after a protracted siege in which scores of thousands perished from hunger and wounds. Seeing Persia in chaos, the Turks invaded from the west in 1723, occupying Tbilisi. The Ottoman sultan threatened war if the Russians sent help to the Georgians or entered the Turkish occupation zone. Driven from his capital, Vakhtang soon lost all hope of effective Russian support: 'While Peter plans to succour Paul, Paul is being skinned.' Eventually, the Russians offered Vakhtang and his followers asylum; the Georgian king died in exile at Astrakhan in 1737.

This setback curtailed Russian influence in Georgia for many years. The next serious *rapprochement* took place during the reign of Erekle II (1744–98), a remarkable man who played in his youth a leading role in the campaigns of the Persian conqueror Nadir Shah, whom he accompanied on his expedition to India between 1737 and 1740. Nadir rewarded him in 1744 with the throne of Kakheti, while his father, Teimuraz II, became King of Kartli. In 1762, Teimuraz II died while on a diplomatic mission to the court of St. Petersburg. Erekle now combined Kartli and Kakheti into one East Georgian kingdom. 'Nervous, brittle and intelligent in his small tumbling world,' to use W. E. D. Allen's graphic phrase, the king 'felt out this way and that for the bricks of some stability.'[17] He strove to enlist the support of European powers, and to attract Western scientists and technicians to give his country the benefit of the latest military and industrial techniques. His vigilance in the care of his people knew no bounds. On campaign, he would sit up at night watching for the enemy, while in time of peace, he spent his life in transacting business of state or in religious exercises, and devoted but a few hours to sleep.

Collapse of the monarchy

The great scourge which afflicted Georgia during Erekle's reign was the insecurity which resulted from raids by Muslim tribesmen of Daghestan, the Lezghis. These marauders were egged on by their Turkish co-religionists just over the border. Georgian peasants could not work at any distance from their dwellings for fear of attack by these ruthless mountaineers, who pounced on their victims in the fields, or dragged them from their huts to sell to the Turks and Persians. It has been reckoned that these raids, together with the various local wars which took place in Georgia, reduced the population by as much as a half during the eighteenth century. By 1800, the combined population of Eastern and Western Georgia had sunk to less than half a million.

This state of affairs had a paralysing effect on the development of industry. When Erekle tried to start an iron foundry in the Borchalo district, he had to close it down owing to the onslaughts of the Lezghis. Caravans of merchants were constantly being waylaid and robbed. The economic situation was also adversely affected by hostility between the Armenian moneyed class and the improvident Georgian gentry. There was a steady outflow of much-needed capital from Georgia as the wealthier Armenian merchants left Tbilisi and Gori to make their headquarters in Moscow or Astrakhan.

In 1768, war broke out between Russia and Turkey. Catherine the Great decided to stage a military diversion against the Ottoman Empire's frontier provinces in the Caucasus. She sent to Georgia an expeditionary force, commanded by a swashbuckling German adventurer named Count von Todtleben. In conjunction with Erekle II and the King of Imereti, Solomon I, the Russians scored a few successes over the Turks. However, Todtleben quarrelled with the Georgian rulers, whom he despised as ignorant orientals, and left them to bear the brunt of the fighting themselves. Relations between Georgia and Russia were subjected to great strain.

36

The Russians take over

The estrangement between the courts of Tbilisi and St. Petersburg was eventually patched up, thanks largely to the vision of Catherine's favourite, Prince Gregory Potemkin. The empress and her lover were aware of the important role which the Christian Georgians might be made to play in furthering Russian designs to partition Persia and the Ottoman Empire. The Georgians on their side entertained high hopes of Russian military and economic aid. In 1783, a treaty between Russia and the Georgian kingdom of Kartlo-Kakheti was signed at Georgievsk.

In signing the Treaty of Georgievsk, Erekle undertook to renounce all dependence on Persia or any other power but Russia; he and his posterity were solemnly confirmed for ever in possession of all territories under their sway; the kings of Georgia, on succeeding to the throne, would request and receive from St. Petersburg their insignia of investiture; Erekle was to conduct negotiations with foreign powers only after securing the approval of the Russian authorities; the empress and her heirs were pledged to treat Georgia's foes as those of Russia; there was to be no interference in the internal affairs of Georgia; the Georgian Catholicos-Patriarch was given the eighth place among the Russian prelates, and made a member of the Holy Synod; the Georgian nobility were to have the same prerogatives as the Russian aristocracy; special facilities were to be afforded to Russian traders in Georgia and to Georgian merchants in Russia. The treaty was to remain in force permanently, and any modification was to be made only by the voluntary consent of both parties. Four additional articles were appended to the treaty. These provided among other things for the stationing in Georgia of two battalions of Russian infantry with four cannon, and the eventual recovery by force of arms of Georgia's ancient territories now in the hands of the Ottoman Turks. In making these grandiose promises, Catherine and Potemkin overreached themselves. The only line of direct communication between Georgia and Russia was the precarious military road over the main Caucasus range via the Daryal pass, a route infested by hostile tribes. The Turks and their allies, the Muslim warriors of Circassia and Daghestan, were still entrenched in large areas of North Caucasia. When Catherine's second Turkish war broke out in 1787, it was decided, despite frantic protests from the Georgians, that the Russian expeditionary force should be withdrawn, and the Georgians left to their own devices.

The dire consequence of this decision was seen a few years later, when a new dynasty, that of the Qajars, seized power in Persia. The head of this royal house, the eunuch Agha Muhammad Khan, resolved to turn Georgia once more into a province of Persia. In vain did Erekle send appeal after appeal to the Empress Catherine at St. Petersburg. The Russians, confronted with the French Revolution and the resulting wars and upheavals in Europe, had other problems to occupy their minds. In 1795, Agha Muhammad and his savage hordes swooped down on Tbilisi. King Erekle, in spite of his seventy-five years, took part in the furious battle which raged before the gates of the city. The Georgians fought like lions at bay, but were decimated and had to give way at last before the overwhelming numbers of the foe. The king narrowly escaped capture, while Tbilisi was sacked and burned by the triumphant Persians. To quote a contemporary, Sir John Malcolm:

'The conquerors entered Teflis: a scene of carnage and rapine ensued pleasing to one who desired to make this city an example for such as dared to contemn his authority. The Mahomedan historian of Aga Mohamed Khan, after describing the barbarous and horrid excesses, observes, "that on this glorious occasion the valiant warriors of Persia gave to the unbelievers of Georgia a specimen of what they were to expect on the day of judgement". It is not easy to calculate the number who perished. Bigotry inflamed the brutal rage of the soldier. The churches were levelled to the ground; every priest was put to death. Youth and beauty were alone spared for slavery. Fifteen thousand captives were led into bondage; and the army marched back laden with spoil.'[18]

The destruction of his capital city was a death blow to Erekle's dream of establishing, with Russian protection, a strong and united Georgian kingdom, into which Imereti and the lost provinces under Turkish rule would all eventually be drawn. The old king died early in 1798.

The next three years were a time of muddle and confusion. Georgian affairs were subjected to the imponderable whims of

Tsar Paul I, the crazy autocrat of Russia, who had succeeded his mother Catherine in 1796. At Tbilisi little more than nominal power was exercised by Erekle's son, King Giorgi XII. This invalid monarch was beset by the intrigues of his step-mother, the Dowager Queen Darejan, whose aim was to deprive Giorgi of the throne in favour of one of her own numerous progeny. The king thus lived in constant fear of being deposed or even murdered by his half-brothers, or of seeing yet another Persian army invading his kingdom. In these circumstances, Giorgi was forced to the conclusion that something more than a formal Russian protectorate was needed to ensure the kingdom's survival. In September 1799, he sent an embassy to St. Petersburg with instructions to surrender the realm of Eastern Georgia into the care of Tsar Paul—'not under his protection, but into his full authority' —provided only that the royal dignity should be preserved for ever in the Georgian royal family of the Bagratids. He was asking, that is to say, for a status comparable to that of native rajahs under the British empire in India, or that enjoyed by many sheikhs, amirs and sultans during the French and British dominion over the Near and Middle East.

But even this modest remnant of autonomy was to be denied to the Georgian kings and their subjects. Tsar Paul, it is true, at first promised to guarantee certain privileges to King Giorgi and the Georgian royal family. However, in November 1800, the emperor wrote to the Russian general in command on the Caucasian front: 'The weakening of the king's health gives ground for expecting his decease; you are therefore immediately to despatch, as soon as this occurs, a proclamation in Our name that until Our consent is received no action should be taken even to nominate an heir to the Georgian throne.'[19] The following month, Paul signed a manifesto declaring the kingdom of Kartlo-Kakheti annexed to the Russian crown.

Neither Tsar Paul nor King Giorgi were fated to see these measures put into effect. On 28 December 1800, before his emissaries had returned from St. Petersburg, Giorgi XII died. The commandant of Russian troops in Tbilisi set up a temporary administration, but on 15 January 1801, Giorgi's eldest son, Prince David, declared himself Regent of Georgia. Before the succession problem could be finally settled, Tsar Paul was himself assassinated in St. Petersburg during the night of 11–12 March 1801.

The Georgian question confronted the new emperor, Alexander I, with something of a dilemma. His more liberal advisers urged him to repudiate his despotic father's policy of unilateral annexation which, as they justly reminded him, contravened the Russo-Georgian treaty of 1783. In their view, the perpetration of so flagrant a wrong against the Georgian royal house would be a blot on the emperor's honour. The difficulty was that the Georgians themselves were bitterly divided on the succession to the throne. At Tbilisi, the Dowager Queen Darejan incited her own sons to open revolt against the Prince-Regent David, her stepson; one of Darejan's sons, Alexander Batonishvili, even fled the country and offered his services to the new Shah of Persia, Fath-'Ali, successor of the eunuch Agha Muhammad who had ravaged Georgia only five years previously. This violent discord within the Bagratid house was adroitly utilized by some of Tsar Alexander's less scrupulous intimates, who focused his attention on the rich mineral resources of Georgia, on the country's vital military position as a springboard for invasion of the Middle East, and strongly urged him not to miss this unique opportunity of joining the land to the Russian empire.

After much high-minded vacillation, Alexander decided to throw scruples to the winds. A manifesto couched in grandiose terms was drawn up, announcing Eastern Georgia's annexation, and repudiating any suggestion of self-interest on the Russian side. The Tsar cited the defenceless state of Georgia, the menace of civil war, the unanimous appeals which had been received from the Christian population for protection against the Persians and Turks. Alexander undertook to turn over the country's entire revenues to its own use, and to preserve the rights and prerogatives of all classes of the community, except, of course, those of the dethroned royal house. Each social order would have the opportunity of taking an oath of allegiance to the emperor. This manifesto was published in Moscow on 12 September 1801, three days before Alexander's coronation. For over two hundred years, the Tsars of Russia had styled themselves 'Lords of the Iberian land and the Georgian kings'. Now this honorific title had become reality with a vengeance; having entered voluntarily into the bear's embrace, the kings of Georgia now found the breath hugged out of them altogether.

Following the abolition of the Bagratid monarchy of Kartlo-Kakheti in Eastern Georgia, the liquidation of the branch of the dynasty ruling in Western Georgia was only a matter of time. King Solomon II of Imereti defended his independence as long as he was able. Taken under Russian suzerainty in 1804, Solomon later revolted and was deposed and captured by armed force in 1810. The smaller independent principalities of Western Georgia were gradually absorbed into the administrative framework of the Caucasian Vice-royalty. Guria was taken over in 1829, Mingrelia in 1857, Svaneti in 1858 and Abkhazia in 1864.

The decision of Tsars Paul and Alexander to destroy the independence of a vassal monarchy which they were pledged to maintain was morally indefensible, and was also to prove highly inexpedient in the longer term. Nevertheless, it is certain that Georgia in 1801 was in no position to stand on her own feet. With a population of only 500,000 or less, there was no prospect of a resurrection of the old pan-Georgian monarchy of David the Builder and Queen Tamar. With the royal family of Kartlo-Kakheti convulsed by dynastic feuds and Western Georgia perpetually agitated by civil strife, the disintegration of the state had reached an advanced stage. The raids of the Lezghian tribesmen and the depredations of the Persians and Turks rendered it impossible to build up a viable national economy. Some form of close association with Russia —though not necessarily outright annexation—was clearly essential for the sake of corporate physical survival. The Russia of Alexander I was not, by Western standards, a liberal or a progressive state. But it was a European power, with a European administration of sorts. Russian occupation turned the eyes of the Georgians away from Muslim Asia and gave them a window on to Europe, with all the opportunities which that implied, while the population of their country, surrounded by a ring of Russian bayonets, increased eight-fold in a century and a half.

CHAPTER III

GEORGIA UNDER THE TSARS: RESISTANCE, REVOLT, PACIFICATION: 1801-32

The liquidation of the old order — Prince Tsitsianov — Death of a general — Subjugation of Western Georgia — King Solomon II and Napoleon Bonaparte — The revolt of 1812 — Suppression of the Georgian Church — Economic progress and literary contacts — The conspiracy of 1832

The liquidation of the old order

WHEN TSAR ALEXANDER I published his manifesto of 12 September 1801, declaring the East Georgian kingdom of Kartlo-Kakheti irrevocably joined to the Russian empire, he also made public the outline of a new system of administration for the country. The land was now divided into five districts or *uezdy* on the Russian model, three in Kartli and two in Kakheti, with administrative centres at Tbilisi, Gori, Dusheti, Telavi and Sighnaghi. With the Georgian royal family removed from power, the commander-in-chief on Russia's Caucasian front was now supreme head of the central government at Tbilisi by virtue of proconsular powers conferred on him by the Tsar. Authority on the spot was vested in a council of Russian and Georgian officials headed by the commander in chief's deputy, who received the title of *pravitel* or administrator of Georgia. The administration was divided into four branches or 'expeditions'—the executive, the financial, and the criminal and civil judiciaries. Each branch was to be headed by a Russian official set over four Georgian committee members. Corresponding local administrations were to be set up in the country districts under Russian *kapitan-ispravniki* or district officers. The mountain clans of the Pshavs, Khevsurs and Tush, as well as the Tatar nomads dwelling in the southern borderlands, continued to be governed by Georgian *mouravs* or prefects. For civil litigation, the code of King Vakhtang VI remained in force, while criminal cases were to be judged according to Russian law.

The high-handed way in which Alexander had suppressed the independence of Kartlo-Kakheti did not pass without protest. The late King Giorgi's second son, Ioane, who had come to St. Petersburg, tried to organize a nation-wide petition to be submitted to the emperor, urging him at least to maintain the royal title in the Bagratid line in accordance with the treaty of 1783 and subsequent Russian pledges. Ioane's correspondence was seized by the Russian authorities, and his efforts frustrated. The Georgian envoys who had been sent to St. Petersburg by King Giorgi to negotiate an extension of Russian suzerainty over Georgia protested vigorously at the fashion in which the Russians had devoured their country, without any pretence of negotiation, and without even notifying the Georgian delegation of what was afoot. A number of petitions were received from Georgia, urging the claims of the Prince-Regent David or of his uncle, Prince Yulon, to be retained as titular head of the Georgian administration. It appears also that representatives of Western powers expressed, albeit discreetly, their misgivings at the way in which Georgia's absorption had been effected. But the Tsar stuck to his decision, and refused to make any concession to the Georgians' national pride and susceptibilities.

On 12 April 1802, the Russian commander-in-chief in the Caucasus, General Karl Knorring, published in Tbilisi the imperial proclamation of September 1801, confirming Tsar Paul's earlier decree, and affirming Kartlo-Kakheti to be an integral part of the Russian dominions. The general then administered to the princes and notables of Georgia the oath of allegiance to the Tsar. The effect was somewhat marred by the presence of armed Russian guards around the audience hall, making it clear that any attempt to avoid due compliance would provoke reprisals. A few Georgians who voiced disapproval were taken into custody. This made a poor impression on Russia's new subjects, deemed to have placed themselves voluntarily under the Tsar's benevolent protection.

The new Russian administration was set up in Tbilisi in May 1802. The administrator of Georgia was a certain Kovalensky, who had served as Russian envoy at the Georgian court during the reign of the late King Giorgi XII. This Kovalensky had already made himself obnoxious to the Georgians by his haughty manner and bullying demeanour. They were not reassured to see him back among them, invested with all the authority of the Russian state.

During these first two years of Russian rule, the internal situation in Eastern Georgia left much to be desired. Russian authority was confined to only a small part of Transcaucasia, namely the area centred on Tbilisi, measuring about one hundred and ninety miles long by one hundred and forty miles wide. This bridgehead of Russian power was ringed about by Persian khans, Turkish pashas, wild mountaineers, and un-subdued Georgian princelings, most of them hostile to Russia. Marauding parties of Lezghis on their agile steeds roamed the countryside, defying the less mobile Russian garrisons. The Ossetes who dominated the Daryal Pass, Russia's only supply line over the Caucasus range, held up travellers and convoys. Trade was virtually at a standstill, while the peasantry scarcely ventured out to plough the fields.

The widow of King Erekle II, the redoubtable Dowager Queen Darejan, continued to intrigue in favour of her eldest son, Prince Yulon, whom she wished to see installed as king under the Russian aegis. The nobles and people, while affirm-ing their desire to remain under Russian protection, contin-ually agitated for a prince of their own. The Russian authorities interpreted this natural aspiration as insurrection, and made a number of arrests. Seeing scant improvement in the state of the country, the Georgians lost faith in the Russian govern-ment and its local representatives.

Prince Tsitsianov

The chief administrator in Tbilisi, Kovalensky, was not the man to restore general confidence. He was busy enriching himself by disreputable speculations in the bazaar, and allot-ting key positions in the government to his relatives and friends. The Georgian councillors whose appointment was provided for in the manifesto of September 1801, were never nominated. Corruption and abuse went unchecked. Official documents of the time show that rape and acts of violence were commonly committed by Russian officials and soldiery. Prince Tsitsianov, who later succeeded Knorring as commander-in-chief, alludes in one of his reports to the 'crying abuses of authority committed by the former administrator of Georgia', which had 'gone beyond the Georgian people's limits of patience'. Even the official Russian historian of the Caucasus, A. P. Berzhe, remarks that 'Kovalensky and Company did not remove, but aggravated the abuses from which the Georgian people so grievously suffered. . . . Disappointed hope for improvement turned into ill-will, discontent, and impotent resentment, in fact the very impulses from which derive rebellion and revolt against supreme authority.'[20]

Rumours of Kovalensky's nefarious activities soon reached St. Petersburg. It was reported to the Tsar by one of his trusted advisers, Count Kochubey, that Knorring and Kovalensky 'were committing great exactions; that they were maintaining discord among the peoples of the country in order to be able to pillage them with more ease; and all kinds of similar horrors'.

It can hardly be said that Tsar Alexander was much of a liberal in his dealings with his Georgian subjects. But he was determined at least to keep up appearances, and saw how much Georgia needed a governor with courage and integrity, and some direct knowledge of local conditions and of the mentality and culture of Russia's new citizens.

Fortunately, so it seemed, the ideal man was to hand in the person of Prince P. D. Tsitsianov, a scion of the Georgian noble family of Tsitsishvili. Tsitsianov was an officer with a distinguished record in the Russian Army; he had been a disciple of the illustrious Suvorov. He was also a distant relative of the widow of King Giorgi XII of Georgia, Queen Mariam, who had been a Princess Tsitsishvili. In September 1802, Alexander appointed Tsitsianov commander-in-chief on the Caucasian Line, with viceregal powers over Georgia. He was instructed to introduce order and prosperity into the country, and to show the Georgian people that 'it would never have cause to repent of having entrusted its destiny to Russia'. The Tsar further empowered him to take immediate steps to persuade—if necessary by physical force—the former Georgian royal family to settle in Russia, and thus put an end to all agitation for the Bagratid dynasty to be retored.

Arriving at Tbilisi on 1 February 1803, Tsitsianov's first care was to pack off the remaining members of the old royal family. The former Prince-Regent David and his uncle, Prince Vakhtang, left Tbilisi under escort later in February. There remained the Dowager Queen Darejan, widow of Erekle II, and the widow of the late King Giorgi XII, Queen Mariam, with her seven children. In April, Tsitsianov heard that Queen Mariam was planning to flee to the mountain strongholds of Khevsureti with the aid of loyal clansmen from the hills. He therefore gave orders that the queen and her children should be sent off into exile in Russia under guard the very next morning. To impart an air of ceremony to the proceedings, it was decided that Major-General Lazarev, commander of Russian troops in Tbilisi, should proceed in full uniform to the queen's residence, with a military band and two companies of infantry, and prevail upon her to take her departure forthwith.

Death of a general

Of the ensuing tragedy there are several contemporary accounts, based on the reports of eye-witnesses.[21] Arriving at Queen Mariam's mansion, Lazarev found her in her private apartment, seated on a couch, and surrounded by her seven sleeping children. The general strode brusquely up to the queen and said, through his interpreter: 'Get up, it is time to be off.'

The queen calmly replied: 'Why this hurry to get up? Can you not see my children peacefully asleep round about me? If I wake them up abruptly it might be harmful to them. Who has given you so peremptory an order?'

The general replied that his orders were from Prince Tsitsianov himself.

'Tsitsianov—that mad dog!' Queen Mariam cried out.

At this, Lazarev bent down to drag her forcibly to her feet. The queen was holding on her knees a pillow, beneath which

46

she held concealed the dagger which had belonged to her late husband, King Giorgi. As quick as lightning, she drew the dagger and stabbed Lazarev through the body with such force that the tip of the weapon emerged through his left side. Mariam pulled the dagger from the gaping wound and threw it in the face of her prostrate tormentor, saying: 'So dies anyone who dares add dishonour to my misfortune!'

At Lazarev's expiring cry, his interpreter drew his sword and hacked at the queen's left arm. Soldiers rushed in and beat at the queen with their rifle butts. They dragged her from the house all covered in blood, and hurled her with her children into a carriage. Escorted by a heavy guard of armed horsemen, the party left Tbilisi along the military road leading to Russia over the Daryal Pass. Everywhere the queen's carriage was surrounded by devoted Georgians, who wept as they struggled to bid farewell to the family of their late sovereign. These loyal manifestations were repulsed by the Russian soldiery. When one of the children cried out that he was thirsty, a bystander brought up a jug of water, which the Russian escort hurled to the ground. On arrival in Russia, Queen Mariam was imprisoned for seven years in a convent at Voronezh. She lived to a great age, and eventually died at Moscow in 1850. She was interred at Tbilisi with regal honours.

The Queen Dowager Darejan—'that Hydra', as Tsitsianov delicately termed her—held out until the October of 1803, when she too was bundled off to Russia.

Subjugation of Western Georgia

Having eliminated these obstacles, Tsitsianov rapidly extended Russia's grasp on Transcaucasia. He saw the urgency of securing as rapidly as possible the entire area between the Black Sea and the Caspian. From his headquarters in Tbilisi, he turned his attention westwards to Imereti. Western Georgia was at this time torn by a feud between King Solomon II of Imereti and his nominal vassal, the semi-independent prince-regent or Dadian Grigol of Mingrelia. One of Grigol Dadian's predecessors had sworn fealty to the Tsar of Russia as long ago as 1638. Now, in 1803, his country was taken under direct Russian suzerainty. In contrast to the situation in Eastern Georgia, the local administration was left to the princely house, which retained control under nominal Russian supervision until the dignity of Dadian was finally abolished in 1867. With his principal vassal and foe now under Russian protection, King Solomon of Imereti felt it wise to feign submission. His dominions also were in 1804 placed beneath the imperial aegis, under guarantees similar to those given to the Dadian. However, Solomon remained at heart bitterly opposed to his foreign overlords, and his court at Kutaisi was a hot-bed of anti-Russian intrigue.

Eastwards of Tbilisi, Georgia's internal security was still threatened by the warlike Lezghian tribesmen of Daghestan, and by the independent Muslim khans of Ganja, Shekki and Baku, allies and nominally vassals of the Shah of Persia. Tsitsianov sent several expeditions against the Lezghis, with only partial success. His bravest lieutenant, General Gulyakov, was killed in one of the bloodthirsty engagements which took place. In his dealings with the Muslim potentates of Daghestan, Tsitsianov did not mince words. 'Shameless sultan with the soul of a Persian—so you still dare to write to me! Yours is the soul of a dog and the understanding of an ass, yet you think to deceive me with your specious phrases. Know that until you become a loyal vassal of my Emperor I shall only long to wash my boots in your blood.'[22] With language of this kind, backed by cold steel, Tsitsianov eventually abated the Lezghian menace and improved Georgia's internal security.

On 3 January 1804, Prince Tsitsianov took the important trading centre and fortress of Ganja by storm. Its ruler, Javat Khan, had been a bitter enemy of the Georgian kings, and had helped Agha Muhammad Khan Qajar to invade Georgia and sack Tbilisi in 1795. Javat was now slain on his own battlements. The town was renamed Elizavetpol, in honour of the Empress Elizabeth, consort of Alexander I. (It is the present-day Kirovabad.) This success enhanced Russian prestige to such an extent that for the time being, to use the historian Dubrovin's metaphor, the rulers of neighbouring *khanates* took on a demeanour of lamb-like meekness.[23]

During the reign of King Erekle II, the rulers of both Ganja and the chief city of Armenia, Erivan, had been vassals of the Georgian crown. Having subjugated Ganja, Tsitsianov judged the moment ripe for an expedition to Erivan. He learnt also that the Persians were massing a large army in Azerbaijan to the south, in preparation for an onslaught on the Russian dominions in the Caucasus. Determined to nip this in the bud, Tsitsianov marched against Erivan in June 1804, defeated a Persian force under the Crown Prince, 'Abbas Mirza, and laid siege to the city. A wet autumn, supply difficulties, and skirmishing attacks by the Persian light cavalry, ultimately forced Tsitsianov to raise the siege and retire to Tbilisi.

A contributory cause of this fiasco was a mass uprising which broke out along the Georgian military highway over the Caucasus range, on which the Russians depended for all reinforcements and supplies. This was the first of several spontaneous mass revolts against Russian rule. Its unmistakably popular character distinguished it from earlier movements of protest headed by the Georgian royal house and landed aristocracy.

The immediate reason for the outbreak was the severity of the Russian commandants in the Daryal Pass and Ananuri sectors. The Ossete mountaineers and the villagers of Mtiuleti were forced to toil without payment on the roads and were mercilessly flogged, some dying from their injuries. Others perished from cold in clearing away snow drifts. The peasants broke into revolt and killed the town commandant of Ananuri. The insurgents were joined by contingents of the Khevsurs and other mountain clans. They received encouraging messages from Prince Yulon, who still hoped to win the Georgian throne, and from the Shah of Persia. The rebels defeated a regiment of Don Cossacks sent from the North Caucasian Line, cut communications between Georgia and Russia, and menaced the town of Gori. The onset of autumn and the arrival of Russian reinforcements strengthened Tsitsianov's hand. The insurgents were no match for regular troops, and the revolt was brought under control. Reprisals followed and whole families were shut up in Gori castle and left to perish of hunger and cold.

Despite these difficulties, Tsitsianov did his best to put the social and economic life of Georgia on a sound footing. It had been one of the conditions of the various pacts concluded between Russia and Georgia that the Georgian aristocracy and squirearchy should be confirmed in their traditional privileges, and placed on the same footing as the Russian nobility. Feudalism as practised in Georgia was by no means identical with the Russian system of serf proprietorship, which had reached the high point of its development during the reign of Catherine the Great, and was in many ways indistinguishable from outright slavery. However, Tsitsianov did the best he could to regularise relationships between the Georgian nobles and their vassals, though many grievances and misunderstandings arose under the new dispensation.

Tsitsianov was well aware of the urgency of improving trade and communications, with a view to feeding the Russian garrisons off the land and clothing them from local resources, increasing the customs and excise revenues, and generally making the country self-supporting. The town bourgeoisie were afforded special protection, with inducements to expand their operations. For some years to come, however, the occupation of Georgia entailed a substantial drain on the central Russian treasury. In 1811, for instance, a million silver rubles had to be sent to pay the troops and civil servants stationed in the country.

Education and public amenities were not neglected. Prince Tsitsianov founded a school in Tbilisi for sons of the aristocracy. Special scholarships, notably in medicine, were founded to enable some students to continue their studies at Moscow University. The Georgian printing press which had functioned in Tbilisi until Agha Muhammad Khan destroyed it was now reinstalled. A State-owned apothecary's shop was opened, as well as a botanical garden, since famous throughout Russia. In 1804, a mint was opened in Tbilisi, at which a distinctive Georgian silver and copper coinage was struck until 1834, when the standard Russian coinage was given exclusive currency in Georgia. Public buildings constructed on European lines began to make their appearance in the Georgian capital, while the citizens were encouraged to rebuild those quarters of the town which had been completely laid waste by the Persians in 1795.

With his Georgian ancestry, Tsitsianov fully realized the dangers inherent in over-hasty russification of Georgia's administrative and judicial system. He recommended that the transition from the old oral system of administering justice to the bureaucratic formalism characteristic of Russian official procedure should be brought about by gradual stages. He thought that it would be best to retain the Georgian language as the medium for transacting local official business. However, Tsitsianov set his face firmly against any concession to Georgian national sentiment. Loyalty to the Russian Tsar and his own personal ambition overrode any regard which he might have had for Georgia's glorious past and for her ancient dynasty, the Bagratids. Thus when Count Kochubey, Alexander's liberal-minded minister of the interior, wrote in 1804 to ask whether one of the Georgian royal princes might not after all be set up as a vassal ruler in Georgia under Russian supervision, Tsitsianov at once stifled the project.[24]

The successes won by Tsitsianov and the rapid expansion of Russian influence throughout Transcaucasia were a source of extreme concern to the Ottoman Porte and to the Shah of Persia, as well as to the East India Company and the British Foreign Office. The Shah was at this time in the enviable position of having rival French and British missions in Tehran vying for his favour. In 1805, profiting by Russia's heavy commitments in the struggle against Napoleon in Europe, the Persian crown prince, 'Abbas Mirza, invaded the Karabagh and menaced Elizavetpol. The Russians stood firm, until finally the Shah's forces retired discouraged and without engaging battle.

Prince Tsitsianov now judged the time ripe to extend Russia's dominions to the shores of the Caspian Sea south of the Caucasian range. In January 1806, he marched on Baku. The khan who governed that place as a nominal vassal of the Persian shah feigned submission, and undertook to hand over the keys of the city. As Tsitsianov rode out to meet the khan and his followers, the Persians opened fire and shot him down on the spot. The artillery of the citadel started up a bombardment, and the demoralized and leaderless Russians withdrew. So ended the brief but eventful viceroyalty of this determined proconsul, a renegade to his own people, but a man who, in serving Russia, dealt many a crushing blow to Georgia's traditional enemies.

The decade which followed Tsitsianov's death was less spectacular than these first few years, in which Russian power had spread so rapidly through Transcaucasia. Tsitsianov's successors were less talented than he. The element of surprise which had enabled the Russians to overcome the petty Caucasian states one by one was now lost; the Persian shah and the Turkish sultan were on the alert, and neither the British nor the French could view with approval this Russian wedge being driven down towards Mesopotamia and the Levant on the one side, and towards the Persian Gulf and the Indian Ocean on the other. Furthermore, the Napoleonic wars imposed an immense strain on Russia's resources, and prevented the deployment of large forces in remote Caucasia. Nor can one overlook the deterioration of relations between the native Georgian population and the occupying power, resulting from the exactions of the military commanders and the corrupt ways of Tsarist officialdom.

'Up to 1812,' wrote a staff officer serving at that time in the Russian Army of the Caucasus, 'the Georgians, organized as irregular troops, had served in our ranks virtually as volunteers. A disastrous expedition against Akhaltsikhe, in which they felt themselves to have been sacrificed and abandoned, the resulting misfortunes, combined with requisitions and extortions, drove them to revolt. Rebellion was stifled in blood; but its spirit lived on. Only an entirely new approach can reawaken the fidelity which an odious system has almost extinguished.'[25]

Under Tsitsianov's successors, the war against Persia and Turkey continued with varying success and great ferocity. On the Persian front, Derbent and Baku were at last annexed in 1806, though a second attack on Erivan in 1808 ended in another costly failure. In Western Georgia, the Russians kept up their pressure on the Turks, from whom they took the Black Sea port of Poti in 1809, Sukhum-Kaleh on the coast of Abkhazia in 1810, and the strategic town of Akhalkalaki ('New Town') in south-western Georgia in 1811.

King Solomon II and Napoleon Bonaparte

The remaining independent princes of Western Georgia hastened to accept Russian suzerainty. In 1809, Safar Bey Sharvashidze, the Lord of Abkhazia, was received under Russian protection and confirmed in his principality. Prince Mamia Gurieli, ruler of Guria, was taken under the Russian aegis in 1811, receiving insignia of investiture from the Tsar. Only King Solomon II of Imereti held out to the bitter end.

Encircled by Russian troops, the king strenuously resisted all demands for submission, in spite of the fact that he had earlier, under pressure, sworn fealty to the Tsar. In 1810, the Russians despatched an ultimatum to Solomon, demanding that he hand over the heir to his throne and other Imeretian notables as hostages, and reside permanently under Russian surveillance in his capital at Kutaisi. Solomon refused, and was declared to have forfeited his throne. Hounded by Russian troops and by Georgian princes hostile to him, he sought refuge in the hills, but was soon captured and escorted to Tbilisi. A few weeks later, Solomon staged a dramatic escape from Russian custody, and took refuge with the Turkish pasha at the frontier city of Akhaltsikhe. Inspired by this daring feat, the people of Imereti rose against the Russian invaders. Ten fierce engagements were fought between the Russian forces and the guerillas of Imereti. Famine and plague broke out, and some 30,000 people perished, while hundreds of peasant families sought refuge in Eastern Georgia. Eventually the patriots were crushed by armed force. A Russian administration was set up in Kutaisi, the country placed under martial law.

King Solomon now applied for help to the Shah of Persia, to the Sultan of Turkey, and to Napoleon Bonaparte himself. To the Emperor of the French, Solomon wrote in 1811 that the Muscovite Tsar had unjustly and illegally stripped him of his royal estate, and that it behoved Napoleon, as supreme head of Christendom, to 'take cognizance of the act of pitiless brigandage' which the Russians had committed against him. 'May Your Majesty add to your glorious titles that of Emperor of Asia! But may you deign to liberate me, together with a million Christian souls, from the yoke of the pitiless emperor of Moscow, either by your lofty mediation, or else by the might of your all-powerful arm, and set me beneath the protective shadow of your guardianship!'[26] Napoleon himself was, of course, quite a connoisseur of 'pitiless brigandage'. However, this eloquent plea, which reached him shortly before he set out on his ill-fated campaign to Moscow, provided him with encouraging evidence of the unsettled condition of Russia's Transcaucasian provinces. But as things turned out, Napoleon could not save even his own Grand Army from virtual annihilation, let alone a princeling down in the distant

Caucasus. Without regaining power, Solomon died in exile in 1815, and was buried in the cathedral of Saint Gregory of Nyssa in Trebizond.

The elimination of King Solomon did not bring civil strife in Georgia to an end. No sooner was Western Georgia outwardly pacified than fresh troubles broke out in Kartli and Kakheti. Ten years of Russian occupation had greatly changed the attitude of a people who, a decade before, had welcomed the Russians as deliverers from the infidel Persians and Turks. Called upon to furnish transport, fodder and supplies to the Russian Army at artificially low rates, and regarded by their new masters as mere serfs, the Georgian peasantry looked back wistfully to the bad old days. Under the Georgian kings, though invaded and ravaged by Lezghis, Persians and Turks, their country had at least been their own. Now it was simply an insignificant province, engulfed in a vast, alien empire, whose rulers seemed lacking in sympathy for this cultivated, Christian nation which had voluntarily placed itself under the protection of its northern neighbour.

In their yearning for independence, the Georgians were encouraged by the dauntless personality of Prince Alexander Bagration, son of their great king Erekle II. Alexander, who had sought refuge with the Shah of Persia, was described by a contemporary British traveller as 'a prince whose bold independence of spirit still resists all terms of amity with Russia'. 'It was impossible to look on this intrepid prince, however wild and obdurate, without interest; without that sort of pity and admiration, with which a man might view the royal lion hunted from his hereditary wastes, yet still returning to hover near, and roar in proud loneliness his ceaseless threatenings to the human strangers who had disturbed his reign.'[27]

The revolt of 1812

In 1812, the Persians won some military successes against the Russians in the Karabagh region. When they heard of the Russian setback, the peasants of Kakheti broke into revolt. They wiped out the garrison of Sighnaghi and blockaded Telavi, the capital town of Kakheti. The insurgents proclaimed as king the young Bagratid prince, Grigol, son of Prince Ioane, and grandson of the late King Giorgi XII. In answer to an ultimatum addressed to them by the Russian commander-in-chief, Marquis Philip Paulucci, the rebels replied:

'We know how few we are compared with the Russians, and have no hope of beating them. We wish rather that they would exterminate us. We sought the protection of the Russian Tsar, God gave it to us, but the injustices and cruelty of his servants have driven us to despair. We suffered long! And now, when the Lord has sent us this terrible famine, when we ourselves are eating roots and grass, you violently seize food and forage from us! We have been expelled from our homes. Our storerooms and cellars have been plundered, our stocks of wine uncovered, drunk up and wantonly polluted by the gorged soldiery. Finally our wives and daughters have been defiled before our eyes. How can our lives be dear to us after such ignominy? We are guilty before God and the Russian Tsar of steeping our hands in Christian blood, but God knows that we never plotted to betray the Russians. We were driven to this by violence, and have resolved to die on the spot. We have no hope of pardon, for who will reveal our condition to the emperor? Do we not remember that when we called on the Tsar's name, our rulers would answer: God is on high, the emperor far away.'[28]

The rebellion spread like wildfire. Even the Russian authorities in Tbilisi felt themselves menaced. Prince Alexander Bagration arrived in Daghestan from Persia to mobilize the Lezghis, those inveterate foes of both Georgia and Russia. But Russian reinforcements were hurried to the scene. The rebels lacked cohesion, discipline, supplies. In October 1812, the Russians defeated Alexander and his motley horde at Sighnaghi. A few days later, the daring Russian commander, Kotlyarevsky, crossed the River Araxes and defeated the main Persian Army at Aslanduz, leaving 10,000 of the enemy dead upon the field of battle.

Neither the Russians nor their Persian and Turkish adversaries were in a fit state to continue the struggle. Peace with the Ottoman Empire had already been concluded at Bucarest in May 1812, whereby the Russians handed back to the Turks the Black Sea port of Poti and the strategic town of Akhalkalaki. More favourable to Russia were the terms of the Treaty of Gulistan, concluded between Tsar Alexander I and Fath-'Ali Shah of Persia in 1813, largely through the mediation of the British ambassador to Persia, Sir Gore Ouseley. By this instrument, Russia was confirmed in possession of Eastern and Western Georgia, Daghestan, and the Muslim khanates of Karabagh, Ganja, Shekki, Shirvan, Derbent, Baku and Kuba.

Suppression of the Georgian Church

An event which caused the greatest resentment throughout Georgia, and contributed still further to the deterioration of Russo-Georgian relations, was the suppression in 1811 of the independent Georgian Church. It will be recalled that the Russo-Georgian treaty of 1783 had guaranteed to the Patriarch of Georgia the eighth place among the prelates of Russia and a seat in the Russian Holy Synod. Now, having abolished both the Georgian monarchies, the Russians found that the Church was becoming a focus for Georgian national solidarity. With that same scant regard for treaty rights which it had shown even earlier, the Russian government now sent the Catholicos-Patriarch Antoni II into enforced retirement at St. Petersburg, replacing him by a representative of the Russian Church, the Metropolitan Varlaam, who was given the title of Exarch of Georgia. This complete suppression of a national Church by the government of a friendly Christian power must be without parallel in the modern annals of civilized nations.

Himself a Georgian of noble birth, Varlaam failed to show himself sufficiently obedient to the will of his Russian masters. He was soon replaced by a Russian cleric, Theophilact Rusanov, a man quite alien to Georgian ways. Theophilact regarded his flock as ignorant barbarians, and did his utmost to replace the Georgian liturgy with Slavonic forms of worship. In spite of the Russian bayonets which he had at his disposal, Theophilact encountered strong opposition throughout Georgia. In 1820, the Russians arrested the Archbishops of Gelati and Kutaisi, the principal ecclesiastical leaders of Western Georgia. Archbishop Dositheus of Kutaisi, stabbed and mal-treated by Russian Cossacks, died soon afterwards. Spontaneous uprisings followed these Russian outrages. The insurgents planned to restore the monarchy of Imereti. The upland district of Ratcha was the scene of bitter fighting. The movement also spread into Guria and Mingrelia. An outbreak of civil war in Abkhazia in 1821 further aggravated the situation. The general unrest was not quelled until 1822.

The Russian proconsul in Georgia between 1816 and 1827
was General A. P. Ermolov, one of the heroes of the Napoleonic wars. Ermolov, who had taken part in the battles of
Austerlitz, Borodino and many others, was a man of un-
surpassed courage, spartan in his habits, and adored by his
troops. He declared a war to the death against the Muslim
tribesmen of Daghestan and North Caucasia, and his campaigns, conducted on the good old plan with fire and sword,
the devastation of crops, the sacking of villages, the massacre
of men and the ravishing of women, gave them a lesson which
they doubtless appreciated to the full. Another Russian general
said of Ermolov that 'he was at least as cruel as the natives
themselves'. He himself declared:

'I desire that the terror of my name should guard our frontiers
more potently than chains of fortresses, that my word should be
for the natives a law more inevitable than death. Condescension
in the eyes of Asiatics is a sign of weakness, and out of pure human-
ity I am inexorably severe. One execution saves hundreds of
Russians from destruction, and thousands of Mussulmans from
treason.'[29]

Ermolov's administration resulted in improved public
security within Georgia. A police force was founded in Tbilisi.
Bands of marauding Lezghis dared no longer carry off villagers
into slavery or raid trading caravans. Military and post roads
were built, benefiting trade and communications. Ermolov
had some of the Tbilisi streets paved, and roofed over the
bazaar. The erection of European public buildings helped to
modernize the city's appearance. Similar improvements were
undertaken in Kutaisi, the old capital of Imereti, until now a
decayed and insignificant township.

Economic progress and literary contacts

Now that Russia controlled a stretch of territory extending
from the Black Sea to the Caspian, commerce began to revive.
Odessa in southern Russia was linked by sea with the little
port of Redut-Kaleh in Mingrelia. By this route, manufactured
goods from Russian cities and Western Europe could be trans-
ported via Tbilisi to Baku on the Caspian, or into Persia
overland via Tabriz. Tsar Alexander's edict of 1821 granted to

Russian and foreign concerns operating in Georgia special customs concessions and other privileges for a space of ten years. Tbilisi merchants began to establish connexions with Marseilles, Trieste, and Germany, and to re-export European wares to Persia on a substantial scale. In 1825, Georgian and Armenian traders made purchases totalling over a million rubles at the Leipzig fair; in 1828, the figure exceeded four million. The demand for European manufactured goods was stimulated by the presence in Georgia of a large number of Russian officers and civilian functionaries, with their families. In 1830, an official of the finance department reported from Tbilisi that trade was in the most flourishing condition. British, French and Swiss commercial houses showed interest in this growing market.

Imports of Western manufactured goods, however, far outweighed Georgian exports of raw materials. In 1824, for instance, the Acting French Consul in Tbilisi reported that although Georgia produced timber, cotton, saffron, madder, wax, honey, silk and tobacco, there was little attempt as yet to market these commodities on a large scale. By Western commercial standards, Georgia could not furnish a worthwhile cargo of goods for export at any one time, while acts of piracy by the Circassians and Abkhazians on Black Sea shipping made sea trade hazardous.[30]

General Ermolov did his best to remedy these difficulties. The French Consul, the Chevalier de Gamba, was granted a concession in Imereti to exploit the country's vast timber resources, and to start up cotton plantations. Five hundred families of Swabian peasants from Württemberg arrived in Georgia in 1818. They were encouraged to set up model farmsteads near Tbilisi and elsewhere. They set an admirable example of diligence, thrift and sobriety, which contrasted with the fecklessness of the local inhabitants. But they remained aloof from the population at large, with whom they had nothing in common. They were respected rather than liked, and their influence on the general life and history of Georgia was small. Other branches of industry encouraged by Ermolov were the cultivation of silk in Kakheti, and the production of wine, for which that same province had always been famed. It would, however, be wrong to imagine that Russia benefited financially at this period from her colonization of Georgia. In 1825, her total revenue derived from the country amounted to 580,000 rubles, which did not even pay for the maintenance of the local Russian garrisons and administration.

During the 1820's, the influence of the Russian Finance Minister, Count Kankrin, and the agitation of the Moscow manufacturers led to the triumph of protectionism in Russia generally and the abandonment of any attempt to promote free trade with foreign countries. Tariff walls and similar devices were imposed increasingly for the encouragement of budding home industries. Accordingly, on the expiration of the ten-year customs franchise granted for Georgia by the edict of 1821, this was not renewed; merchandise entering Trans-caucasia was subject now to the same high dues as were levied at Russia's other frontiers. Since no large-scale local factories existed, this return to protectionism simply impoverished the Tbilisi merchants and hampered the growth of Georgian trade. European goods soon began to reach Persia via Trebizond and Erzurum in Turkey, without passing through Russian territory at all. This put a stop for the time being to any increase in Georgia's importance as a stage in the international trade route between Europe and the East.

In the meantime, a series of spectacular events had brought Ermolov's Caucasian viceroyalty to an untimely close. Early in December 1825, news was brought to St. Petersburg of the death of Tsar Alexander I at Taganrog. Immediately, a nation-wide crisis arose over the succession to the imperial throne. The reason for this was that the Grand Duke Constantine, who was governing Poland, had in 1822 formally renounced the succession to the Russian throne in favour of his younger brother Nicholas, though this had been kept a closely guarded state secret. For a time, neither Nicholas nor Constantine would accept the imperial succession, until finally Nicholas was prevailed upon to do so.

Clandestine revolutionary societies had for some years been active among the younger, liberal-minded officers of the Russian army. Many of the conspirators belonged to the fore-most princely families in the land. The unsettled state of public opinion now provided them with what they deemed a propitious moment for their projected coup. On 26 December 1825, when called upon to take the oath of allegiance to the new emperor, Nicholas I, 2,000 soldiers of the Guard formed up outside the Senate building in St. Petersburg, shouting for 'Constantine and Constitution (*konstitutsiya*)' which latter many of the soldiers took for the name of the Grand Duke Constantine's wife. The military governor of St. Petersburg was killed while parleying with the mutineers. Finally, loyal troops were brought up and two volleys of grapeshot cleared the square.[31] The resulting investigation revealed that the conspiracy had wide ramifications throughout Russia. Five of the ringleaders were hanged, and many others exiled to Siberia or sent to serve in the ranks of the army of the Caucasus. Among the many distinguished individuals whose names were mentioned in the course of the enquiry was General Ermolov. In the absence of specific evidence against him, he was left at his post, though under a cloud.

Ermolov was soon under fire from another quarter. In spite of the Treaty of Gulistan, which they had signed under duress in 1813, the Persians had never reconciled themselves to the loss of their Caucasian possessions. In 1825, Ermolov's troops occupied Gokcha, a small and barren frontier district northeast of Erivan in Armenia. This precipitated a crisis. Encouraged by garbled reports of the Decembrist uprising, the Persians decided on an offensive. They were spurred on to action by Prince Alexander Bagration, the exiled Georgian royal prince, whose hatred of Russia overbore any reluctance to subject his native land once more to the horrors of war. In 1826, the Persian Army launched a surprise attack on Georgia and the Karabagh. Pambak, Shuragel and Borchalo were overrun, Elizavetpol (Ganja) captured. Tbilisi itself was menaced.

Ermolov reacted with what can only be termed masterly inactivity. To the urgings of Tsar Nicholas he responded with pleas for reinforcements. The fire seemed to have gone out of the veteran warrior.

It was not long before the dashing General Paskevich arrived to take command in the field. Ermolov was relieved of his post. Paskevich soon routed the Persians completely. The cities of Erivan, Tabriz and Ardebil fell to his victorious army. In February 1828, the Russo-Persian Treaty of Turkmanchai was signed, establishing Russia's frontier on the River Araxes, where it has ever since remained fixed.[32]

The treaty of Turkmanchai eliminated Persia as a factor in Caucasian politics. The warlike tribes of Daghestan were cut off from direct contact with their co-religionists in the Islamic world outside the borders of the Russian Empire. In future, the Muslims of the Caucasus were to look to the Turks alone for support. But the successes won by such commanders as Paskevich meant that the Ottoman Empire, once a mighty world power, was fighting a losing battle to hold the passes giving access to the inner homeland of Anatolia. During the century following the Caspian campaign of Peter the Great, the main chain of the Caucasus mountains had lost its old importance as an impregnable bastion shielding the Middle Eastern lands against invasion from the north. Caucasia had become a base from which Russian political and military power could be directed westward across Anatolia towards the Mediterranean, southward across Persia towards the Indian Ocean, and eastward across the Caspian into the heart of Central Asia.[33]

The conclusion of peace with Persia set Paskevich free to concentrate on Turkish affairs. A general war between Russia and the Ottoman Porte was in prospect. The main Russian objectives were the expulsion of the Turks from the Black Sea coast, and in particular from the ports of Anapa, Poti and Batumi; the reconquest of the former Georgian province of Samtskhe, which had for centuries now been governed by the Turco-Georgian pashas of Akhaltsikhe; and the establishment of a satisfactory frontier which would round off Russia's Transcaucasian dominions and be defensible against Turkish incursions.

The campaign opened in May 1828, with the surrender of the Turkish garrison in Anapa to a combined expedition of the Russian fleet and troops from the Caucasian Line. Relieved of anxiety on the score of his communications with Russia, Paskevich then marched on the famous fortress of Kars, which he captured by storm in June. The next month, the Georgian towns of Khertvisi and Akhalkalaki fell to the Russians, as well as the port of Poti. The key city of Akhaltsikhe was captured in August, while the Turks in Ardahan surrendered without fighting. With autumn coming on, Paskevich suspended operations and retired into winter quarters. He left garrisons in the captured Turkish strongholds, and withdrew with the bulk of his weary forces into bases within Georgia.

During the winter, Paskevich visited his imperial master in St. Petersburg, and impressed upon him the potentialities of an all-out offensive in Asia Minor. The general proposed first to conquer Erzurum and overrun the Armenian highlands; next, to launch a combined operation against Trebizond, with the support of the Russian Navy; and thirdly, to advance into the heart of Anatolia by way of Sivas.

Two untoward events delayed the campaign of 1829. On 11 February, the Russian mission to Tehran, headed by the playwright Griboedov, was hacked to pieces by a frenzied mob of fanatical Persians. Only a display of unwonted moderation by the Russians prevented a fresh outbreak of war with Iran. This moment, too, was chosen by the Turks to launch a counter-offensive in the course of which they reoccupied Ardahan and laid siege to the Russians who manned the citadel of Akhaltsikhe. At the beginning of June, Paskevich resumed the offensive. His brilliant strategy and forceful leadership soon reduced the Turks to a state of demoralization. Within a month, the Russians were before the great Turkish fortress of Erzurum, which the Ottoman seraskier made haste to surrender together with the remnants of his army, one hundred and fifty fortress guns, and vast stores. The conclusion of the Treaty of Adrianople in September 1829, forestalled the complete execution of Paskevich's ambitious plan. The terms of this treaty, dictated by wider issues of European politics, were relatively moderate in regard to the Ottoman Porte's Caucasian dominions. The Russians gained the strongholds of Adsquri, Akhalkalaki and Akhaltsikhe. But the provinces of Erzurum, Bayazid and Kars reverted to the Turks, who also regained Batumi and parts of Guria. The Russians received the ports of Poti and Anapa. The loss of Anapa cut off the Turks from direct access to Circassia, over which the Porte formally renounced all claim to suzerainty.

These spectacular campaigns had the effect of making Georgia an important focus of international affairs. Intellectual life began to revive as Tbilisi became more and more of a cosmopolitan centre. There were frequent contacts between the Georgian aristocracy and visitors from the outside world, both Russians and travellers from Western Europe. The first Georgian newspaper, *Sakartvelos gazeti* or *The Georgian Gazette*, was published between 1819 and 1822. The Russian-language *Tiflisskie vedomosti* or *Tiflis News* started to appear in 1828, with a supplement in Georgian. Associated with this venture was the Georgian publicist Solomon Dodashvili, otherwise known as Dodaev-Magarsky (1805–36), who had attended the University of St. Petersburg and was now a teacher at the government school in Tbilisi. Also prominent in the intellectual life of Georgia was Prince Alexander Chavchavadze (1787–1846), father-in-law of the Russian dramatist Griboedov. Chavchavadze's house in Tbilisi was a meeting place for the cream of Georgian and Russian society. He won renown as a lyric poet, as did Prince Grigol Orbeliani (1800–83), both of them being high-ranking officers in the Russian Army.

After the abortive Decembrist conspiracy of 1825, the Caucasus was used by the Tsar as a milder alternative to Siberia for political offenders. Many of the exiled Decembrists served in the ranks of Paskevich's army. Several of these were poets and novelists of distinction, who found the hospitable atmosphere of Georgia highly congenial. The prevailing cult of Byronism in Russia encouraged a mood of romantic enthusiasm for the snow-capped peaks of the Caucasus, and their valiant, picturesque denizens. As the Russian critic Belinsky observed, 'The Caucasus seems to have been fated to become the cradle of our poetic talents, the inspiration and mentor of their muses, their poetic homeland.' In one of his lyrics, Griboedov describes the charm of Kakheti, 'where the Alazani meanders, indolence and coolness breathe, where in the gardens they collect the tribute of the purple grape.' He started work on a romantic tragedy to be entitled *Georgian Night*, based on a theme from national legend. The great Pushkin was in Georgia in 1829. He was royally feted in Tbilisi, and wrote several lyrics on Georgian subjects. His travel journal, *A Journey to Erzurum*, gives an account of his visit to the marchlands of Turkey in the train of the victorious Paskevich; it contains glimpses of Georgian life, music, poetry and scenic beauty. Some of the brilliant inspiration of the great romantic

M. Yu. Lermontov came to him from Georgia. The poems *Mtsyri* and *Demon* have a Georgian setting, while his ballad *Tamara* presents a lurid if historically false image of the great queen. In another of his poetic works, Lermontov sketches a portrait of a drowsy Georgian countryman, recumbent in the shade of a plane tree, languidly sipping the mellow wine of Kakheti.

But neither the Russian romantic cult of the Caucasus, nor the hospitable welcome extended by Tbilisi society to Russian officers and poets, could efface the deep-seated antagonism which the experience of a generation of Russian rule had implanted in the Georgian nation. There were observers who saw with concern the effect which foreign misrule was having on the Georgian population. One eyewitness, Colonel Rottiers, a Belgian in the Russian service, went so far as to recommend that Russian officials be removed altogether from service in Georgia.

'The Georgians,' he wrote, 'would submit to a governor from among their own nation. They would be happy to see punished, or at least recalled, the officials of whom they have had the most to complain. They ask for an administrative system which extends beyond questions of criminal, civil and commercial law, and would like to have laws based as far as possible on the code of their ancient kings. It is wrong to despise as barbarians a people whose aspirations testify at once to their love of abstract justice, and to so pronounced a sense of nationality. . . . They desire, finally, to be eligible according to merit to posts which up to now have been bestowed by favour alone, and, furthermore, they would like themselves to elect their municipal magistrates, their *mouravs* or justices of the peace. "But," you may say, "these folk are as good as demanding a constitution!" And why not? Those who have seen them at close quarters deem them ripe for this privilege. When it is a question of bestowing liberty on a nation, that is the crucial point at issue.'[34]

The conspiracy of 1832

The moral climate of the 1820's was conducive to romantic nationalism and to movements of revolt against imperial systems. Throughout Europe, the ideals typified by the Holy Alliance and the policies of Metternich and the Russian autocrats were being called in question by thinking men. The activities of the Carbonari in Naples, the liberation movement in Greece, the abortive Decembrist rising in Russia, the Paris revolution of 1830 and the general insurrection in Poland, were all symptoms of a general malaise.

The Georgians had not forgotten their chivalrous days of old, and the general mood of romantic effervescence found response in their hearts. There were also material causes of grievance. Even the higher aristocracy were discontented, especially as the Russian administration had curtailed the landlords' feudal jurisdiction over their peasants and ousted them from participation in local government, as well as questioning the titles of nobility of some of the leading princely families. Continual wars had bled the country white. The Russian writer Griboedov commented in 1828 that 'the recent invasion by the Persians, avenged by Count Paskevich-Erivansky with so much glory for Russia, and the triumphs which he is now winning in the Turkish pashaliks, have cost the Transcaucasian provinces enormous sacrifices, above all Georgia, which has borne a war burden of exceptional magnitude. It is safe to say that from the year 1826 up to the present time she has suffered in the aggregate heavier losses in cereal crops, pack animals and beasts of burden, drovers, etc., than the most flourishing Russian province could have sustained.'[35] The prevailing mood was aptly summed up in a quatrain by Prince Ioane Bagration, son of the last king of Kartlo-Kakheti, Giorgi XII:

> The Scythians [i.e., Russians] have taken from us the entire land, and not even a single serf have they given to us.
> Not satisfied with Kartli and Kakheti, they have added to them even Imereti.
> We have grown poor in misfortune, and have no advocate to whom to turn.
> We ask justice from above; we shall see how God decrees!

A striking portrayal of the results of a generation of Russian rule over Georgia is contained in the report submitted by two Russian senators, Counts Kutaysov and Mechnikov, who carried out an official inspection of Georgia in 1829–30. The state of affairs displayed in this document resembles that so effectively pilloried in Gogol's comedy, *Revizor*, or *The Inspector-General*.

'Not in a single government chancellery in Transcaucasia is there a shadow of that order in the forms and procedure of transacting business which is prescribed by law. In some chancelleries, this is because of their defective organization; in others, because of the incapacity and lack of experience of the officials posted for service there, and the complete absence of personnel capable of efficient work.... The quantity of unresolved lawsuits turned out to be beyond calculation. They had piled up, not because they were submitted in great quantities, but because no efforts were made to bring them to a prompt settlement.'

According to these two senators, Russian officials were volunteering to serve in Georgia simply in order to benefit by the advancement in rank automatically granted as an incentive to undertake a tour of duty in the Caucasus. On arrival there, they spent their period of service in wandering idly from one department to another, and waiting impatiently for the moment to return home. Arbitrary caprice rather than observance of official regulations governed the administration of justice. Thus, the Governor of Tbilisi, P. D. Zavaleysky, and his colleagues, had deprived some proprietors of their lands, and granted these to others, just as they saw fit. 'In Imereti', the senators went on, 'we found abuses of power and acts of extortion.' The main culprits were the head of the local administration, State Councillor Perekrestov, and his colleagues. The senators removed these persons from office and committed them for trial. The general muddle was further aggravated by the right which the Russian commanders-in-chief at Tbilisi had arrogated to themselves of acting as supreme judges of appeal, and sometimes forcing local tribunals to give verdicts against the canons of Russian law, in which nobody therefore had any faith. 'Although certain provinces have been joined to Russia for about thirty years,' the senators continued, 'the administration in Transcaucasia still bears the stamp of the irresponsible, capricious and vague methods of government practised by the former rulers of this country.' This applied particularly to the basis of land tenure and the system of serfdom. 'Some peasants exercise rights of ownership over other peasants, as if they were themselves members of the gentry class. . . . The princes there possess nobles as their vassals, and dispose of their persons as well as of their property.' The dues and services rendered by the peasants to their proprietors were innumerable, and not defined by any law. The lot of the farmers was rendered intolerable by the behaviour of Russian quartermasters. When grain and other supplies needed for the troops were commandeered, often at artificially low prices, payment was frequently withheld and embezzled by the military commanders themselves. There were even cases where the authorities acted as receivers of stolen property, and protected the thieves from prosecution by the rightful owners.

Senators Kutaysov and Mechnikov went on to underline the backward state of the social services and public amenities in Georgia. There were no charitable foundations, orphanages, almshouses, homes for incurables, or lunatic asylums. One small, wretched hospital served the needs of the entire population. Public hygiene and the study of tropical diseases demanded urgent attention. The towns were still dirty and squalid in appearance. There were no regular travel facilities or posting stations. The income of the Georgian Exarchate was not being spent, as it should have been, in keeping the churches under its authority in good repair. The churches in both Eastern Georgia and Imereti were in a wretched and dilapidated condition. Some of these, which the senators recognized as possessing outstanding architectural merit and historical interest, were literally falling down; others had holes in the roof, through which rain poured down upon the worshippers. The senators concluded by informing the emperor that they had uncovered in the administration of Transcaucasia abuses, malpractices and oppression of the people, and had endeavoured to put an end to these once for all. They hoped that the state of Georgia would swiftly take a turn for the better.[36] This hope, as it turned out, was a trifle premature.

It was natural, given these conditions, that the Georgians should have yearned for the removal of Russian dominance and the return of the house of Bagration. The senior members of the Georgian royal family were by now dead, or else for the most part resigned to exclusion from power. An exception was Prince Alexander Bagration, who was still living among the Persians, and ever on the alert for a chance of action against the hated Russians. Within Russia, the spirit of Georgian nationalism was kept alive principally by Okropir Bagration, a younger son of King Giorgi XII and the heroic Queen Mariam, and also by his cousin, Prince Dimitri, son of Yulon. Okropir and Dimitri used to hold gatherings of Georgian students at Moscow and St. Petersburg, and attempted to inspire them with patriotic feeling. A secret society was formed in Tbilisi to work for the re-establishment of an independent kingdom under Bagratid rule. Okropir himself visited Georgia in 1830, and held talks with the principal conspirators, who included members of the princely houses of Orbeliani and Eristavi, as well as the publicist Solomon Dodashvili. They hoped to enlist the support of Western Georgian nationalists who had been active in the revolt in Imereti in 1820. The young Constantine Sharvashidze, a scion of the ruling house of Abkhazia, was also believed sympathetic.

The Georgian conspirators of 1830-32 were not liberal republicans, but rather monarchists and nationalists. Their projected plan of action was melodramatic rather than practical. It was proposed to invite Baron Rosen, who had succeeded Paskevich as commander-in-chief in Georgia, and other members of the garrison and administration, to a grand ball in Tbilisi. At a given signal, they would all be assassinated. The conspirators would then seize the Daryal Pass to prevent reinforcements from arriving from Russia. Prince Alexander Bagration would return from Persia to be proclaimed king of Georgia. Plans for seizing the arsenal and barracks were drawn up, as was the composition of a provisional government.

This rather wild project proved unacceptable to the more moderate members of the group. Many of the Georgian nobles had, after all, friends or relatives by marriage among the Russian residents. The publicist Dodashvili quitted the conspiracy altogether, while the patriot and poet Alexander Chavchavadze refused to support a scheme which depended on the support of Prince Alexander Bagration and his infidel Persians, the murderers of his son-in-law Griboedov. These waverers refrained, however, from disclosing their knowledge to the Russian authorities.

The ball at which the Russian officers were to be assassinated was scheduled for 20 November 1832, the day of the meeting of Georgian princes and nobles at Tbilisi for the election of deputies to the Provincial Assembly of the Nobility. This session was unexpectedly postponed, first to 9 December, then to 20 December.

Early in December, the whole affair was revealed to the authorities by one of the conspirators, who turned 'King's Evidence'. Extensive arrests were made. Commissions of enquiry were set up at Tbilisi and in St. Petersburg. Although ten of the accused were sentenced to death, they were all reprieved. Some of them were deported for a few years to provincial centres in Russia, or enrolled in the ranks of the Russian Army. The writer Dodashvili, already a consumptive, was posted to Vyatka, the harsh climate of which place soon brought him to the grave.

The Emperor Nicholas was perturbed by the well-founded grievances revealed by the commissions of enquiry, and ordered a thorough investigation into the causes of discontent. Most of the conspirators were later allowed to resume their official careers, and one of them, Prince Grigol Orbeliani, rose to be Governor of Tbilisi. The failure of the plot of 1830–32 marks the end of an epoch in Georgian history. All hope for a restoration of the Bagratid dynasty was now lost. The Georgian aristocracy came more and more to identify their own interests with those of the Russian autocratic régime. Georgia sank gradually into a mood of torpid acquiescence, until the economic and intellectual revival which occurred during the viceroyalty of Prince Vorontsov, between 1845 and 1854, paved the way for a fresh upsurge of national consciousness.

CHAPTER IV

TSAR NICHOLAS AND
VICEROY VORONTSOV: 1832–55

*The Murids of Daghestan — Russian reverses — Georgian feudalism
and Russian serfdom — Deus ex machina — Attempts at reform
— Formation of the Caucasian Viceroyalty — Industrial progress —
Decline of the old aristocracy — Literature and the theatre — The
Crimean War — Passing of an autocrat*

The Murids of Daghestan

IT WAS a misfortune for Georgia that the Russian government,
in view of the Polish uprising of 1830, had found it necessary
in the following year to recall Prince Paskevich-Erivansky
from the Caucasus and send him to take charge of operations
in Poland. Paskevich was an exceptionally talented man, who
enjoyed—a rare advantage—the confidence of his captious
imperial master. To quote a British observer, Paskevich
possessed an instinctive knowledge of character, and he completely trusted those whom he employed.

'In his attention to the civil administration he was indefatigable,
and he put a stop to the abuses which had so long disgraced and
ruined Russian affairs. Men of every rank and class had free access
to him; they might bring their own interpreter, and be sure of having justice quickly administered. His loss was deeply felt in Georgia,
which he was rapidly getting into order, and he had nearly succeeded
in bringing the tribes of the Caucasus into pacific relations with the
Russian Government by employing a portion of their troops and
not interfering with their internal government—the only system of
policy, as I often heard from his own lips, that he thought likely
to succeed.'[37]

Paskevich's successor, Baron Grigory Vladimirovich Rosen,

70

was a run-of-the-mill general officer, with no special talent for administration, and no direct access to the emperor. He took over responsibility for both the military command and the civil administration of the Caucasus at a crucial moment; knowing little or nothing about the country, he found himself plunged immediately into a sea of difficulties. The government at St. Petersburg was at this time disturbed by the abuses revealed by the report of Senators Kutaysov and Mechnikov, extracts from which have been quoted already. Then came the abortive conspiracy of the Georgian nobles in 1832, the main victim of which was to have been Rosen himself. On top of this came intensified hostile activity among both the Muslim tribes of the eastern Caucasus, and the Circassians towards the Black Sea.

The Russian annexation of Transcaucasia in the early decades of the nineteenth century helped to excite the militant religious faith of the motley clans of Daghestan. In their Holy War against the Russian invaders, these tribes became involved in a politico-religious movement with puritanical features which, under the name of Muridism, united for a time the majority of the inhabitants of Daghestan and neighbouring Chechnya. Ermolov's ruthless policy of war and extermination helped to instil in these wild mountaineers the courage of desperation; the infidel foreigner became the alien oppressor, and the desire for spiritual reformation was heightened by the urge for temporal liberty.

The first militant leader of the Murids of Daghestan was the Imam Qazi Mullah, who issued in 1829 a general appeal in favour of a Holy War. He set Avaria alight, invaded the north-eastern Caucasus by way of Tarku, and laid siege to the Russian stronghold of Vnezapnaya in Chechnya. He soon afterwards defeated a Russian army under General Emanuel. South of the mountains, Hamzat Bek, afterwards the second Imam of Daghestan, was stirring up rebellion among the Jaro-Belak-anis on the borders of Georgia. The Russians under General Strekalov were severely defeated at Zakatali, and some units were seized with panic and fled for their lives. In 1831, Qazi Mullah and his followers laid siege to Derbent, and then made a daring and successful raid on the town of Kizlyar on the Lower Terek. As Rosen reported to the Russian War Minister,

71

'I arrived here at a time of very great disturbances. Never were the mountain tribes so insolent or so persistent in their undertakings. They are exasperated at what has taken place, and the fact that our actions either resulted in failure, or, when successful, were not followed up, has emboldened them and given scope to Qazi Mullah's false teaching.'

Taking the offensive in 1832, the Russians raided the important *aul* or mountain village of Dargo, on the borders of Chechnya and Daghestan. Qazi Mullah met his death in a Russian attack on the Murid stronghold of Gimri, and was succeeded as Imam by Hamzat Bek. Two years later, in 1834, the new Imam sought to extend his authority by massacring the ruling khans of Avaria and making himself master of their capital, Khunzakh. But retribution soon overtook Hamzat, who was shot down in a mosque by a party of loyal Avars intent on avenging their dead rulers.[38]

Russian reverses

Hamzat was succeeded by a yet more formidable leader, the Imam Shamil, who was to keep the armies of Russia at bay for a quarter of a century. Shamil was a leader whose puritanism and insistence on obedience and sacrifice inspired his followers with fanatical courage. At the same time, the native population not numbered among the Elect often grumbled at being exposed to Russian reprisals, while Shamil's radicalism alarmed the conservative *beks* or tribal chiefs of Daghestan, some of whom were driven out of their estates by the Murids and forced to seek refuge with the Russians.

Shamil began his rule by strangling the boy prince of Avaria and throwing his body over a cliff. Early in 1837, his followers inflicted a severe reverse near Gimri, on a detachment under General Kluge von Klugenau. In the summer, Baron Rosen decided to send an expedition against Shamil's headquarters at Ashilta, which the Russians took in face of the Murids' desperate resistance. A truce was then concluded between the Russians and Shamil. But while the Russian commander alleged that Shamil himself begged for a respite, in reality it was the Russians who were compelled to withdraw owing to the disorganization of the expeditionary corps, the enormous loss in personnel, and the want of ammunition. However, such glowing accounts of this campaign were sent to St. Petersburg that the Emperor Nicholas, when he visited the Caucasus in the autumn of 1837, quite expected to be met by a suppliant Shamil in person. The letter which eventually arrived from the Murid leader was a rude disappointment. 'From the poor writer of this letter, Shamil, who leaves all things in the hand of God. . . . This to inform you that I have finally decided not to go to Tbilisi even though I were cut in pieces for refusing, for I have ofttimes experienced your treachery, and this all men know.'[39] The Tsar was annoyed at this fiasco, responsibility for which he laid at poor Rosen's door.

Rosen's period of command coincided also with a marked revival of anti-Russian activity among the Circassians, in the north-western Caucasus region. Any hope that the Treaty of Adrianople had put an end to Turkish ambitions in that area were speedily dispelled. Although the British Foreign Office refrained from adopting an openly anti-Russian policy, successive British ambassadors to the Sublime Porte, such as Ponsonby (1833-41) and Stratford Canning (1842-58) were on the alert to stir up trouble for Russia all round the Black Sea and in areas adjacent. The Turks were well versed in the intricate politics of the mountain tribes and succeeded in interesting influential Englishmen in the struggle waged by the Circassians against the spread of Russian domination. The British adventurers Longworth and Bell made several trips across the Black Sea to establish contact with the Circassians, to whom they held out hopes of material help and diplomatic support from the British government. Arms and ammunition were smuggled in from Turkey under the noses of Russian gunboats, while the impetuous British diplomat David Urquhart helped to set up a Cherkess political centre in Istanbul.

The Russian governor of Western Georgia, with some 12,000 troops, joined forces in 1835 with General Velyaminov, the commander in northern Caucasia, in an expedition to subdue the Abkhazians and Circassians, and prevent the Turks from landing arms and launching pirate raids on Russian shipping. The effectiveness of the Russian Army in this sector was weakened by the presence within it of thousands of deported Poles who, abominably treated, were constantly on the verge of mutiny. In 1836, the Russians proved unable to protect Kislovodsk in North Caucasia from a raid by some eight hundred Circassians, who also attacked the town of Pyatigorsk. Foreign observers commented on the extravagant losses in blood and in money which the Russians incurred in their efforts to subdue these freedom-loving clansmen by force of arms, when better results could have been secured with time by conciliation and peaceful penetration.

Nor was Baron Rosen very successful in improving the economic and social condition of the Caucasian peoples. He was handicapped, of course, by the withdrawal of the special tariff concession granted for Georgia by the Russian government in 1821. Rosen's attempts to have this renewed met with failure. Thus, instead of being the hub of a trade network connecting Europe with Asia via the Black Sea and the Caspian, Tbilisi became for the time being a commercial backwater, and the Caucasian market served mainly as an outlet for the inferior products of Russian manufacturers. Although a Society for the Encouragement of Rural and Manufacturing Industries and Trade was set up in Tbilisi in 1833, the French Consul there calculated that the total imports of Russia's Trancaucasian provinces sank in value from 12,000,000 francs in 1830 to 5,610,000 in 1834, while exports declined from 5,000,000 francs in value to 1,500,000.[40]

Georgian feudalism and Russian serfdom

As Georgia was a predominantly agricultural country, the peasant question, serfdom, and problems of land tenure were always to the fore. Following the report of Senators Kutaysov and Mechnikov, and the enquiry arising from the abortive conspiracy of 1832, the Russian government tried hard to conciliate the landed proprietors, whom they regarded as the most reliable bulwark of the Russian autocratic system in Georgia.

Baron Rosen unfortunately proved incapable of implementing intelligently the measures decreed by the authorities in St. Petersburg. An example of this occurred in 1834, when the Russian Senate decided that peasants from Western Georgia (Imereti and Mingrelia) who had run away from their masters and taken refuge in Eastern Georgia should, after due investigation, be handed back to their owners. Now the majority of the Imeretian peasants in Eastern Georgia had been there for nearly thirty years. Many had come there during the famine and plague which ravaged their country in 1811-12, often with the active encouragement of their then lords, who had no means of feeding them. In spite of these factors, Rosen carried out the Senate's orders to the letter. Peasant families settled in Eastern Georgia for more than twenty years were forcibly uprooted from their homes by landlords whom they had never met in their lives, and dragged off into a country they had never seen.

'The Imeretian proprietors and the agents of the ruler of Mingrelia, taking advantage of the strict implementation of the above-mentioned measures, resorted during the removal of Imeretian and Mingrelian peasants from Georgia to the most oppressive methods, reducing them to complete ruin through the loss of their property and possessions, so that the majority of these resettled peasants were without clothing or footwear, and were dragged along in winter time together with their wives, babes in arms and other offspring.'[41]

In this way, the Russian authorities endeared themselves to the landed gentry of Western Georgia, though at the expense of the wretched serfs.

As a result of wars, raids and economic stagnation, Georgia was still very under-populated. To remedy this, as well as to rid Russia of troublesome sectarians, the government settled in Transcaucasia a number of dissenting communities such as the Molokans or 'drinkers of milk'. Some of these were exiled to the Black Sea area of Western Georgia, and condemned to certain death in the murderous malarial climate of Mingrelia. Later on, the Molokans were joined by several thousand of the famous sect of the Dukhobors, some of whom settled down near Akhalkalaki, in a region only lately recovered from the Turks. Until the disturbances and persecutions which afflicted the Dukhobor colonies at the end of the nineteenth century, they did sterling work in reclaiming land which had been little better than a wilderness.

In spite of the painful incidents we have cited, the life of the Georgian peasantry at this period was not one of unrelieved oppression and misery. A French observer wrote in 1835 that 'if slavery is a state contrary to nature, and in opposition to modern ideas, in Georgia at least it is fortunately mitigated by the humane character of the masters, who in general treat their men with extreme mildness'. This writer added that Georgian lords hardly ever beat their serfs, since such behaviour was condemned by public opinion; it was even rarer for a Georgian nobleman to have one of his vassals punished by the Russian police, as national pride forbade him to subject his fellow-countrymen to chastisement at the hands of foreigners.[42]

At its best, indeed, the old Georgian feudal system could provide a benevolent, patriarchal way of life. The Georgian poet, Prince Akaki Tsereteli (1840–1915) writes in his auto-biography:

'The relationships which had been introduced long ago in con-nexion with the system of serfdom had entered into the people's very marrow and were treated as law, the breaking of which was deemed a sin. In our country, in contrast to other lands, the feudal relationship was conditional and limited. Serfs knew what their obligations were, masters, what they could require of their serfs, and both sides carried out their duties meticulously. Not all serfs were taxed the same amount by way of quitrent. Some peasant families paid less, some more; certain ones, having paid off their quitrent, received manumission. For instance, the quitrent of one of our peasants was equivalent to half an egg. This peasant used to arrive in the courtyard at the beginning of Shrovetide, would cook his egg in the kitchen, peel off the shell, cut the egg into two equal halves with a horse hair, and hand one half to his lord as his quit-rent. This half-egg quitrent so burdened the peasant that he more than once begged his lord: "Let me off the quitrent, and I will bring you a cow."

'But his master retorted: "The quitrent was fixed by our fore-fathers. I will not cancel it for the sake of a cow, or everyone will say that I was inspired by greed. . . . But if you show your devotion in some other way, perhaps I will remove this quitrent. . . ."

'The peasants themselves firmly insisted on the precise fulfilment of mutual obligations—they were ready to die rather than pay any-thing extra.'[43]

Other landowners were less indulgent. Among the various dues and services which might be required of the peasant were working a stipulated number of days on the lord's private land, helping to build the lord's house or barns, handing over a share of the harvest or of flocks and herds, offering hospitality to the lord's guests and their retinue, gathering and delivering firewood, and providing food for the lord's table at weddings and church festivals. Serfs were debarred from selling property or incurring debts without their master's permission, though this applied only to such transactions as the sale or leasing of houses, fields, and so on, and not to the marketing of farm or garden produce. Particularly irksome was the need to secure the master's consent before a serf was allowed to marry. No journey, needless to say, could be undertaken without the master's permission.

In spite of all this, the Georgian feudal system had its positive features, especially in times of insecurity. Every serf or vassal was to some extent a member of the lord's family or household. When raiding and oppression were rife, this fact helped to compensate for the absence of any effective police system. In sickness or want, it was considered shameful for any landowner not to provide for the dependents of his men. In some cases, both landlords and peasants united in face of the unpopular Russian administration. Baron Rosen once urged some of the Georgian princes to free their vassals, offering them a cash indemnity as inducement. The princes, however, refused to comply, alleging the undertaking given by Tsar Alexander I to respect and preserve Georgia's traditional institutions. They suspected, not without good grounds, that one object of this proposal was to introduce into Georgia the Russian system of conscription, which would be easy to put into effect once the liberated serfs had no lord to defend their interests. Up to that time, the Georgian peasant was called upon to take up arms only when his own village was menaced, and then solely when summoned to battle by his own prince. Faith in the Russian government's sincerity in regard to the abolition of serfdom was somewhat impaired by the behaviour of Baron Rosen himself, who purchased negro slaves in Egypt and brought them to Tbilisi to wait on him in his palace.

Moral questions apart, a charge which could be brought against serfdom in Georgia, as indeed against serfdom gen-erally, was that it impeded the growth of the economy. A French consular report on the commerce and agriculture of Georgia during the year 1836 stresses the continuing lack of agricultural manpower, due to wars, to raids by the Turks and the Caucasian mountaineers, and to the persistence in Western Georgia of trade in captives who were exported to Turkey. Serfdom, the consul considered, encouraged idleness and lack of enterprise, while the primitive construction of Georgian ploughs and other agricultural implements hampered the oxen and retarded improvement in farming methods. The Russian provincial governors and their subordinates were 'vampires who sucked the blood of the peasants, and often that of the hard-pressed local princes'. Government subsidies to agriculture were squandered and misappropriated, and corruption was rife. Areas inhabited by the Caucasian Muslims were better cultivated than those belonging to the Georgian Christian population, perhaps because serfdom had never taken root in the Islamic world.[44]

Observers of the time unite in characterizing Baron Rosen's administration as a period of venality and self-indulgence. The general, a good-natured *bon viveur*, was powerless to check the rapacity of his subordinates. Among the greediest of these was Rosen's own son-in-law, the Georgian prince, Alexander Dadiani, who commanded the Erivan Regiment. This officer made a fortune by hiring out his soldiers as forced labourers and pocketing their wages. In the local offices of the justice department, a regular tariff of bribes existed, nicely graduated in accordance with the value of the service required.

'What can one expect of an administration in which the subordinate officials have no other aim but to enrich themselves, and in which besides there is never the least question of supervision? Each district or province is a satrapy destined to augment its governor's private fortune, just as each regiment is, for its colonel, a collection of men whose various skills he exploits for his own benefit.'[45]

Deus ex machina

Rumours about this state of affairs eventually reached the central government in St. Petersburg. In 1837, the Senator Baron Paul von Hahn, a learned German who had been Governor of Courland, was sent to Georgia on a tour of inspection. In the same year, to the horror of Rosen and his associates, it was learnt that Hahn would soon be followed by his imperial master in person.

The impending arrival of Tsar Nicholas in Tbilisi had an effect similar to that produced on the corrupt mayor and officials in Gogol's comedy *Revizor* by the visit of the Inspector-General from St. Petersburg. Houses were painted, roads hastily mended. In anticipation of the Tsar's arrival, large buildings were swiftly run up to complete unfinished squares. The Georgian princes and notables wanted to arrange a grand ball in the emperor's honour, but found themselves short of 18,000 rubles, which Rosen declined to lend them.

At the end of September 1837, Baron Rosen and his suite set off to meet the Tsar at the little Black Sea port of Redut-Kaleh. Nicholas soon showed that this visit was to be no formal parade. He was determined to see everything and go everywhere himself. So rapid were his movements that his companions found time neither to eat nor to sleep. According to a British visitor,

'The road which leads through the marshy forests of Mingrelia being axle deep in mud, the Emperor had become impatient, and, ordering the escort of Cossacks to dismount, had mounted with his own staff, and proceeded on horseback, riding on a Cossack-saddle, and wearing the black felt *yaponcha* of the natives. All his suite, and the poor old Baron Rosen, had to accompany him. I heard also that the Mingrelian fleas had not respected the person of the Emperor, and had driven him, on one occasion, to take refuge for the night in his carriage.'[46]

After visiting Kutaisi, the capital of Imereti, the Tsar turned southwards towards the city of Akhaltsikhe, taken from the Turks during the war of 1828-29. Near this place, the inhabitants of an entire village were seen kneeling on the road in silence as the emperor drove past, and this circumstance recurred several times. Nicholas enquired of the people what this signified. They replied that the Russian officials had forbidden them to approach him with petitions or complaints. Nicholas told them that this ban was quite unauthorized, and that they might fearlessly present him with their petitions. Thereupon the people poured forth to meet the Tsar in such numbers that during his journey between Akhaltsikhe and Erivan alone, about 1,400 formal complaints were proffered to him.

From Erivan, the chief city in Armenia, Nicholas proceeded

to Tbilisi, where he received from Baron Hahn a report highly critical of Rosen and his methods. Amid the festivities and parades arranged in his honour, the Tsar performed an act designed to strike terror into malefactors in high places. After the dress parade held on 11/23 October 1837, Nicholas formed up all the officers in a circle, into which he summoned Rosen's son-in-law, Prince Alexander Dadiani, colonel of the Erivan Regiment, who was an imperial aide-de-camp and one of the chief profiteers. 'Colonel,' exclaimed the Tsar, 'I am acquainted with all your infamies. You have dishonoured your aide-de-camp's aiguillettes, and are henceforth unworthy to bear them.' Turning to the military governor, Nicholas said: 'General, tear off his aiguillettes, take his sword from him, and have him sent off within two hours to the fortress of Bobruisk.' To the petrified company, the Tsar declared: 'Gentlemen, mark well that this is my first act of justice in Georgia; and it will not be my last.'

Petitions from the nobility and common people continued to pour in. An extent of corruption and injustice was revealed which induced the Tsar to arrest the Tbilisi chief of police and dismiss several generals. Shortly after Nicholas's visit, Rosen was himself relieved of his command, which was entrusted to General Golovin. Baron Hahn stayed behind in Georgia to prepare a scheme for a reorganization of the civil administration of the Caucasian provinces.

During the administrations of Rosen and Golovin, progress was made towards absorbing the remaining autonomous principalities of Western Georgia. In 1833, Michael (Tatarkhan) and Nicholas (Tsiokh) Dadeshkeliani, *mtavars* or ruling princes of Western Upper Svaneti, signed a treaty of protectorate with Russia. Seven years later, in 1840, Eastern Upper Svaneti (the so-called *Free Svaneti*) also became a Russian protectorate. The districts of Dsibelda and Samurzaqano, on the border between Mingrelia and Abkhazia, were also taken over in 1840. Samurzaqano had since 1758 constituted a separate principality, and its last ruling prince was Manuchar Sharvashidze. Not long afterwards, the Dadian or ruling prince of Mingrelia was deprived of his powers of criminal jurisdiction, which he had retained since becoming a vassal of the Tsar in 1803. The criminal code of Mingrelia involved the physical mutilation of offenders. All this was now abolished, and Mingrelian criminal cases were from then onwards dealt with by the Russian tribunal in Imereti at Kutaisi.

Attempts at reform

Baron Hahn returned in due course to St. Petersburg and secured imperial approval for his new scheme of government for Georgia and adjoining provinces. In 1840, he returned to the Caucasus with a mandate to put his system into operation. He stayed for several months and did what he could to cleanse the Augean stables left behind by the previous régime. Unfortunately, Hahn's ideas on administration were ill-adapted to the outlook of the local people. Bred in the traditions of German and Russian bureaucracy, Hahn was all for administrative uniformity and adherence to protocol and procedure. He abolished the use of the Georgian code of King Vakhtang VI as a guide for civil actions, and forced everyone to be governed by Russian laws which were unintelligible to the people. Some of Hahn's ideas were praiseworthy in themselves, but their execution was paralysed by a lack of honest functionaries capable of putting them into effect. The rogues whom Hahn purged were replaced by still worse ones. The new commander-in-chief, General Golovin, was reputed to be an honest man, but was constantly hoodwinked by his underlings. 'It is a state of general pillage,' the French consul reported in despair.[47]

Hahn's attempt to regulate and standardize the amount of dues to be rendered by peasants to their feudal masters proved unpopular. Hahn tried to replace payments in kind and compulsory labour by a cash levy of some seven rubles per head. This measure helped to provoke a general uprising in the Western Georgian province of Guria. The reigning princess of Guria, Sophia, had been driven out by the Russians during the war of 1828–29, and took refuge in Turkey. The principality was annexed to Russia, but the Gurians were far from reconciled to the new order. They now rose *en masse*, expelled the Russian officials, and were only subdued after a violent struggle against 3,000 Russian troops. Tsar Nicholas soon became as impatient with poor Hahn as he had been with old Baron Rosen. Hahn's system was in part abandoned, and its deviser disgraced. Hahn retired in dudgeon to his native Germany, while the Tsar set up in St. Petersburg a special Transcaucasian Committee, the members of which included the Grand Duke Alexander Nikolaevich (the future Tsar Alexander II) and the Minister of War.

During the five years of General Golovin's command, little progress was made in the fierce struggle against the Caucasian mountaineers. In Circassia, forts were built along the coast to cut off the tribesmen from their outlets to the Black Sea. However, almost every month brought news of some Russian detachment that had been cut to pieces by these intrepid horsemen. A general insurrection flared up in 1840, and was not put down without heavy Russian casualties. Further to the east, Shamil's struggle against the Russians continued. There were also rebellions in Kuba and the Karabagh. Between 1840 and 1842, the Russians lost about 5,000 men in numerous encounters with the fanatical Murids. General Grabbe made a successful raid on Shamil's headquarters at Ahulgo, but the Imam made his escape and was able in 1843 to resume the initiative. By that time, General Golovin's army in Daghestan was being depleted through casualties at the rate of 12,000 men a year, apart from the loss of scores of guns and other valuable equipment. The emperor, thoroughly vexed at the course of events, recalled Golovin in December 1842. The Caucasian command was entrusted to the Governor of Moscow, General Neidhardt, an officer who proved no more capable than his predecessor of mastering Shamil and his dogged followers.

Formation of the Caucasian Viceroyalty

Weary of all these muddling mediocrities, as the fuming Tsar regarded his long-suffering Caucasian generals, Nicholas decided at long last that the time had come to appoint a first-class man to take over both military and civil responsibility for the entire area. His choice fell in 1844 upon Count Michael Vorontsov, who had been since 1823 Governor-General of New Russia (i.e. the Ukraine and Crimea) and Bessarabia. Vorontsov was appointed to be both commander-in-chief of the Russian armies on the Caucasian front, and Viceroy of the Tsar with overall administrative authority over the Caucasus.

He was the first of Georgia's governors to be officially invested with the viceregal title.

By his character, reputation and past record, Michael Vorontsov towered above most of his contemporaries. His father, Count Simon Vorontsov, had been for many years Russian ambassador to England, and was noted for his adherence to British Tory principles and his attachment to the younger Pitt. Brought up in London, Michael Vorontsov was a complete Westerner in outlook and education. He won his spurs as a young officer in the Caucasus under Prince Tsitsianov, and went on to distinguish himself against the Turks and in the Napoleonic wars. After Napoleon's defeat, Vorontsov commanded the Russian occupation force in France. Later, as Governor-General of Russia's Black Sea provinces, he was responsible for the rapid development of Odessa. His appointment was well calculated to restore the faith of the Russian public in the prospects of bringing the Circassians and Shamil's highlanders to heel, as well as to instil much-needed confidence into the Georgians and other Caucasian peoples who had suffered under the rule of Vorontsov's mediocre forerunners.

But first Nicholas demanded of Vorontsov some spectacular military action against the insufferable rebels of the mountains. The Tsar's impetuosity drove the viceroy to undertake an ill-fated expedition to Shamil's stronghold of Dargo. The Imam lured the unwieldy Russian force into the ravines and forests of southern Chechnya. Vorontsov occupied Dargo without much difficulty. But he had ventured into a trap. When, without having brought his foe to battle, he attempted to return through the beech forests of Chechnya to his base at Grozny, he found Chechen sharpshooters lurking behind every tree. Horses and baggage were abandoned, and the numbers of wounded and dead grew daily. When finally Vorontsov extricated himself and the famished and threadbare survivors of his force from enemy territory, it was with a loss of 4,000 men, including three generals and 200 other officers. However, he had punctually carried out the orders of his august sovereign, for which he was awarded the title of Prince of the Russian Empire.

Emboldened by this Russian fiasco, Shamil took the offensive himself. His idea was to invade the Kabarda and effect a junction with the Circassians in north-western Caucasia. To do this, he needed to cut the Georgian military highway which led over the Caucasus Range through the Daryal Pass and down to Tbilisi. In the spring of 1846, Shamil set out in force from his highland fastnesses, and crossed the military highway and the River Terek to the north of Vladikavkaz. The Kabardians, however, failed to respond as Shamil had hoped, and their anticipated rising *en masse* against the Russians did not materialize. Owing to the hostility of the local Ossete clansmen, who remained loyal to Russia, the Murids were unable to occupy the Daryal Pass itself. When Shamil and his followers had almost reached Nalchik, the arrival of a Russian force under the vigorous command of General Freitag forced him to retreat south-eastwards to his home base, though without much loss of life on the Murid side. For the next few years, both the Russians and Shamil's men were more or less on the defensive. Shamil remained in possession of most of Daghestan, including Avaria, and of the greater part of Chechnya. Prince Vorontsov, aware that he was not strong enough to deal the Murids a mortal blow in existing conditions, contented himself by strengthening his lines on all sectors pending resumption of a more aggressive policy.

Industrial progress

Meanwhile, he turned his great ability and energy to reforming the civil administration of the Caucasus, in which he achieved notable success. Recalling the period around 1860, it was said by one of Georgia's foremost poets that 'in these years the lustrous memory of Vorontsov lived on still in the hearts of the Georgians.' 'Until the memory of Georgia itself vanishes from the earth, the name of Vorontsov will remain alive,' was a phrase which he had often heard repeated in conversation in the Georgia of those days.[48] Members of the Georgian aristocracy would go out of their way to visit Odessa and call on Prince Vorontsov's widow, *née* Countess Elizabeth Branitskaya, a gracious lady who had in her youth attracted the admiration of the poet Pushkin.

To what, it may be asked, did the Vorontsovs owe this devotion which they inspired among the Georgians, who had usually so little affection for Russian proconsuls sent to govern them in Tbilisi?

The answer is that Vorontsov was one of those few highly-placed Russians who genuinely enjoyed being in Georgia, derived pleasure from the company of Georgians, and evinced a real interest in their language, culture and national past. 'Georgia,' he said on one occasion, 'is a garden, but one which is not like other gardens. A gardener of special talents is needed to tend the flowers which grow in this garden.' Again, he would declare: 'This little Georgia will become in time the most beautiful, the most durable piece of gold brocade woven into the many coloured patchwork of mighty Russia. We must simply give her the chance to develop freely as well as guiding and helping her, but without infringing her primordial customs.'[49] He would receive deputations from the various peoples and communities dwelling under his aegis, listen patiently to their point of view, and do his best to satisfy their grievances and aspirations. All the Georgian nobility was assured of a warm welcome at the viceregal palace. In 1848, that same Georgian aristocracy which had plotted together less than two decades previously to exterminate the Russian garrison and administration was sending a loyal address to the Tsar, protesting undying attachment to the Russian fatherland.

Vorontsov was no social reformer. The iron hand of Tsar Nicholas the autocrat gave him no scope in this direction, even had he been so inclined. But more than reform, Georgia needed justice, prosperity, order, education. Here Vorontsov excelled. He instilled some efficiency into the Russian bureaucratic machine, and punished corruption. He built bridges and roads, and improved communications. He patronized schools, had a theatre built in Tbilisi, and vastly increased the output of journals, newspapers and books, both in Russian and in Georgian. He encouraged the founding of the Tbilisi Public Library and the Caucasian branch of the Russian Geographical Society.

Vorontsov devoted much attention to commerce. He persuaded the Russian Finance Ministry to restore the customs concessions facilitating transit trade through Georgia between Europe and the East. He supported the merchant and craft guilds of Tbilisi and Gori, while at the same time enabling entrepreneurs to start up several modern factories. A trading depot was established at Tbilisi in 1847 by a syndicate of Russian manufacturers, as well as warehouses and showrooms. The number of industrial organizations in Georgia grew between 1843 and 1850 by 94 per cent., while their total output went up by 105 per cent. There thus existed in Georgia in 1850 some 132 industrial enterprises, with a total production valued at 256,000 rubles. Growth over the next few years continued at a rapid rate, so that by 1864, when serfdom was abolished in Georgia, there existed 465 factories and industrial concerns of various kinds, with a production worth over 860,000 rubles.[50] Vorontsov also tried to improve methods of farming, viniculture, cotton planting and silk raising. A branch of the Russian Agricultural Society was founded in Tbilisi.

Decline of the old aristocracy

As usually occurs during the transition from an agricultural and pastoral to an industrial society, the landed proprietors began to feel the pinch. In 1852, Prince Vorontsov reported that 'the nobility have constantly had to sell their estates because of inability to pay extortionate rates of interest on debts incurred with private usurers, so that many of the most ancient and honoured of the local aristocratic houses have gradually sunk into poverty'. Prince Vorontsov was himself sometimes accused of having deliberately sapped the power and prosperity of the Georgian nobility by encouraging them to attend balls, theatrical displays and public functions, and by introducing into Georgia all manner of European luxuries which they could not afford. It is doubtful, however, whether the convivial Georgians required much inducement to engage in social activities and enjoy the good things of life. In reality, the causes of their impoverishment lie far deeper, being bound up with the economic evolution of the Russian Empire, indeed of Europe as a whole. It was during the reign of Nicholas I, which lasted from 1825 to 1855, that the industrial revolution really got under way in Russia. Landed property ceased to be the sole source of wealth and influence. In spite of the shortage of free labour, and the shackles of serfdom, Russia's industrial production quadrupled in thirty years.

It was industrial progress as much as humanitarian considerations which made feudalism and serfdom appear burdensome relics of a vanishing age.

The landed gentry in Georgia were not equipped, either by temperament or by upbringing, to cope with the changing order of things. The traditional occupations of a gentleman were hunting and fighting. The amassing of money and attention to household or industrial management were beneath his dignity, while a rustic simplicity characterized the lives of even the most exalted families. The satirical book by Prince Ioane Bagration (1772–1830), called *Kalmasoba* or *The Alms-Collecting Tour*, contains an account of a visit to the Dadian or ruling prince of Mingrelia, who liked to spend the fishing season in a roofless, floorless house by the River Rioni, which afforded him shelter only from the wind. The Dadian observing that sixty days' more rain fell in Mingrelia than in any other country, one of the characters exclaims: 'Sir Dadian! In that case you, the ruler of this land, are excused from building any bath-houses!' In the good old days, a Georgian noble was provided with all necessities of life by the resources of his own estates and the offerings of his vassals and serfs. Without spending a penny in hard cash, he received unlimited food, drink, clothing, footwear, arms, cattle, furniture and so on. Some landed proprietors even numbered among their followers Armenian and Jewish hawkers, who supplied them gratis with tea, sugar, coffee, rice, candles and olive oil. The possession of money was considered plebeian. Akaki Tsereteli the poet relates in his reminiscences how, as a young cadet, he once rejected out of pride a pocketful of gold ducats offered to him as a gift by Princess Vorontsov herself. It is scarcely surprising that the wealth of the country passed as time went on into the pockets of the new middle-class merchants and entrepreneurs, including many Armenians, Russians, Muslims and Jews, who were burdened by no such delicate scruples.

Symptomatic of the social and economic trends of the time is the remarkable novel *Solomon Isakich Mejghanuashvili* by Lavrenti Ardaziani (1815–70). The hero, a Caucasian Scrooge or Shylock living in the Tbilisi Armenian milieu, starts modestly as a small tradesman, and then turns to money lending. 'Six years went by,' he says, 'and through all Kartli, on both banks of the

Kura, there was not one village left which did not owe me money.' Later, the aristocracy also fell into his clutches. From then on, Solomon became an honoured pillar of the establishment. Like Molière's Monsieur Jourdain, his aim was now to become accepted in high society and have his daughter marry a prince. The story of his chequered career, with its realistic portrayal of social life in old Tbilisi, is full of satirical touches. A contrast to the character of Solomon is provided by the well-bred aristocrat, Prince Alexander Raindidze, an enlightened man who believes in treating serfs humanely, but cannot bring himself to favour freeing them altogether.

Literature and the theatre

The decline of old patriarchal and heroic patterns of life, the imposition of alien rule, and the growth of a new economic order fostered the nostalgic, elegiac mood characteristic of several of the outstanding Georgian poets of this period. The all-pervading cult of Byronism, combined with pride in Georgia's glorious past, produced a spirit of defiant, romantic patriotism, tinged at times with morbid gloom, at others with radiant hope in a better future.

The poetic genius of the Georgian romantics shines brightest of all in the work of the young bard Nicholas Baratashvili (1817–45), whose verse is full of profound philosophical thought and a deep sadness, inspired both by the destiny of his country and his own unhappy life. His soul melts in tears in his poems, the vanity of life drives him almost to despair. But he is no passive fatalist, no pessimist; his faith in a better future stands out clearly in his verse. Most famous of his works, perhaps, is *My Steed* (*Merani*), in which the poet's mood of restless turmoil finds vigorous expression.

It runs; it flies; it bears me on; it heeds no trail nor spoor;
A raven black behind me croaks with ominous eyes of doom.
Speed thee on and onward fly with a gallop that knows no bound,
Fling to the winds my stormy thoughts in raging darkness found.
Go onward! onward! cleaving through the roaring wind and rain
O'er many a mount and many a plain, short'ning my days of pain.
Seek not shelter, my flying steed, from scorching skies or storm;
Pity not thy rider sad, by self-immolation worn.

88

I bid farewell to parents, kin, to friends and sweet-heart dear
Whose gentle voice did soothe my hopes to a hot and bitter tear.
Where the night falls, there let it dawn, there let my country be;
Only the heavenly stars above my open heart will see.

The sighs that burn, that rend the heart to violent waves I hurl;
To thy inspired, wild maddened flight love's waning passions
   whirl.
Speed thee on, and onward fly with a gallop that knows no bound,
Fling to the winds my stormy thoughts, in raging darkness found.

In foreign lands thou lay me low, not where my fathers sleep,
Nor shed thou tears, nor grieve, my love, nor o'er my body weep;
Ravens grim will dig my grave and whirlwinds wind a shroud
There, on desert plains where winds will howl in wailings loud.

No lover's tears but only dew will moist my bed of gloom;
No dirge but vultures' shrieks will sound above my lowly tomb.
Bear me far beyond the bounds of fate, my Merani,
Fate whose slave I never was, and henceforth—ne'er shall be!

By fate repulsed, oh bury me in a dark and lonely grave.
My bloody foe, I fear thee not—thy flashing sword I brave.
Speed thee on and onward fly with a gallop that knows no bound,
Fling to the winds my stormy thoughts in raging darkness found.

The yearnings of my restless soul will not in vain have glowed.
For, dashing on, my steed has paved a new untrodden road.
He who follows in our wake, a smoother path will find;
Daring all, his fateful steed shall leave dark fate behind.

It runs; it flies; it bears me on; it heeds no trail nor spoor;
A raven black behind me croaks with ominous eyes of doom.
Speed thee on and onward fly with a gallop that knows no bound,
Fling to the winds my stormy thoughts, in raging darkness
   found.[51]

From this period also dates the birth of modern Georgian
drama. In 1845, a Russian theatre with professional repertory
company was opened in Tbilisi. This stimulated the Georgians
to emulation. With the encouragement of Prince Vorontsov, a
Georgian amateur dramatic society was formed, under the
direction of the talented playwright Giorgi Eristavi. On 2
January 1850, in the great hall of the Tbilisi High School, the
company made its debut in Eristavi's comedy *The Share-out*
(*Gaqra*), a play which gave a humorous satirical view of life
among the Georgian squirearchy. This venture was greeted

with great enthusiasm, so that in May, Eristavi staged another of his comedies, *The Lawsuit* (*Dava*). Eristavi then formed a professional company, which was granted a subsidy of 4,000 rubles a year, and the use of the Russian theatre building. The professional company's first night took place on 1 January 1851. Later on, it was able to stage its performances in the fine new theatre in Erivan Square, which held seven hundred spectators. The repertoire was composed largely of original plays by Eristavi and other contemporary Georgian writers, as well as a few dramas translated from the Russian, and an adaptation of Molière's *Le Médecin malgré lui*.

The bold satirical tone of some of the original plays put on by the young Georgian troupe annoyed diehards among both the Georgian landowners and the Russian bureaucrats. Eristavi eventually resigned. After Prince Vorontsov's departure from Tbilisi in 1854, the company fell on evil days. Two years later, official coolness and the clamour of unpaid creditors brought this first Georgian professional theatrical company to an untimely end. But its period of activity marks an important stage in Georgian literary and social history, as well as in the reawakening of Georgian national consciousness.

Another significant trend in Georgian intellectual life at this period was the revival of scholarly interest in the country's historical past. Among the pioneers in this movement were Prince Ioane Bagration and his brother Teimuraz, sons of the last King of Eastern Georgia, Giorgi XII. Prince Teimuraz (1782–1846) composed a history of Iberia (i.e. Georgia), and was elected an honorary member of the Imperial Academy of Sciences in St. Petersburg. He was a friend and collaborator of the French scholar Marie-Félicité Brosset (1802–80), who worked for over forty years in Russia and placed the study of Georgian and Armenian history on a scholarly footing. Brosset translated and edited Prince Vakhushti's classic geographical description of Georgia, as well as the entire corpus of the Georgian annals. He visited Georgia during the viceroyalty of Prince Vorontsov, who joined with local notables in encouraging his work, helping him to search out and edit ancient charters and record inscriptions on churches and ancient monuments.

Other noteworthy Georgian scholars of the time included David Chubinashvili or Chubinov (1814–91), Professor of

Georgian at St. Petersburg University, who brought out valuable Georgian dictionaries and an anthology of Georgian literature, and assisted M.-F. Brosset in editing the Georgian annals; also Platon Ioseliani, the Tbilisi antiquary, who wrote a brief history of the Georgian Church, a life of King Giorgi XII, and studies of ancient Georgian cities. On a broader plane, interest in the history and civilization of Georgia was stimulated by the launching of the Georgian magazine *Tsiskari (The Dawn)*, the Russian magazine *Kavkaz (The Caucasus)*, and the invaluable annual almanach *Kavkazsky Kalendar (Calendar of the Caucasus)*. These Tbilisi periodicals set a very high standard.

The Crimean War

In 1853, during the last months of Vorontsov's viceroyalty, Georgia was once more involved in the alarums of battle. The inadequacies of Russia's military machine and backward economic and social system were now to be revealed in a conflict with a rearmed Ottoman Empire supported, albeit inefficiently, by a concert of Western powers. In the Crimean War, as in other Russo-Turkish wars, events on the Caucasian front played an important, if secondary role. In anticipation of the outbreak of armed conflict, the Turks had fortified Trebizond, Erzurum and Batumi. Special attention was paid to Kars, which, commanded by Colonel Fenwick Williams of the Royal Engineers, was turned into a fortified camp of great strength. During the summer of 1853, the Turks concentrated substantial forces along their Caucasian frontier. In addition to keeping watch on this line, the Russians had large bodies of troops tied down in north-western Caucasia, to counter activity by the Circassians, and in the eastern Caucasus, in expectation of renewed forays by Shamil and his Murids against the Russian garrisons in Chechnya and Daghestan, and against the Eastern Georgian province of Kakheti.

The first important engagement was in fact an attack on Kakheti by the Imam Shamil with 10,000 or more mountaineers in August 1853, but this was beaten off by a Russian force under Prince Argutinsky-Dolgorukov. At the end of October, the Turkish offensive began in earnest. Parts of Guria were occupied, but attacks on the towns of Akhaltsikhe, Adsquri and Akhalkalaki were repulsed. On 1 December, Prince V. O.

Bebutov with 10,000 men, including a large contingent of Georgian troops, signally defeated a Turkish army some 36,000 strong, and sent the survivors streaming back into Kars. This engagement occurred the day after Admiral Nakhimov destroyed the Turkish fleet at Sinope on the Black Sea, thus precipitating the entry of Britain and France into the war.

As the new year of 1854 opened, the septuagenarian viceroy felt his physical powers to be waning. In March, Vorontsov left on sick leave for Western Europe, never to return. He submitted his resignation to the emperor the following October, and died, full of honours, in 1856.

On the Russo-Turkish border, the campaign of 1854 was largely indecisive, except for a defeat inflicted by the Russians on the Turks at the village of Kurudere, between Kars and Alexandropol. At the eastern end of the Caucasus, Shamil and his Murids were emboldened to launch another assault on Kakheti. They descended into the Alazani valley, but failed to capture any of the Russian posts guarding the Lezghian line. On 16 July, Prince David Chavchavadze routed the Murid horde at Shilda. Shamil's only success in this operation was his raid on Prince Chavchavadze's mansion at Tsinandali, whence he abducted the prince's wife and her sister, Princess Orbeliani, as well as slaughtering or kidnapping other members of their family and entourage. A few months later, the surviving captives were handed back in exchange for Shamil's own son Jamal-al-Din, who had been taken prisoner by the Russians in 1839 and brought up at St. Petersburg with honour and distinction. The young man had been made colonel of a regiment and aide-de-camp to the Tsar; restored reluctantly to the savage life of his primitive compatriots, he soon pined away and died.

Under the new viceroy, Count N. N. Muraviev, military operations on the Caucasian front in 1855 took on a more active look. After bloody and desperate fighting, the great fortress of Kars capitulated to the Russians in November. But meanwhile the Russians had been taken in the rear by Turkish forces under Omar Pasha, who landed at Sukhumi in Abkhazia and occupied a strip of Western Georgia's Black Sea littoral. Omar Pasha occupied the Mingrelian capital of Zugdidi and prepared to advance on the main city of Western Georgia, Kutaisi. But he had reckoned without the torrential rain and pestilential vapours typical of the Mingrelian climate. Soon his troops were without bread and his animals without forage, and his army was bogged down in the Mingrelian quagmire. The local princes and their predominantly Christian peasantry showed no inclination to rise in revolt against the Russians and join the Turks, from whom they had suffered much tyranny in earlier periods. In spite of the incompetence of the local Russian commander, who was the Georgian prince Ivane Bagration-Mukhransky, Omar's campaign gradually petered out. The signing of the Treaty of Paris, which concluded the Crimean War in 1856, prevented Muraviev from following up his success at Kars, and redeeming the disgrace inflicted on Russia by the fall of Sebastopol in the Crimea.

Passing of an autocrat

Nicholas I, martinet that he was, claimed to have given Russia prosperity and good order at home, power and prestige abroad, and predominance in the affairs of Europe and the world. The disasters of the Crimean War dissipated these fond illusions. 'War,' a contemporary remarked, 'opened our eyes, and things appeared to us in their true guise.' In February 1855, the autocrat caught a chill; on March 2, he was dead. As Nicholas admitted on his death-bed, he was handing over command to his successor in a pretty bad state.

Thanks largely to Prince Vorontsov, the closing years of the reign had, for Georgia at least, their brighter side. Now that most of the country had been thoroughly subjugated from a military viewpoint, it could be peacefully assimilated into the Tsarist system, and the old arbitrary methods of military government replaced by more civilized methods of administration. These years, viewed in historical perspective, mark a turning point in the country's economic and social life. The decay of the old feudal system became daily more apparent. The growth of capitalism, combined with changes in public opinion produced by contact with European ideas, showed that traditional forms of agrarian and manorial economy, based on serf labour and the individual craftsman, were doomed. The spread of education combined with resurgence of national pride to produce a new and vigorous Georgian intellectual life which was to manifest itself increasingly during the second half of the century.

CHAPTER V

SOCIAL CHANGE AND NATIONAL AWAKENING: 1855–94

Alexander II and the liberation of the serfs

RUSSIA'S NEW SOVEREIGN, Alexander II, was at heart an honest conservative, forced by the logic of events to place in the forefront of his programme the liberation of the serfs. The humiliations of the Crimean War had exposed the bankruptcy of the old order, while the growth of industry in Russia underlined the chronic shortage of free labour. Enlightened public opinion, both at home and abroad, clamoured for the abolition of a system which reduced the bulk of the population of a European state to a condition similar to that of the mediaeval villein, or even to that of negro slaves on the American plantations. In 1856, on announcing the conclusion of peace, Alexander directed all thoughts to reform.

'May Russia's internal welfare be established and perfected; may justice and mercy reign in her law courts; may the desire for instruction and all useful work grow everywhere with new strength; and may everyone enjoy in peace the fruits of honest labour under the shelter of laws equally just to all, equally protecting all.'

To the Governor-General of Moscow, who expressed alarm at

the implications of these amiable generalities, the Tsar replied: 'Better to abolish serfdom from above than to wait till it begins to abolish itself from below.'[52] For the next five years, both government and public opinion in Russia were occupied with preparations for the peasant reform of 1861 which, after some delay, was to be applied also to Russia's dominions beyond the Caucasus.

Shamil capitulates

In the meantime, there remained in the Caucasus defiant tribes who preferred their own native brand of liberty to any which the Russian Tsar might graciously provide. The termination of the Crimean War set free the Russian military command to terminate once for all the menace of the warrior Shamil and his Murids. Prince Baryatinsky, who succeeded Count Muraviev as viceroy of the Caucasus in 1856, worked out a systematic plan for the reduction of Daghestan. Its rapid success took the Russians themselves by surprise. Shamil's authority had for some time been waning, so that the Russians, who had greatly improved their communications system, were able to cut off the Murids from their sources of supply and gradually to squeeze them out of one redoubt after another. In August 1859, after a quarter of a century's desperate resistance, the terrible Imam was brought to bay. Surrounded on the rocky brow of Gunib, the surviving five hundred Murids put up a determined fight until, seeing the situation to be hopeless, Shamil surrendered to the Russian viceroy in person, and was sent into honourable exile at Kaluga in Russia.

Simultaneously, the Russians were actively extending their grip over those areas of western Caucasia which still retained some vestige of independence.

The integration of Western Georgia

It was at this period that Mingrelia, the Colchis of the ancients, finally lost its autonomy. It will be recalled that the Dadian or ruling prince of Mingrelia had been placed under a Russian protectorate in 1803, but had retained a large measure of authority as a vassal of the emperor. During the Turkish invasion under Omar Pasha in 1855–56, the Regent of Mingrelia, Catherine Dadiani, showed attachment to the Russian cause, and organized a militia to help drive out the intruders. This invasion imposed a severe strain on the Mingrelian economy, and particularly on the peasants. When the Turks withdrew, the landowners attempted to reimpose their authority on their serfs, but were met with defiance. A peasant revolt broke out, led by a blacksmith named Utu Mikava. Most of Mingrelia was reduced to a state of turmoil. In the end, both parties welcomed Russian intervention—the landowners to safeguard their lives and property, the serfs in the hope of being guaranteed a status approximating to that enjoyed by crown peasants in Russia. Fate thus played into the hands of the Russian authorities, who sent in 1857 a commission to Mingrelia, and removed the Regent Catherine from office. A Russian-dominated Council of Regency was set up, nominally in the interests of the youthful heir, Nicholas Dadiani. In 1867, when Nicholas attained his majority, he was compelled to cede all his sovereign rights to the Tsar in exchange for 1,000,000 rubles, a grant of estates in Russia, and the title of Prince Dadian-Mingrelsky. The principality of Mingrelia thus became an integral part of the Russian empire.

A like fate soon overtook the free mountaineers of Upper Svaneti, high up in the Caucasus range looking down over Imereti and Mingrelia. The Russians had long been irked by the rebellious attitude of the Svanian princes, who spent their ample leisure in prosecuting blood feuds against one another, and in intrigues with Omar Pasha's invading Turks. In 1857, Prince Baryatinsky ordered Svaneti to be subdued by armed force, despite the existence of the treaties of 1833 and 1840, which established a protectorate over the principality of Western Upper Svaneti and the self-governing tribal area of Free (Eastern Upper) Svaneti. The ruling prince of Western Upper Svaneti was exiled to Erivan in Armenia. On his way to banishment, this Svanian prince, Constantine Dadeshkeliani by name, came to Kutaisi for a farewell audience with the Governor-General of Western Georgia, Prince Alexander Gagarin, a jovial man and a good administrator, who had built a boulevard and two bridges over the Rioni at Kutaisi and embellished the town with a public garden. At this interview, Constantine Dadeshkeliani suddenly drew his dagger and stabbed to death the Russian general and three of his staff.

When captured, he was summarily tried by court martial and shot. In 1858, the whole of Upper Svaneti was annexed to the Russian viceroyalty of the Caucasus. Thus ended the independent existence of this renowned nation of fighters and hunters, mentioned with respect by Strabo and the ancients, but sunk in more recent times into squalor and ignorance from which contact with European ways has only lately begun to redeem them.

The Russians were now able to subjugate Abkhazia, the autonomous principality situated immediately north-west of Mingrelia along the Black Sea coastline. It will be recalled that the Lord of Abkhazia, Safar Bey or Giorgi Sharvashidze, had been received under Russian protection as long ago as 1809, and confirmed in perpetual possession of his domains. In the intervening period, Abkhazia had been frequently involved in the Russian campaigns against the Circassians, with whom the Abkhaz, many of them Muslims, had cultural, ethnic and linguistic connexions. During the Crimean War, the Turks stirred up the Abkhaz against Russia at the time of Omar Pasha's invasion of Mingrelia. Turkish envoys who arrived at the Abkhazian capital, Sukhumi, found the ruling dynasty of the Sharvashidzes divided: the Christian princes adhered to the Russian interest, but Iskander (Alexander), a Muslim, was prepared to help the Turks in return for permission to annex the neighbouring Mingrelian district of Samurzaqano. Omar Pasha had subsequently landed at Sukhumi, from which he advanced south-eastwards into Mingrelia. After the Crimean War was over, the Russians looked for a chance of extending their direct rule to Abkhazia. In 1864, they deposed the ruling prince, Michael Sharvashidze, and annexed his country by force of arms. Two years later, the Abkhaz staged a general revolt against their new masters, and recaptured their capital, Sukhumi. The Russians had to send 8,000 troops to quell this rising, which was suppressed with heavy loss of life.

The subjugation of Abkhazia coincided with Russia's annihilation of the national existence of the Circassians, that valiant North Caucasian people who had for a century been a thorn in the side of Tsarist colonialism. Cut off since the Crimean War from contact with Turkey and the Western

European powers, the Circassians were no match for Russia's military might, especially after the surrender of Shamil and the Murids of Daghestan. In Chechnya and Daghestan, the Russians were satisfied with the submission of the local population to Russian law. But on the Black Sea coast, their plans involved the seizure of the wide and fertile Cherkess lands to provide for a part of the wave of Russian peasant migration which resulted from the emancipation of the serfs in 1861. The Russian government conceived the drastic project of enforcing the mass migration of the Circassians to other regions of the empire or, if they preferred, to Ottoman Turkey. The last shots in the long series of Russo-Circassian conflicts were fired in 1864. Rather than remain under infidel rule, some 600,000 Circassian Muslims emigrated to various regions of the Ottoman Empire, where their descendants may be found to this day. Many of the Russian, German, Greek and Bulgarian colonists who were endowed with the tribal lands of the Circassians near the Black Sea coast proved unable to endure the sub-tropical climate, and the wilderness invaded the orchards and gardens once cultivated by prosperous and highly civilized Circassian communities.

The peasant question in Georgia

While the emancipation of the serfs in European Russia did not for the time being affect conditions in Georgia and other regions of Caucasia, its application there was seen to be only a matter of time. We have already spoken of the economic and social changes which took place in Georgia towards the middle of the nineteenth century, and which gathered momentum under the viceroyalty of Prince Vorontsov. Patriarchal customs unchallenged over the centuries were breaking down as the Georgian people came into contact with European ways and acquired new tastes and habits. In 1858, the port of Poti was opened for Black Sea shipping, replacing the inferior anchorage of Redut-Kaleh. Agricultural exhibitions were held with increasing frequency, and silk, tobacco and cotton produced in substantial quantities. More corn had to be brought in to feed the growing population, while maize and wine were exported in bulk. From the 1840's onwards, the Georgians grew potatoes, cabbages and tea—the latter being introduced from

China in 1845. Foreign capital was put into silk farms in Western Georgia. Iron foundries, brick works, glass works, a steam sawmill, helped to provide new occupations for the townsfolk. Landowners often loaned out their serfs to factories and plantations on a seasonal basis, in return for a cash payment. Many peasants were able to save up and purchase their freedom. There was an increasing tendency for feudal dues in labour or in kind to be commuted into a money payment. The basis of the old manorial economy was correspondingly weakened, while the improvidence of the Georgian gentry resulted in the forced sale or mortgaging of a large portion of their estates.

The steady increase in the population of Georgia meant that by the 1850's, land hunger was becoming acute. It is reckoned that at the beginning of the nineteenth century, the average peasant holding amounted to from ten to twenty *desyatins* (one *desyatin* = 2·7 acres); by the time the Georgian serfs were freed, in 1864, the average holding had sunk to between five and six *desyatins*. The position was made worse by the seizure of communal lands, forests and pastures by the State and by powerful landowners. A class of rich peasants or *kulaks* was starting to emerge, with the inevitable concomitant of a poverty-stricken rustic proletariat. The so-called 'class struggle' in the Georgian countryside resulted in sporadic revolts and deeds of violence. Peasant unrest broke into disorders in Imereti in 1857, in Guria in 1862, in the Ksani valley and around Surami in Kartli in 1863, and near Tbilisi itself in 1864.

The rise of the Georgian intelligentsia

The Georgian peasant had vigorous champions among the younger generation of intellectuals, many of whom belonged to leading aristocratic families. The freer access to Russian universities which was one of the beneficial consequences of the educational policy of Alexander II in his early years made it possible for Georgian students to study at Moscow and St. Petersburg. Contact with the writings of such pioneer radicals as Belinsky and Herzen, and the personal influence of the fearless progressives Chernyshevsky and Dobrolyubov, soon produced in these Georgian students a state of mind highly critical towards Tsarist autocracy, the institution of serfdom, and the patriarchal ways which they had taken for granted in their native Georgia. These young Georgian intellectuals were known as 'Tergdaleulis', signifying 'those who had drunk from the River Terek', i.e., had crossed the Terek and gone for their education to Russia; among them were Ilia Chavchavadze, Akaki Tsereteli, Niko Nikoladze, Raphael Eristavi, Iakob Gogebashvili—in fact, almost all the young men who were to lead Georgia's literary, political and scholarly life during the following half century. Several of them joined with the Russian students at St. Petersburg University in the political demonstrations of 1861, and paid for their audacity with a few painful months in Kronstadt fortress.

The first notable production of the new school in Georgian literature was the short novel *Suramis tsikhe (Surami Castle)* by Daniel Chonkadze (1830–60), who was the son of a poor priest who had himself begun life as a serf. For censorship reasons, this remarkable tale was given a mediaeval setting. Its message was none the less clearly understood by contemporaries. Serfdom as practised in Georgia is depicted by Chonkadze, not without a measure of exaggeration, as the rule of darkness and superstition, brutal violence and unchecked wickedness. The princes refuse to recognize peasants as human beings. 'They imagine that we are incapable of loving or hating, they deem us without hearts or the faculty of thought.' In one chapter, a prince seizes a poor woman who has tried to escape from his clutches, drags her home, yokes her to a plough with the oxen, and then forces her to drag along a heavy threshing board, flogging her the while until she falls dead to the ground. The poignancy of this vividly written tale is more effective than any social moralizing. Chonkadze's story may be compared in this respect with *Uncle Tom's Cabin*, or with Turgenev's *Huntsman's Sketches* or *Mumu*.

After Chonkadze's early death, his message was taken up by several other brilliant poets and writers of the young generation. Prince Raphael Eristavi, who had witnessed the Mingrelian peasants' revolt in 1857, composed a poem called *The Suppliant to his Judge*, in which justice was demanded for the peasant class. Ilia Chavchavadze and Akaki Tsereteli, both offspring of leading princely families, published in the journals *Tsiskari (The Dawn)* and *Sakartvelos moambe (The Georgian*

Messenger) a number of remarkable articles and essays on social themes. Several of Akaki's early poems, such as *Glekhis aghsareba* (*The peasant's confession*), showed indignation at the lot of the serfs. Indeed, Akaki was denounced as a traitor to his class, and on one occasion an enraged diehard, Prince Mikeladze, made a violent physical assault on the young poet.

Ilia Chavchavadze's devastating novel *Katsia adamiani?* (*Do you call this a man?*), published in 1863, was another important literary expression of the crisis in Georgian society. The motto of the book—'Criticize your friend to his face, your foe behind his back'—shows the author's intention of depicting the seamy side of Georgian life in the hope of stirring his countrymen to mend their ways. Ilia's novel may be compared with Gogol's *Dead Souls* or with the savage rustic satires of Saltykov-Shchedrin. The writer shares Gogol's disgust with the *poshlost*—the triviality and sordidness of life in the dim backwaters of the Tsarist Empire, and his description of the domain of Prince Luarsab Tatkaridze, a feudal lord of Kakheti, is one of the most picturesque pages of Georgian literature. Dirt, indolence, dilapidation are the prevailing features of the princely economy. 'The yard was as dirty as the soul of a superannuated bureaucrat. To reach the proprietor without getting filthy or collecting some kind of choice odour in the process was a great achievement.' The aristocratic interior was equally squalid, His Highness's sitting room being furnished with sofas spread with carpets kept in such a condition that every excellent movement of Their Excellencies' excellent limbs sent clouds of dust into the air, thus mercifully obscuring other sordid features of the apartment. Chavchavadze pokes fun at all kinds of hallowed features of Georgian life. His account of how the slow-witted Luarsab is tricked into marriage with the ugly Darejan, daughter of the most noble Prince Moses, son of Noshrevan, provides a hilarious commentary on the activity of the village match-maker. Little wonder that Luarsab and Darejan Tatkaridze became proverbial figures of fun, or that many a Georgian squire should have cursed Ilia and his clever young friends as harbingers of ruin and destroyers of traditional values. Indeed, at a meeting where Ilia was advocating the prompt emancipation of the peasants with their land, an outraged proprietor armed with a *kinzhal*—the deadly Caucasian dagger—hurled himself at the orator shouting: 'Let me get at him! I'll kill him on the spot!'

Land hunger and peasant discontent

In spite of much opposition, the Georgian nobility were eventually prevailed upon to accept a scheme for the liberation of the peasantry with an allotment of land to former serfs. The manifesto of 1864 proclaimed the emancipation of serfs in the Tbilisi area, while those of Imereti (Western Georgia) were freed the following year. The Mingrelian peasants were liber-ated in 1867, those of Abkhazia in 1870, and those of Svaneti in 1871. In Georgia, as in Russia, the peasantry were saddled with redemption payments of fantastic magnitude to be paid off by instalments to their former owners, pending which they remained in an equivocal status known as 'temporary obliga-tion'. In addition, about a third of each peasant plot was detached from the holding and handed back to the landowner by way of additional compensation. The peasantry lost their free access to forests and communal pasture lands. Former landless serfs, domestic bond serfs, and an important category of migrant agricultural labourers known as *khizani* were excluded from the settlement, and were condemned to an impoverished existence. Even after the reforms of 1864, the lot of the Georgian peasant could be summed up only too often in the poignant lines of Raphael Eristavi's poem, *Sesia's Thoughts*:

> Dust am I, to dust I cling;
> A rustic born, my life is one
> Eternal strife and endless toil,
> And endless woe . . . till life is gone.
> I plough, I sow, I labour on,
> With muscles strained, in sun and rain.
> I scarce can live on what I earn,
> And tired and hungry I remain.
> The owner of the land torments me;
> Even the tiny ant's my foe.
> For townsfolk, priests and native country
> In blood-like sweat I plough and sow . . .
> How long, O God, this endless grind,
> This life of sorrow and of toil?
> Alas! I fear that death alone
> Will bring me rest within this soil![53]

The land settlement imposed on the newly conquered Abkhaz proved particularly onerous. The Russian authorities failed to distinguish adequately between the various categories of free, semi-free and serf peasants which had existed in that somewhat primitive tribal society. Under the arrangements imposed in 1870, the landowners received up to two hundred and fifty *desyatins* apiece, while the peasants got only from three to seven per household, much of this being unfit for cultivation. Contemporary Russian officials admitted that the Abkhaz peasantry were left with little more than rocky mountain slopes and low-lying bogs. It is only fair to add that the Abkhaz peasantry had shown little disposition to co-operate with the Russian land commission sent to work out the details of the new arrangements, finally waylaying the commissioners and exterminating them. After a series of insurrections, many of the Abkhaz eventually joined the Circassians in exile in Turkey.

The edicts of 1864

Whereas the freeing of the peasantry marked a decided, if belated step forward in the evolution of Georgian society, the country still lagged behind metropolitan Russia in the matter of civil rights and local government reform. Georgia reaped no benefit from the Zemstvo law of 1864, which laid the basis of voluntary local government throughout European Russia. Instead, the peasant communities had village councils headed by a rural bailiff who was responsible to the Russian district authority for collecting taxes and carrying out compulsory work assignments. These village councils had little in the way of status, and were at the beck and call of the local Russian military commanders and police. The Georgians were likewise refused the benefit of the jury system as adopted in Russia in 1864. Legal business continued to be transacted exclusively in Russian and judgement enforced by administrators sent from St. Petersburg.

The Viceroy of the Caucasus from 1862 until 1882 was the Grand Duke Michael, brother of Tsar Alexander II. The future Russian Prime Minister Sergius Witte, who in his boyhood knew the Grand Duke personally, described Michael as a broad-minded and dignified man with gentlemanly instincts. He made himself extremely popular throughout the Caucasus, being a complete stranger to the narrow-minded chauvinism which developed in Russia towards the end of the nineteenth century and found expression in pan-Slavonic jingoism, anti-Jewish pogroms and other unlovely manifestations. The Grand Duke considered rather that since many of the Caucasian peoples had entered the Russian empire voluntarily and were serving with loyalty in Russia's army and civil service, there was no distinction to be made between them and the inhabitants of European Russia.[54] The viceregal palace was always open to the Georgian aristocracy, while marriages between Russian noblemen serving in the Caucasus and Georgian princesses were of frequent occurrence.

The War of 1877–78

An important event of the Grand Duke Michael's viceroyalty was the recovery during the Russo-Turkish war of 1877–78 of substantial areas of former Georgian territory which had been under Ottoman sway since the sixteenth century. With their Georgian and Armenian auxiliaries, the Russians had gained brilliant successes on this front during Paskevich's campaign of 1828–29, and had acquitted themselves very creditably here during the Crimean War. Each time, however, the complications of great power politics had wrested the fruits of success from the Russians' grasp during the subsequent peace settlements. This time, however, the Russians were able to turn their victory on this front into a territorial gain which they held until the collapse of the Tsarist Empire in 1917. While the main Russian and Turkish forces were locked in their usual massive combat on the Balkan front, the Grand Duke Michael captured Kars in November 1877, and blockaded Erzurum. The Congress of Berlin confirmed Russia in possession of extensive tracts of territory which had centuries before formed part of the mediaeval Georgian kingdom: Atchara-Kobuleti, with the port of Batumi, Shavsheti, Klarjeti, Kola-Ardahan, and the northern portion of Tao, comprising the district of Oltisi. From the military viewpoint, great importance attached to Russia's acquisition of the fortresses of Kars and Ardahan, controlling the approaches into Turkish Anatolia.

Commerce and industry

The last thirty years of the nineteenth century saw the beginnings of a minor industrial revolution in Georgia. This was accelerated by improved communications. Roads were built, and the main towns of Transcaucasia connected by the telegraph in 1870. Two years later, a regular service was inaugurated on the new Poti-Tbilisi railway. A branch line to Kutaisi was opened in 1877. Following the Russian annexation of the Black Sea port of Batumi after the war of 1877-78, a line between Batumi and Samtredia was opened in 1883, while Tbilisi was simultaneously connected by rail with the great Caspian oil town of Baku. The whole of Russian Transcaucasia was now spanned by rail from the Caspian to the Black Sea coast. In 1886, a further rail extension was built to link Kutaisi with the rapidly expanding coal-mining town of Tqibuli in upper Imereti. The manganese industry set up at Chiatura in 1879 soon attained international importance. By 1892, Chiatura manganese represented 38 per cent. of the entire world production of this essential mineral. Baku being on the land-locked Caspian, Batumi became the main outlet for Baku oil. In 1888, 21 per cent. of the world supply of oil passed through that port on its way to Russia and other consumer countries.

The population of Georgia continued to increase. In 1866, it totalled 1,300,400, in 1886, 1,731,500, in 1897, 2,034,700. There was a constant drift from the countryside to the towns. Between 1865 and 1897, the population of Tbilisi more than doubled —from 71,051 to 159,590. The capital of Georgia became more and more of a cosmopolitan city, complete with European amenities such as hotels, a horse tramway, new bridges, paved streets, a piped water supply, schools, and other municipal and government institutions, housed in imposing stone buildings.

Economic change brought with it changes in social relationships and habits of mind. Many Georgian intellectuals greeted these readjustments with approval, and were glad to see the old ruling class stirred from its torpor into fruitful enterprise. In 1874, the liberal journalist Sergei Meskhi noted 'a new and general trend and impulse' throughout Georgia, manifested as a craze for business activity and money-making.

'So long as the feudal system persisted in our land, everyone relied on the peasants' unpaid labour and concentrated on living in a carefree way. The landlord proudly declared: "What do I want with business, what do I want with money? My peasants' labour is my money!" Since the abolition of serfdom, our circumstances have altered: the erstwhile feudal lord has been deprived of his unpaid labour force and with it, of his effortless income and the means of living a carefree life. The smaller proprietors have come to feel with special acuteness, on their own hide, the impact of the fact that those days have passed away for ever when what they termed "business" consisted in hunting and revelry, and when they had need of cash only to gratify their desires in the direction of superfluous luxuries. Everyone has come to feel that the era when it was possible to live an insouciant, idle existence at the expense of other people's efforts has vanished completely, or is at least on the way out. . . . Times have changed indeed!'

Latterly, Meskhi went on, everyone has been engaged in a mad rush to think up some lucrative enterprise which will enrich him in a few years. One man is building a wine warehouse to supply the city with drink, another is trying to make a fortune out of milk—there is no limit to these bright ideas, and all their promoters are naturally keen to secure financial backing from the bank! In the wake of this mad bustle, there must be many disappointments, many false starts. But in the end, this burst of feverish activity may have the good effect of teaching the Georgians that there is no substitute for diligent learning, steady work and the careful thinking out of feasible projects and undertakings.[55]

If the 1870's were, for Russia as for Georgia, a time of new ideas and new possibilities, they were also a period of frustration and disillusionment. The reign of Alexander II was drawing to its tragic end. The emperor whose accession and early reforms had aroused the most sanguine hopes, who had freed the peasants from servitude and carried through so many promising reforms, was spending his last years hunted like a beast by revolutionaries, and hiding in his palaces in a vain effort to ward off their bombs and guns. The landlords had never forgiven him the reform of 1861, while the peasants found that the yoke of serfdom had been replaced by the burden of poverty and debt. The intelligentsia, whose evolution Alexander's early reforms had done much to foster, were seething with resentment at the dead weight of autocracy which excluded them from participation in government, and deprived public opinion of all influence on the course of affairs. Symptomatic of this frustration was the Narodnik or Populist movement of the 1870's, in the course of which thousands of idealistic students and intellectuals abandoned homes and professions and tried to settle as peasants among the country folk to enter into communion with them and prepare them for the coming of the revolutionary utopia. But the *muzhik* refused to respond to the advances of these town-bred zealots, most of whom were rounded up and imprisoned or deported to Siberia. The hard core of the revolutionary intelligentsia turned to terrorism and conspiracy. One group of the *Land and Freedom* party broke away and formed a new body, known as *The People's Will*. In 1879, a rapid succession of spectacular acts of violence took place, in which the Governor of Kharkov was shot dead, and the Tsar narrowly escaped two attempts on his life. Neither arrests, executions, deportations, nor the prospect of constitutional concessions could save the emperor from his fate. In 1880, a workman blew up the imperial dining room at the Winter Palace. The following year, on 1 March, the bombs of the Nihilists reached their targets and Alexander II, the Emancipator, died a ghastly death.

Thinking people in Georgia could not avoid being affected by the general tension and malaise affecting Russia. 'What has come over us, what has happened to us?' asked the veteran poet and administrator Prince Grigol Orbeliani on the morrow of the war of 1877–78.

'What invisible agency has been exercising so lamentable an effect upon us, so that we are all heading for general ruin precisely at that moment when the external enemy no longer exists for us? From every side, from every household is heard nothing but the sound of weeping and wailing. Misery has stricken everyone, down to the lowest class of society. Where are we to look for a deliverer? This terrible thought keeps sorrowing me and adding to my weight of years.'[56]

Russian Pan-Slavism and the lesser breeds

Particularly ominous for Russia's minority peoples was the alarming growth of official chauvinism, which came at a time

when the intensification of self-conscious and articulate
nationalism among the subject nations of the great multi-
racial empires—Austro-Hungary, Ottoman Turkey and Russia
—confronted governments with new problems and demands.
The liberation of Italy from Austrian rule had been a great
fillip to this movement, while increasing restiveness was
shown by the Hungarians as well as by the Czechs, Poles and
other Slavonic peoples under Hapsburg rule. The Ottoman
Empire, long in decline, faced continual trouble in the Balkans,
where nationalist sentiment was inflamed by agents of imperial
Russia spreading the sacred message of Orthodoxy and Pan-
Slavism. Within Russia itself, the authorities lent their support
to a sort of mystical Messianism, designed to enhance the
prestige of the imperial dynasty and of 'Holy Russia' as champions of Christendom, and to stifle heresy and dissent at home
and abroad. Pan-Slavism inside Russia was an ugly growth.
Poles, Ukrainians and other Slavonic lesser breeds were
coerced into conformity with Muscovite ways and ideas, while
every attempt was made to assimilate Russia's Asiatic subjects
and bring them into line. These efforts, needless to say, had
scant success in the long run. The pride of the minority peoples
was offended by official refusal to countenance use of local
languages as the media for education or state business, and by
the scorn poured by the dominant race on the cultural heritage
of the smaller brethren.

Such resentment was especially keen in Georgia which had,
after all, formed an independent and highly civilized kingdom
within the Greco-Roman world when the ancestors of the
Russians were still nomads wandering about the draughty
steppes. The Georgians had accepted Christianity more than
six centuries before the Russians, had been a bulwark of
Christendom in the East for a millennium and a half, and had
entered voluntarily under the Russian sceptre—only to be
treated now as if they were barbarians. Thus, from 1871 the
study of Georgian language and literature in State Schools was
replaced by compulsory Latin and Greek. Admittedly, Georgian could be studied as a voluntary extra, but it was deprived
of its place on the official time-table. In 1872, an inspector
arrived from St. Petersburg and banned the use of Georgian
as medium of instruction in the Tbilisi Theological Seminary,

the main training college for the Georgian priesthood. The seminary thereafter became more and more a centre for nationalist resistance to Russian rule. It gained nation-wide notoriety in 1886, when an expelled student named Laghiash-vili assassinated the rector, Chudetsky, a bigoted Russian who described Georgian as 'a language for dogs'. In his rage at this incident, the Russian Exarch of Georgia cursed the Georgian nation with a wholesale anathema. A venerable Georgian writer, Prince Dimitri Qipiani, who ventured a protest against the prelate's intemperate mouthings, was deported to Stavropol in the North Caucasus, where he was soon afterwards murdered in mysterious circumstances.

Ilia Chavchavadze and Georgia's re-awakening

Georgian patriotic resistance at this period was headed by Ilia Chavchavadze (1837–1907), the poet, novelist and orator, who had gained prominence as a firebrand at the time of the liberation of the serfs. With growing maturity, Ilia's stature as a responsible public figure rapidly increased. In 1875, he was elected Chairman of the newly founded Land Bank of the Nobility in Tbilisi, an institution designed to put the impoverished landed gentry on their feet by providing credit and capital, as well as fulfilling ordinary day to day banking functions. From then onwards, Ilia's life was devoted to practical activities of all kinds. In 1879, he helped to found the Society for the Spreading of Literacy among the Georgians. He financed new schools and supported the Georgian national theatre. In 1877 he launched the newspaper *Iveria,* an organ which played an outstanding part in reviving Georgian national consciousness. The Tbilisi gendarmerie could report with truth that

'the principal leader of the movement which aims at the intensifying of nationalistic trends is Prince Ilia Chavchavadze, Chairman of the Tbilisi Bank of the Nobility. . . . Prince Chavchavadze is a man of exceptional intellect and standing, and enjoys great ascendancy over the Georgians in general, and over free-thinking elements in particular.'[57]

Ilia Chavchavadze and his associates were known as the *Pirveli Dasi* or *First Group,* to distinguish them from the more radical *Meore Dasi* or *Second Group,* founded in 1869 by Giorgi

Tsereteli and Niko Nikoladze. Both these early Georgian social and literary movements were, however, far more moderate in their aims than the young Marxists who later banded themselves together as the *Mesame Dasi* or *Third Group*, and formed the basis of the Georgian revolutionary Social-Democratic Party.

Chavchavadze's ideology at this stage of his career could justly be described as bourgeois-nationalist. One of his objects, which aroused criticism in radical circles, was to reconcile the various classes of Georgian society in the interests of national solidarity. In a series of articles which appeared between 1877 and 1881 under the title *Life and Law*, Ilia preached that the antagonisms which existed in other countries between rich and poor, high and low, either did not exist in Georgia, or could be easily dispelled thanks, apparently, to some superior, moral qualities vouchsafed to the Georgian nation. There was, Ilia taught, no real obstacle to a complete understanding between the different social classes. After Ilia's vigorous campaign on behalf of the serfs against their feudal masters not two decades previously, this doctrine appeared to many as novel and disconcerting. As one contemporary put it, Chavchavadze's aim was apparently to turn prince and peasant into brothers and inspire them both with a single common purpose—the peasant to ministering to the prince's stomach, the prince to ministering to his own stomach. This happy consummation would indeed remove all conflict of interest between them.[58] Such an interpretation of Chavchavadze's ideas does them less than justice. Ilia's real aim, which under the Tsarist censorship could not be proclaimed in print, was to unite his fellow countrymen, regardless of social status, into a closely knit national community capable one day of winning independence from the Russian overlord.

The efforts of publicists and authors like Ilia Chavchavadze were powerfully seconded by the new generation of Georgian school teachers and pedagogues. While forced to instruct their flock in the uncongenial idiom of Russian, the teachers drummed into their pupils contempt for alien ways and pride in their native Georgian heritage.

The most remarkable of these teachers was Iakob Gogebashvili (1840–1912), who studied at Kiev University and became familiar with Darwin's evolutionary theory and the political ideas of Russian radicals such as Herzen, Belinsky and Chernyshevsky. Returning to Tbilisi, Gogebashvili taught arithmetic and geography in the ecclesiastical school and later in the seminary. In 1868, he was appointed inspector of the ecclesiastical school, but was dismissed a few years later on orders from the Synod in St. Petersburg.

From then onwards Gogebashvili became a free-lance and devoted his energies to spreading education and enlightenment among his fellow-countrymen and their children. He played a prominent part in the work of the Society for the Spreading of Literacy among the Georgians. He was intensely proud of Georgia's language and literature, and wrote essays in which he urged people to show themselves true patriots in the educational sphere. He contrasted Georgian patriotism with the chauvinism of the great powers, and particularly with the Russian reactionary Pan-Slavists, whose ideal Russian patriot was a man who would crush all the smaller nations which Russia had annexed, and enslave all countries of Europe situated outside the frontiers of the Tsar's domains.

'Our patriotism is of course of an entirely different kind: it consists solely in a sacred feeling towards our mother land; . . . in it there is no hate for other nations, no desire to enslave anybody, no urge to impoverish anybody. Our patriots desire to restore Georgia's right to self-government and their own civic rights, to preserve their national characteristics and culture, without which no people can exist as a society of human beings.'

For Gogebashvili, there could be no revival of self-respect among his fellow-countrymen without a revival of interest in the Georgian language. 'The status of the Georgian tongue in Georgian scholastic institutions may be compared with that of a wretched foundling, deprived of all care and protection. Georgia's native language is treated just as a spiteful stepmother treats her stepchild.'[59] Throughout his life, Gogebashvili spared no effort in remedying this situation. His masterly introduction to Georgian for children, *Deda Ena* (*Mother Tongue*) has been republished several dozen times since its first appearance in 1876, and in modified form serves to this day as a manual in Georgian schools.

Alexander III and Russian reaction

After the assassination of Tsar Alexander II and the accession of Alexander III (1881–94), relations between the Russians and their Georgian subjects continued to be strained. A feature of Alexander III's reign was an increased persecution of everything which diverged from the officially accepted national type. Dissenting sects, the Uniat Church and the Lutherans in the western provinces, Lamaist Kalmuks, Buryat Mongols, and especially all Jews, suffered a systematic campaign of persecution and denigration. Under the influence of reactionaries like Katkov and Pobedonostsev, the Russian Press was effectively muzzled. Every effort was made to stifle the growing revolutionary movement and destroy the remnants of the revolutionary organizations. All manifestations of independent public opinion were treated as signs of sedition.

The intensification of Russian reaction had unpleasant repercussions in Georgia. Added obstacles were placed in the way of the Georgians' progress towards full civic rights. The government in St. Petersburg habitually sent to Georgia the dregs of the Russian civil service. Oliver Wardrop, one of the English pioneers of Georgian studies, visited the Caucasus in 1887. Most Georgians, he noted, knew Russia only as a foreign power that sent them tax-collectors, justices of the peace and other bureaucrats, many of them obnoxious. Russian magistrates, according to this observer, were arrogant when sober and odious when drunk. Wardrop himself once witnessed the reception accorded to a fine, tall mountaineer who came humbly to present a petition to a puny, besotted Russian magistrate. 'The representative of law and order was drunk, hopelessly drunk, and treated the suppliant in such a manner that I blushed to be in his company.'[60]

In Western Europe at least there were signs of growing sympathy with Georgia and her people. Arthur Leist in Germany and Professor Morfill at Oxford were influential advocates of Georgian literature and culture. A special place in the affections of the Georgians is occupied by Oliver Wardrop's sister Marjory, who translated into English one of the most nobly conceived of Ilia Chavchavadze's poems, *The Hermit*, and later, Shota Rustaveli's classic epic, *The Man in the Panther's Skin.* In 1894 we find Ilia writing to Marjory Wardrop:

'The renowned land of England knows little enough about our unfortunate country and orphaned people, which at one time had its own heroes, scholars, writers and poets, and through their endeavours steadfastly resisted the barbarian enemies of enlightenment.

'Every Georgian will feel gratified that you and your respected brother have conceived a love for our universally forgotten land, and desire to convey to your countrymen its bad and good sides, with all that affection and sympathy which so adorn a human being and are the priceless consolation of those who are oppressed by fate. It is to be wished that the noble and powerful people of England should know that even in our little country, the mind functions and the heart beats in a human way; that even here, men have their longings and their hopes; that even here, there exists faith and painful striving towards better days; and that this people of ours feels nothing human to be alien to it.

'All this has permeated our little literature, in so far as our burdensome situation permits . . .'[61]

Great Georgian writers of the late nineteenth century

Despite official discouragement, the last decades of the nineteenth century witnessed a Georgian literary revival in which there emerged writers of a stature unequalled since the Golden Age of Rustaveli seven hundred years before. Ilia Chavchavadze himself excelled alike in lyric and ballad poetry, in the novel, the short story and the essay. Apart from Ilia, the most universal literary genius of the age was Akaki Tsereteli. Known as 'the immortal nightingale of the Georgian people', he was as versatile as Ilia, and also a prominent public figure. Many of his lyrics have been adopted as folk ballads and popular drinking songs. In his historical lay *Tornike Eristavi*, he conjured up the heroic days when Georgian arms played a part in the mighty wars of Byzantium. Akaki lost no occasion of expressing his contempt for Tsarist autocracy. In 1871, Ilia Chavchavadze devoted one of his most fiery poems to the downfall of the Paris Commune, which he mourned as a victory for tyrants and oppressors of the people. Ten years later, Akaki Tsereteli greeted with enthusiasm the news of the assassination of Alexander II, whom the Georgians by now regarded as among the chief tyrants of the age. 'Today a swallow brushed with its wings against my window. Spring! Spring! its bird-like chatter seemed to say, and hope sprang up afresh within my heart.' These verses were part of a poem entitled *Spring* which appeared in a Tbilisi paper, and within a few days was being recited all over Georgia. The Russian authorities, waking up too late to the true significance of the verses, threatened to send the audacious bard to Siberia. Later on, Akaki translated into Georgian *The Internationale*, the revolutionary hymn of the proletarians, and greeted the 1905 uprising with militant poems and slogans.

Another important poet of the period was Vazha-Pshavela (1861–1915), a true child of nature, who spent the greater part of his life in a small village in the Georgian highlands. The majestic mountain scenery, the ways and customs of the hill folk, their virile, jealous and combative spirit, and their rich folk-traditions, were important elements in Vazha-Pshavela's artistic inspiration. In his epics and heroic lays, Vazha-Pshavela depicts human characters of titanic power, locked in elemental struggle with supernatural forces, and torn by profound psychological conflicts. With unerring and often sublime touch, he transmuted the popular idiom of folk poetry into artistic form. In different vein, he excelled as author of nature stories, many of which have become children's classics.

The development of the Georgian romantic novel received powerful stimulus from the work of Alexander Qazbegi (1848–93). Qazbegi was a scion of the princely family which for centuries held sway over the upland region near the Daryal Pass and Mount Kazbek, where the Russian military road passes over the Caucasus range. Sent to complete his education in Moscow, he fell into bad company, and returned disillusioned and broken in health to his native mountains. There he sought refuge from worldly temptations by taking to the life of a simple shepherd, in which condition he passed seven years. Then followed a period of success and literary renown in Tbilisi, after which Qazbegi took to acting and travelled round Georgia as a strolling player. Overtaken in the end by poverty, he went out of his mind, and died after four sad years in Tbilisi asylum. Among his best-known novels are *Elguja* and *Khevisberi Gocha*. The setting of the former is the Georgian

The Land and the People

1   Highland Georgia: a farm in upland Svaneti

2 Old Tbilisi: the Citadel and Muslim quarter

3 Modern Tbilisi: the main pavilion in the Stalin Park at the summit of the funicular railway

4   Old Tbilisi: houses on a cliff overlooking the River Kura

5　Modern Tbilisi: Baratashvili Bridge. In the background are the funicular railway and the mast of the Georgian State Television transmitter

6   The Georgian Military Highway crosses the main Caucasian range between Tbilisi and Dzaujikau (Orjonikidze)

7   Wine-growing is an important feature of Georgian agriculture. Grading grapes at Tsinandali State Farm in Kakheti

8 Women take part in the traditional game of *tskhenburti* or 'horse-ball'

9 Modern Tbilisi: the Sports Stadium

10 A choir of centenarians, who sing regularly at the Peoples Art Club at Sukhumi, Abkhazian ASSR

11 The 'Mother and Son' sanatorium at Tsikhis-dziri, Ajar ASSR

12 An old Laz peasant, belonging to a people of Georgian stock now resident in Turkey

13 Georgia's Muslim neighbours: A village in the Daghestan ASSR, whence in olden times Shamil's Murids would swoop down on and raid Christian Georgia

Historical Background

14, 15 King Erekle II of Georgia (1744–98) and his Consort, Queen Darejan

17 Giorgi XII (1798–1800), last king of Eastern Georgia. An invalid, he sought to save Georgia by placing it under direct Russian suzerainty

ft) The treaty concluded *83* between King Erekle Catherine the Great of ia, showing Great Seal Georgia and Erekle's *ture*

18, 19 Georgian national costumes as worn by the nobility in the late nineteenth century

20 Marjory Wardrop (1869–1909), an English poetess who devoted her life to studying the Georgian people and their culture, and translated Rustaveli's epic into English prose

21 Oliver Wardrop (1864–1948), brother of Marjory, and also a noted Georgian scholar. He is shown here at the British Mission in Tbilisi as Chief Commissioner to Transcaucasia, 1919

22   Metekhi fortress jail, Tbilisi, was built by the tsars for detention
of political prisoners

23 The Georgian national poet, Akaki Tsereteli, was arrested by Russian police in 1907 after writing a lampoon on the Russian Governor of Tbilisi

24 A 500-ruble note current under the independent Georgian republican régime, 1918–21

25 Order of Queen Tamar: This medal was designed for issue to Georgian *émigrés* serving with the German and Turkish armies, 1915

The Soviet Era

26   An official portrait of I. V. Stalin (Ioseb Jughashvili) as Marshal of the Soviet Union

27   The Stalin Museum at Gori, Stalin's Georgian home town

L. P. Beria, Georgian chief
the NKVD and a Vice-
resident of the Soviet Council
Ministers

29   The Institute of Marxism-Leninism at Tbilisi

Industrial Development

30　The hydroelectric station at Zemo-Avchala opened by President Kalinin in 1927

31   Blast-furnaces at the Transcaucasian Metallurgical Works at
Rustavi, near Tbilisi

32   The tube-works at the Transcaucasian Metallurgical Works,
Rustavi

Culture and Education

(a)

(b)

(c)

33 Authors and public figures: Soviet stamps depicting:

(a) Shota Rustaveli, Georgian national poet; he flourished about A.D. 1200 and wrote a romantic epic, *The Man in the Panther's Skin*

(b) Sulkhan-Saba Orbeliani (1658–1725), author of witty and fantastic *Book of Wisdom and Lies*

(c) Akaki Tsereteli (1840–1915), noted patriotic poet

(d) Vazha-Pshavela (1861–1915), poet of nature and the Georgian highlands

(e) Sergo Orjonikidze (1886–1937), the Georgian Bolshevik leader and one-time friend of Stalin

(d)

(e)

34 This beautiful specimen of Georgian calligraphy in the old Georgian alphabet is from a 1,000-year-old Gospel manuscript preserved on Mount Sinai

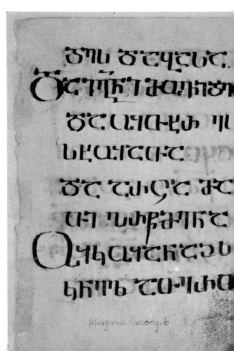

35 Church of Saint David, the Pantheon of Georgian writers, on
the hill above Tbilisi

36 A Georgian dance ensemble gives a spirited performance

38   Modern Georgian art: *Tandila's Dream* (1931), by Lado
Gudiashvili (born 1896)

39 A youth ball given by Georgian students in national costume

40 The Faculty of Physics and Mathematics, Tbilisi State University

peasant uprising of 1804, in which the hill clansmen wreaked vengeance on their Russian oppressors. *Khevisberi Gocha* is an historical novel set in seventeenth-century Georgia; it exalts the concepts of liberty, patriotism and moral duty. Gocha, a patriarchal figure of heroic stature, slays his own son rather than forgive a betrayal of the national cause, even though that betrayal arose from weakness and not from any traitorous intent. In his descriptions of the wild and grandiose scenes of the Caucasus mountains, Qazbegi evokes with masterly power the inner conflict of the human soul. This tormented genius created many characters which live on in the minds of the Georgian people, as symbols of the days when free men and women loved and died among the eagles and the snow-capped peaks of the Caucasus. He also wrote several fine dramas. Like virtually every important Georgian man of letters of those days, he was constantly harried by the Russian censorship, which prevented some of his best works from being published during his life time.

Between 1855 and 1894, during the reigns of Alexander II and III, the revival of Georgian national consciousness proceeded with rapid strides. The emancipation of the serfs dealt a massive blow to the decaying feudal order. The growth of capitalism, the spread of education, and the emergence of a vocal intelligentsia focused attention on the inadequacies of Tsarist rule, and heightened popular dislike for alien domination. The appearance of magnificently gifted writers gave the Georgians a new intellectual self-confidence. All this helped to pave the way for active participation by the Georgians in the revolutionary struggle which culminated in the events of 1917.

CHAPTER VI

THE STORM GATHERS: 1894–1904

*Tsarism under pressure — Accession of Nicholas II — 'Gri-Gri'
Golitsyn — A Georgian anarchist — Populists and Marxists —
The Third Group — Sweated labour — Stalin's revolutionary
youth — 'Legal Marxism' and the fighting underground — 'Down
with autocracy!' — Plehve and the Black Hundreds*

Tsarism under pressure

ALEXANDER III died in 1894. By sheer strength of character and by refusal to make any concession to the new social
forces and political trends stirring in the Russian empire,
Alexander had succeeded in maintaining some semblance of
order and stability. At the same time, he left a legacy of resentment among both the masses and the élite which was finally to
bring down in ruins autocracy itself. The government had
seemed to take pleasure in humiliating the educated classes. In
1884, the University Statute of Alexander II had been replaced by another which robbed the universities of their
autonomy. Student clubs and fraternities were banned, on
pain of conscription into the ranks of the army. Political
trustworthiness was made a criterion for the granting of
bursaries, while the children of the 'lower orders' were excluded from secondary schools. The censorship brooded over
the Press, and the law courts fell more and more under government control.

In rural Russia, the growth of the population resulted in
acute land hunger among the peasantry. Particularly vexatious
to the mass of the peasants was the law of 1889 instituting the
land captains. These officials were appointed by the Minister
of the Interior from among the poorer gentry, and charged with
supervising every detail of peasant life and activity. The land

captains were justly regarded as agents of a new system of serfdom. They took over the functions of justices of the peace and controlled the decisions of the peasant judges and village elders, who ruled their fellows not by common law, but by communal custom. To deal with rural unrest, the government evolved a code of 'exceptional' or 'abnormal' law. There were three grades: 'exceptional protection', 'increased protection' and martial law. Scarcely ever was there not some province of Russia under one or other of these states of emergency.

During the second half of the nineteenth century, Russia's retarded industrial revolution gathered pace. The growth of industry created a factory class, the nucleus of a true urban proletariat. Conditions in the factories run by Russian and foreign entrepreneurs were bad. The industrialists of Moscow, where hordes of workpeople poured in from the surrounding countryside, paid low wages. The workmen were ignorant and clumsy, so that productivity was low; in fact, it often took three or more persons to carry out tasks which a trained Western worker could perform single-handed. Between 1882 and 1886, the enlightened Finance Minister, N. Kh. Bunge, enacted a series of factory laws designed to suppress the more scandalous forms of exploitation, restrict the hours worked by children and progressively remove causes of unrest and discontent. Under pressure from the employers, Bunge was driven from office on the charge of promoting 'socialism', and there was a return to full-scale *laissez-faire*. Children of ten to twelve years of age could now be employed on night work, while the manufacturers could resort to abuses such as substituting payments in kind for wages in cash, imposing arbitrary fines, and forcing workers to buy their supplies from the factory shop.

Such conditions provided a natural breeding ground for radical agitation. The world of the factory, where masses of men and women are herded together, and the spirit of disaffection can spread with lightning speed to produce strikes and civil commotion, is more congenial to revolutionaries than the rustic environment of the village community. The Populists of the 1870's had discovered to their cost how difficult it was for the town-bred intellectual to win the confidence of the *muzhik*, whose main aim in life was to turn himself into a petty-bourgeois proprietor rather than contribute to the consummation of any socialist utopia. The concentration in urban centres of hosts of underfed and disgruntled factory workers provided a hotbed, in which the seeds of sedition were not slow to take root.

Accession of Nicholas II

On succeeding to the Russian throne in November 1894, Nicholas II took over no comfortable heritage. Not devoid of courage and integrity, Nicholas had been overshadowed all his life by his domineering father, and had become in many respects vacillating and easily influenced. He had the fatal knack of following wrong-headed or biased counsel and would sometimes dismiss loyal ministers in obedience to some whim of his foolish consort, the Empress Alexandra. In January 1895, he received from the *Zemstvo* or provincial assembly of Tver a congratulatory address on his marriage, in which the hope was expressed that the voice of the people would be listened to, and that the rule of law would stand above the changing views of the individual instruments of the supreme power. Under the influence of his mentor Pobedonostsev, Nicholas in his reply denounced 'senseless dreams as to the participation of the Zemstvos in the internal affairs of the State', and reaffirmed his unswerving adherence to the principle of absolute rule.

Pronouncements such as these, far from intimidating the Russian public, merely exacerbated opinion. Liberals, moderate socialists and clandestine revolutionaries alike set to work with a will to undermine the Russian leviathan and topple it from its throne.

The development of a revolutionary situation in metropolitan Russia necessarily affected Georgia and the Caucasus generally. Unrest when it arrived was bound to assume an acute form in this imperfectly pacified area, where Orthodox Georgian, Gregorian Armenian and Muslim Tatar had a long tradition of mutual dislike, though sharing for the most part a common animosity towards the alien overlord. In Georgia, of course, there had been many sporadic rebellions against Russian rule, as well as peasant insurrections against the landed proprietors. At the close of the nineteenth century, there were many who had witnessed or heard tell of the conspiracy of 1832, the Gurian uprising of 1841, and the Mikava revolt in

Mingrelia in 1857. Several leading Georgian writers had been imprisoned for their part in the student demonstrations at St. Petersburg in 1861. The movement of national revival headed by Ilia Chavchavadze, Akaki Tsereteli, Niko Nikoladze and others naturally fostered an attitude of mind highly critical of Russian autocracy.

'Gri-Gri' Golitsyn

Nicholas II and his advisers brought trouble upon themselves by a particularly inept choice of Governor-General for the Caucasus. When the Grand Duke Michael retired from the viceroyalty in 1882, Alexander III down-graded the post and appointed Prince A. M. Dondukov-Korsakov to be merely Governor-General and Commander-in-Chief in the Caucasus. Dondukov-Korsakov was succeeded in 1890 by General S. A. Sheremetev, whose governorship continued until 1896. Both these administrators were well acquainted with the spirit of the Caucasian peoples and made themselves popular in Tbilisi by gracious behaviour and lavish entertainments. Prince Grigory Golitsyn, who was appointed governor-general in December 1896, was an individual of very different stamp: nicknamed 'Gri-Gri' in St. Petersburg society, he was a man of the narrowest upbringing and outlook, owing his appointment to the personal patronage of a member of the imperial family. He had no understanding of the multiracial structure of Caucasian society and of the flexible tactics needed to maintain peace and harmony. His one idea was to russify the Caucasus politically and culturally, not by persuasion and example, but by the crudest police methods. Within a few years Golitsyn was as much loathed as his forerunners had been respected, and the basis of Russian rule in the Caucasus was fatally undermined.

By the time Golitsyn was appointed, the roots of the Georgian revolutionary movement were already strong.

A Georgian anarchist

One of the first Georgian professional revolutionaries was the anarchist Varlam Cherkesov or Cherkezishvili[62] (1846-1925), a native of Kakheti. As a student at St. Petersburg, he associated with Karakozov, who made an abortive attempt on the life of Tsar Alexander II in 1866. Later he joined the Nechaev group, who planned a nation-wide plot against the government. Tried with eighty-six others, Cherkesov was sentenced to forced labour in Siberia. Escaping in 1876, he made his way to Switzerland and joined in the literary and conspiratorial work of the Russian émigrés there. However, he parted company with his Russian associates over the issue of Georgian independence. He became a great friend and disciple of Prince Kropotkin the anarchist. Cherkesov favoured the anarchist creed because it promised greater freedom to small nations than did Marxist dictatorship and centralist rule. From 1903, he and Kropotkin assisted another Georgian revolutionary, Kamando or Giorgi Gogelia, alias 'K. Orgeiani', to edit one of the first Russian anarchist papers, *Khleb i Volya* or *Bread and Liberty*. Smuggled into Russia, this paper had an influential following. Its open advocacy of terrorism later alarmed Kropotkin, who had relapsed in his old age into a more abstract and contemplative approach to the revolutionary question. In 1907, Cherkesov helped to organize a mass petition of the Georgian people against Tsarist oppression, which was presented, though with scant result, to the International Peace Conference at The Hague. Cherkesov and his Dutch wife, Freda, had many friends in English society and in European political circles. An uncompromising critic of the doctrines of Marx and Engels, he is excluded today from the Russian revolutionary pantheon. He died in London at an advanced age.

Populists and Marxists

During the 1870's, the Russian Populist or Narodnik movement made considerable progress in Georgia, where the Populist dream of social progress via the destruction of the Tsar's government and the realisation of the moral and economic potentialities of the peasant class seemed highly attractive. The Tbilisi Narodnik group held meetings in 1872 which were attended by students and others, who studied forbidden political tracts, particularly the writings of the Russian Populists. By 1874, the group counted about a hundred members; they had a small secret printing press on the bank of the River Liakhvi, in the quarters of a priest named

Samadashvili, who had learnt type-setting at the Tbilisi Theological Seminary. In 1876, the Georgian Narodniks held a conference at which, according to police reports of the time, speakers proclaimed the impending destruction of the autocratic régime, following which everyone would be equal, and all property would be shared out equally.—Why, the Narodniks demanded, should the famished masses bow down to kings, and themselves groan in poverty and squalor? They should get rid of the Tsar and his agents and laws, and then no one would extort taxes from them any more. Nor should the priests be believed when they asserted that the Tsar was a protector set over the people by God. This was a monkish lie inspired by the priests' desire to curry favour with the government. In furtherance of their programme, emissaries of the Tbilisi Narodniks visited outlying districts, particularly in Mingrelia and adjoining areas, and urged the peasantry to hold themselves in readiness for a general uprising. This movement was, however, soon nipped in the bud. At the end of 1876, the government arrested over fifty of the Georgian Narodniks, and many were exiled to Siberia.

Those Narodniks who escaped exile turned from radical agitation and conspiratorial plotting to more peaceful methods of furthering their ideals. They briefed advocates to defend peasants who were oppressed by their squires, and campaigned actively against individual perpetrators of injustice. In 1881, the Georgian Narodniks started to publish a journal under the title *Imedi* (*Hope*), in which they inveighed against the liberal bourgeois intelligentsia headed by Ilia Chavchavadze, whose ideas they regarded as outmoded. The advance of Russia and Georgia along the path towards modern capitalism and an industrial society eventually rendered obsolete the ideology of the Narodniks themselves, who were increasingly thrust into the background by the more sophisticated adepts of Marxism. However, many of the Narodnik ideas were subsequently revived by the Russian and Georgian Socialist-Revolutionary parties. The 'S.-R.s', as they were called, to distinguish them from the Marxist Social-Democrats or 'S.-D.s', were later to feature prominently as champions of peasant ownership of the land, and opponents of the town-bred Marxists and their schemes of forced industrialization.

The Third Group

The first systematic Georgian Marxists were a band of young intellectuals known as the *Mesame Dasi* (*Third Group*), which set out to supersede both the so-called *First Group*, the movement headed by Ilia Chavchavadze and his contemporaries, who had led the crusade against serfdom a generation before, and the liberal *Second Group* of Giorgi Tsereteli and Niko Nikoladze. Among the leaders of the *Mesame Dasi* were Silibistro (Sylvester) Jibladze, an erstwhile pupil at the Tbilisi Theological Seminary, expelled for assaulting the Russian rector of that institution; Nikolai ('Karlo') Chkheidze, who was to become the Menshevik President of the Petrograd Soviet in 1917; and Noe Zhordania, the future President of independent Georgia.

In later years, Zhordania published informative memoirs, which provide a wealth of insight into the mental evolution of Georgian radical youth of that period.[63] Born in 1868 near Ozurgeti (now Makharadze) in the south-western Georgian province of Guria, Zhordania came of a well-known local family of petty gentry. Like Stalin after him, he received his education at the Tbilisi Theological Seminary; but although destined for the priesthood, he early lost faith in Christianity and found himself drawn step by step into the role of a political agitator and reformer. He recalls how, at the age of sixteen, he chanced on a Russian treatise on natural philosophy, which convinced him that

'God is Nature herself; as for a white-bearded deity, seated upon a throne, such a personage simply does not exist'. 'I thought to myself: If Nature's lord and master is Nature herself, then who is the rightful lord and master of mankind? The general opinion was that the Tsar was lord over the people, and that the Tsar was himself appointed by God. But if God did not exist any more, the Tsar could not be His representative. I was therefore at a loss to understand by whose command and authority he sat upon his throne.'

While still a prey to doubt, Zhordania made the acquaintance of the Tbilisi publisher Zakaria Chichinadze, who lent him two numbers of Herzen's *Kolokol* (*The Bell*). The fiery utterances of that stormy petrel of Russian radicalism dispelled the

Georgian student's last misgivings. 'The Tsar, I now realised, was just as much a faked-up authority as God, and I looked upon them both with the same sceptical eyes. Atheism and republicanism commended themselves to me as twin doctrines of equal validity.'[64]

While continuing with his classes at the Tbilisi Seminary, Zhordania joined various clandestine discussion groups and took a leading part, together with the future Bolshevik leader Philip Makharadze (1868–1941), in student strikes and demonstrations against the Russian management. To begin with, he and his friends came under the influence of the agrarian socialism of the Narodniks. He read with avidity such books as Chernyshevsky's famous revolutionary novel *Chto delat'?* (*What is to be done?*). But somehow the doctrine of the Narodniks failed to satisfy him. In Russia, as Zhordania saw it, rural life revolved round the peasant commune of the *mir* or *obshchina*; in Georgia, all the emphasis among the peasantry was on individual private proprietorship of the land. The Narodniks' mission was to preach the gospel of peasant revolt against the established hierarchy. But the peasant himself was nearly always a monarchist at heart, a petty bourgeois in mentality, incapable of response to the revolutionary vision of a new, socialist society. In short, the achievement of democratic socialism through the agency of a mass of benighted *muzhiks* seemed to the young Zhordania a highly dubious undertaking.

A like dilemma had already helped to produce a split within the revolutionary movement in metropolitan Russia. In 1879, a secret conference of the Narodniks held at Voronezh divided into two factions. One stuck to the time-honoured agrarian programme; the other, led by G. V. Plekhanov, set out to graft on to the Russian revolutionary movement the ideas of Western industrial socialism. Plekhanov soon established himself as the foremost exponent of Marxist philosophy and sociology in Russia. He became the teacher of Lenin and of a whole generation of Russian, as well as of Georgian revolutionaries. Plekhanov foretold that capitalist industrialism was about to invade Russia and destroy the patriarchal-feudal attitudes and relationships and the primitive rustic communes on which the Populists desired to base their socialism. An urban proletariat would arise in Russia, which would embark on a struggle for industrial socialism very much on the Western European pattern. The vision of a peculiarly Slavonic rural socialism springing straight from pure feudalism and serfdom Plekhanov dismissed as utopian. The revolutionaries, he urged, must prepare themselves without delay to organize the urban working class of the future.

These ideas soon spread to the outlying regions of Russia, especially to Georgia. During the 1880's, the Georgian intelligentsia began to study Marx's *Das Kapital*. The book was read even by Georgian political prisoners exiled to Siberia. In 1886, the Georgian journal *Teatri* (*The Theatre*) published a favourable review of the second volume of Marx's great book. Plekhanov's own writings also became known in Tbilisi, where they provoked lively discussion among the young intellectuals.

Meanwhile Noe Zhordania ended his studies at the seminary. Refusing to enter the priesthood, he went instead to Warsaw to attend the veterinary institute there. One of his fellow students introduced him to the writings of Karl Kautsky, the German socialist. Kautsky's writings helped to produce a radical change in Zhordania's outlook. 'I now realized for the first time that Russian socialism was a thoroughly utopian and reactionary movement, and that if it should ever be put into operation anywhere, we should be plunged back into barbarism.' In Tbilisi, there existed only the rudiments of a working class, its habits and outlook still coloured by the traditions of the Oriental bazaar world. In Warsaw, on the other hand, Zhordania found himself in a Western environment, where he could see with his own eyes something of the life and manners of the industrial working class of which Marx and Engels had written. Again, the Poles' deep-rooted antagonism to Russian ways, language and religious dogma, more intense than anything Zhordania had seen in Georgia, made him see that 'in subjugated countries there must first of all take place a political revolution; democracy must be established first, and only afterwards, by the furtherance of economic progress and by extensive organizational work, can we proceed towards social revolution'. The failure of the Narodniks to reach any form of understanding with the inherently passive and bourgeois-minded peasantry made it imperative to operate first on the more receptive mind of the factory worker. Once the town worker was indoctrinated with the new ideas, he could himself propagate them among his rustic cousins in terms they could understand.[65]

From Warsaw, Zhordania kept up a clandestine correspondence with friends in Georgia, such as Sylvester Jibladze and the proletarian writer Egnate Ninoshvili (Ingoroqva), whom he also kept supplied with Russian subversive political literature. With Philip Makharadze, Zhordania formed a socialist group among the young Georgians living and studying in Warsaw. Other Georgian student groups operated in the various Russian university centres. In 1892, a conference of Georgian students was held at Kutaisi in Western Georgia. In the following year, they founded a *League for the Liberation of Georgia*, whose programme sought to reconcile the 'bourgeois-nationalist' and the Marxian 'class-struggle' trends in Georgian progressive thought.

Zhordania returned to Tbilisi in August 1892. After what he had seen in Poland, he brought with him the conviction that the Georgians must make common cause with their Russian and Polish brethren and work towards revolution on an all-Russian scale. By herself, Georgia could never vanquish the Russian dragon. There was no sense in struggling in isolation against the common foe—the Tsarist imperial régime.

In December 1892, there took place at Zestafoni in Western Georgia the first meeting of the so-called *Third Group*, out of which was to grow the *Georgian Social-Democratic Party*. The main organizer of the conference was Egnate Ninoshvili, the young Georgian radical novelist. Ninoshvili, whose real name was Egnate Ingoroqva, occupies an important place in Georgian literature and social thought, as the first truly 'working-class' writer, in which respect he may be compared with Maxim Gorky in Russia. Born in 1859 of a poor Gurian peasant family, Ninoshvili worked for a time as a village schoolmaster. He then moved to Tbilisi and became a type-setter in a printing house. After many setbacks, he left Tbilisi for Batumi on the Black Sea, where he worked as a dock-labourer and then in the Rothschild oil-drum factory. A contemporary who saw him at work there was shocked to see this frail young intellectual dragging great planks about the factory, with blood dripping from his torn fingers. Later on, Ninoshvili was employed as a clerk at the manganese works at Zestafoni, where the fumes and dust finally undermined his health. Meanwhile, Ninoshvili had been working at his remarkable stories, which he used to read aloud to his fellow-workers. Their publication won him fame, and permitted him at last to enjoy a little relief from manual labour. But it was too late to save his life. In 1894, he returned desperately ill to his native village in Guria, where he died in the same year from tuberculosis.

Ninoshvili's stories give a vivid picture of the life of the Georgian workers and peasants of that time and of their struggle against bailiffs, landlords and officials. His historical novel, *The Revolt in Guria*, brings to life the events of the Gurian peasant uprising in 1841 directed against the feudal magnates and the Russian occupying power. The story, *Gogia Uishvili*, tells of a poor peasant flogged for defending his wife and children from insult at the hands of the police, and then committing suicide rather than survive such shameful punishment. Other tales treat of such themes as a peasant knocked down and run over by a train while engaged on forced labour on the railway, and of boatmen drowned while shipping timber over a lake during a storm. The story, *A Hero of Our Land*, tells of a parasitical debauchee squire, by name Tariel Mklavadze, who finally meets his just deserts at the hands of a poor village school-teacher for whose wife's death this Mklavadze is responsible. It is hard to read Ninoshvili's stories without a feeling of indignation against the system which produced such abuses and injustices. There is no doubt that they helped to produce in public opinion a state of mind receptive to the socialist ideas which Zhordania and his associates, with the active encouragement of Ninoshvili himself, were preparing to propagate in Georgia.

At that first gathering of the *Mesame Dasi* at Zestafoni in December 1892, the Narodnik element gained the upper hand. The majority of the group felt unable to share Zhordania's confidence in the possibility of effecting revolution through the medium of the yet immature Georgian proletariat, and stuck to the old Populist formula of socialism via the peasant commune. Undeterred by this, and encouraged by the support of Ninoshvili and Jibladze, Zhordania wrote a comprehensive exposé of Marxist economic doctrine, as applied to specifically

Georgian conditions. This document, entitled *Economic Progress and the National Question*, was presented to the next meeting of the group at Tbilisi in February 1893, and met this time with unanimous approval.

'The current evolution of Georgia,' Zhordania wrote, 'involves two aspects, both of them fundamental, and closely interdependent —namely the economic and industrial development of the various regions of Georgia, together with a growing inequality in the material living standards of the Georgian people. Both of these trends arise from the stimulus of commercial and capitalistic enterprise. In the early stages, a nation achieves unity on the basis of the ideology of self-conscious nationalism; subsequently, however, that same nation is bound to find itself divided through self-conscious economic sectional interest. These two trends are born the one from the other; the first summons the second into being, while the second contributes to the development of the first. . . . The core of our present-day life consists in economic growth, which in its turn has given birth to national unity as well as to social cleavage. Georgia is one and indivisible; nevertheless, she is divided into two sections in regard to wealth and to poverty. If on the first point we are united, on the second we are divided. If on questions relating to our internal way of life we are at loggerheads, nevertheless we stand united against the external foe. . . . Capitalism has changed the customs and manners of nations, destroyed the ancient juridical and political framework, overturned idyllic patriarchal relationships, united each individual nation as a separate entity, and brought the nations into contact with one another. On the other hand, that same capitalism has divided the nation into two factions— rich and poor, landowner and landless peasant, bourgeois and worker—and implanted social friction, given birth to the class struggle and summoned the working class into the political arena.'

Zhordania went on to stress that in the new conditions created by capitalism, it was the town and not the village which led the way towards economic progress and social change. Once new ideas took root in the towns, they would soon spread out into the villages of their own accord. Georgia, he foresaw, was entering on the age of urban capitalism. This did not mean that the peasant and the village community had no part to play. But it had to be recognized that even village life was becoming to some extent coloured by urban influences. The life of the Georgian people generally was being Europeanized.

This meant that Georgians must think increasingly in terms of new social philosophies—such as Marxist socialism—which had been born in the economically more advanced West, but were becoming steadily more relevant to Georgian conditions.

No sooner had Zhordania's programme been adopted as an ideological basis for the new revolutionary school in Georgia than its author was forced to flee the country. The Warsaw police rounded up many Georgian and Polish students there on suspicion of subversive activity. Zhordania received warning in time, and sailed from Batumi to Europe in May 1893, some weeks before a warrant arrived for his own arrest. He remained abroad for over four years, until his return to Georgia in October 1897. He visited Switzerland, one of the main refuges for Russian revolutionaries, and met Plekhanov and the redoubtable Vera Zasulich in Geneva. In 1895, he went to Paris and worked at the Bibliothèque Nationale, as well as making the acquaintance of Jules Guesde, Paul Lafargue and other French socialists. Later he went to Stuttgart to visit Karl Kautsky, who became an enthusiastic supporter of the Georgian socialist movement. 'Kautsky,' Zhordania recalls, 'made a deep impression on me by his modesty, simplicity, clarity of thought and great knowledge.' Zhordania also made the acquaintance of the political adventurer and financier Alexander Helphand, known as Parvus, who was to play a leading part in international politics during the World War and the revolutionary period. Early in 1897, Zhordania left Germany for London, where he met the Georgian revolutionary Varlam Cherkesov, whose anarchist views did not entirely coincide with his own; he also frequented the British Museum. He sent back to Georgia favourable reports on the British way of life, some of which were printed in the Tbilisi journals, and contrasted the benevolent British policemen with their less kindly counterparts in Russia.

Wherever he went on his travels, Zhordania was seeking for solutions to Georgia's many political and social problems, such as the national question, land tenure, the political role of the urban proletariat and so on. Much of what he saw was irrelevant to Georgian conditions. The countries of Western Europe (apart from special instances like that of Alsace-Lorraine) were free from foreign domination and the handicap of a colonial régime. Individual liberty and national independence were, broadly speaking, assured. Like other visitors before and since, Zhordania found the structure of English society particularly baffling. Where were the peasants? He found dukes and aristocratic *grands seigneurs,* middle-class farmers who looked and behaved like members of the bourgeoisie, and hordes of farm-labourers who were merely rustic proletarians. But of true peasants on the Russian or Georgian model, no sign was to be seen. However, Zhordania's years in Western Europe had considerable significance for the future development of socialism in Georgia. The personal contacts which he made enabled the Georgians to drink direct from the wellsprings of European socialism, rather than simply imbibing the muddy puddles of Russian revolutionary ideology. He brought back with him the conviction that Georgia's political and economic progress could not be assured without direct contacts with Western European culture, and a break with the mingled Persian, Turkish and Russian influences in which the people and even the intelligentsia had for so long stagnated.

Within Georgia, the young Marxist intellectuals were in the meantime gaining strength and adherents. They embarked both upon open literary work of a more or less innocuous nature, and upon the formation of clandestine Marxist study circles and revolutionary societies among workers and students. When Egnate Ninoshvili died in 1894, his funeral was turned into a public demonstration at which Sylvester Jibladze and other leaders of the movement boldly expounded their social and economic theories and set forth the remedies they proposed for the ills of Georgia. The liberal writer Giorgi Tsereteli, prominent as leader of the so-called *Meore Dasi* ('*Second Group*'), declared that a new epoch in Georgian social and intellectual life had begun, and hailed the birth of this new school of economic and political thought—the *Mesame Dasi* or '*Third Group*'. Within a decade, this group was to occupy a dominant position in the country's whole political and social evolution.

Sweated labour

It may seem strange at first sight that a people so largely made up of peasants and mountain clansmen, with a small industry and a comparatively negligible and uneducated proletariat, should be attracted to Marxian socialism. However, there were several factors which contributed to this leaning. Following the abolition of serfdom and the break-up of feudal and patriarchal forms of social organization, Georgia, along with other regions of the Caucasus, was undergoing commercial development on an increasing scale. As Lenin put it, 'The country, sparsely populated in the years after the Reform, inhabited by highlanders and staying aloof from the development of world economy, aloof even from history, was becoming a country of oil industrialists, wine merchants, grain and tobacco manufacturers.'[66] The rich manganese ore deposits of Chiatura and the oil industry of Baku and Batumi were being developed, largely by foreign capital. Whereas in 1886–87, the total value of industrial production in the regions of Tbilisi and Kutaisi amounted to little more than 10,000,000 rubles, by 1891–92 the figure had risen to 32,000,000. In the same short period the number of full-time industrial workers rose from 12,000 to 23,000, in addition to those employed on the railway. By 1900, the number of Georgian industrial workers was reckoned at about 35,000, or up to 50,000 if one includes the railwaymen. It may be reckoned therefore that industrial workers with their families formed scarcely a tenth part of the population. But the fact that the workers were concentrated at key centres of transport and communications gave them an importance out of all proportion to their numerical strength. Tbilisi was the main junction on the railway connecting the Caspian coast with the Black Sea. The railway yards of Tbilisi and the oil-fields of Baku were the birthplace of the militant proletariat of Transcaucasia. As Tbilisi and Baku were also the leading cities of the land, strategic hubs of administration, education, journalism, publishing and commerce, they were places from which industrial unrest could be stirred up and socialist propaganda diffused in a most effective manner.

The conditions of work in the mines and factories of Georgia themselves fostered dissatisfaction and discontent. A twelve-hour working day was common. Workers were often forced to clean and repair their machines and tools in their own time and without extra payment. Many workshops were situated in ill-ventilated, noisome cellars or overcrowded sheds, without adequate lighting or heating. Canteen and rest-room facilities were non-existent, and the workers ate and rested beside their machines. All the classic abuses of old-style capitalism flourished unchecked. Arbitrary fines were imposed by the management for minor misdemeanours; the factory hooter was sounded half an hour before the official time in the morning, an hour late at closing time in the evening; vouchers for monopoly-owned factory shops were issued in lieu of wages in cash. Pitiable was the lot of the manganese miners of Chiatura, who worked their seams with primitive instruments down narrow shafts, in the light of open, unguarded kerosene lamps, and on a diet of bread and water and maize porridge. Many observers commented on the squalor prevalent in the Tbilisi match and cigarette factories, the dye works, tanneries, and weaving mills, where frequent epidemics undermined the workers' health. With unguarded and ill-maintained machinery and overtired, underfed workers, accidents were common. The Batumi correspondent of Ilia Chavchavadze's paper, *Iveria*, reported in 1890 that 'not a day goes by without one or two workers being maimed and losing an arm or a foot. The crippled victim is mercilessly kicked out into the street, like a piece of useless old rubbish. . . .'[67] The active working life of a Georgian industrial labourer averaged little more than fifteen years. Trade unions were proscribed, strikes forbidden and suppressed by the police and militia. The appeal of the 'class struggle' was reinforced by feelings of national solidarity. Few of the Caucasian industrial magnates were Georgians. It was therefore all the easier to whip up hatred of the Armenian merchants and money-lenders, the British, French and Jewish capitalists, and the Russian officials who, so it was represented, formed an unholy alliance to exploit the Georgian workers and peasants, and draw fat dividends from their sweat and tears.

It is true that industrialization affected as yet only a relatively small proportion of the population and that Georgia was still a predominantly agricultural and pastoral land. But the agrarian problem itself had revolutionary potentialities. The reforms of the 1860's, while abolishing serfdom as an institution, did virtually nothing to improve the peasant's economic lot. A striking proof of this is the fact that the system of 'temporary obligation'—a form of servitude to which a peasant was subject pending final settlement of redemption dues in respect of land acquired from his former lord—was not abolished until as late as 1912, many years later than in metropolitan Russia. In 1891, the peasants of Eastern Georgia possessed 134,796 *desyatins* of land (1 *desyatin* = 2·7 acres), whereas the landowners had 961,502; the peasants of Western Georgia owned 210,779 *desyatins*, the landowners 815,321. This was at a time when the peasantry formed 85 per cent. of the population of Eastern Georgia and 86 per cent. of that of Western Georgia. The landowning gentry, on the other hand, made up only 2·89 per cent. and 6·78 per cent. of the populations of Eastern and Western Georgia respectively.

However, the largest landlord of all in Georgia was the Russian crown. In 1900, after just a century of occupation, the Russian government had swallowed up more than half the landed estates in the country. Statistics of the time reckoned Georgia to contain some 6,120,000 *desyatins* of exploitable land, or about 16,524,000 acres. This was distributed as follows:

Russian government:	3,535,544 *des.*
Landowners:	1,914,214 *des.*
Peasants:	382,697 *des.*
Merchants and others:	148,885 *des.*
Russian imperial family:	116,299 *des.*
Church domains:	22,361 *des.*
	6,120,000 *des.*

These figures show that the Russian imperial government owned some 58 per cent. of the land, the landed proprietors 31 per cent.; of the remaining 11 per cent., a substantial slice, as will be seen, belonged personally to individual members of the Russian imperial family. The peasants, forming some 85 per cent. of the population, had to content themselves with just over 6 per cent. of the land, and were weighed down into the bargain by redemption payments, tithes and sundry taxes. They were in fact caught in a vicious circle. For the most part, they could afford neither to increase their holdings nor to introduce improved methods of cultivation. Pauperization of the villages was accompanied by a drift of dispossessed peasants into the slums of the towns, where they lent a ready ear to socialist agitators. Nor did the attitude of the Georgian landed gentry do much to alleviate the position. To quote a present-day Georgian writer by no means friendly to Communist ideas:

'If our princes and country squires had renounced their sectional interests in time, and risen to the occasion by making some genuine response to the general interests of the nation, Marxist ideas could never have taken root. Our aristocracy prepared the ground for socialism by its own policy. Its many oppressive acts cleared the way for Socialist propagandists. In the end, the impoverished squirearchy itself became the backbone of this movement, in the person of its most eminent representative, N. Zhordania.'[68]

Like many middle-class socialists, however, Zhordania and his associates failed to realise that the 'class struggle', for the intensification of which they enthusiastically campaigned, would result in a holocaust of which they themselves would be among the victims.

Under the promise of an amnesty, Zhordania had returned to Georgia from Western Europe in 1897. He and his friends soon gained control of the liberal newspaper *Kvali* (*The Furrow*), which became the regular organ of Georgian 'legal Marxism'. In this paper Zhordania and his disciples proclaimed that bourgeois capitalism had already taken root in Georgia, and that the country was thus in the intermediate stage between feudalism and socialism. They criticized the older generation of Georgian patriots who concentrated their efforts on a revival of the use of the Georgian language, on cultivating Georgian literature, and on supporting the Georgian national Church as a focus for the country's moral and spiritual life. The young socialist zealots depicted even the great Ilia Chavchavadze as a dyed-in-the-wool reactionary and criticized the management of such institutions as the Land Bank of the Nobility, the Society for the Spreading of Literacy among the Georgians, the National Theatre and the independent, voluntary Georgian schools as 'bourgeois' or 'aristocratic'. In Zhordania's view, the idea of a Georgian national revival within the framework of Russian tsardom was absurd. The salvation of Georgia lay, he believed, in solidarity between the Georgian and the Russian and international working classes. Implicit in Zhordania's reasoning—

though such ideas could not be expressed openly in print—was the conclusion that only after the overthrow of the Russian imperial system could Georgia hope to achieve national fulfilment through democratic socialism, in which 'effete elements' such as princes, priests and capitalists would have no share.

Such views were anathema to Ilia Chavchavadze and the other leading Georgian nationalists, who were not slow in taking up Zhordania's challenge. In a series of outspoken articles, published pseudonymously in 1900, Ilia roundly castigated Zhordania and his followers, whom he declared to be ignorant, illiterate, conceited and infantile. Zhordania, in Ilia's view, was nothing but a charlatan, a man claiming to be 'sent into the world to alter the axis on which the globe revolves, and make heaven and earth turn according to his will and pleasure'.[69] It is ironic therefore to note that while reeling under Ilia's thunderbolts, Zhordania, Chkheidze and the other 'legal Marxists' who formed the majority of the *Mesame Dasi* group were simultaneously being assailed by the extremist wing of their own party as lukewarm intellectuals, unable and unwilling to lead the nation in an active revolutionary campaign against Tsardom. They were wrong, it was said, to bide their time while limiting themselves to the peaceful propagation of Marxist ideas, and to ignore the need for setting up illegal, revolutionary printing presses, instigating violence, and organizing a massive political upheaval of the working classes against the Tsar and the bourgeoisie.

Stalin's revolutionary youth

Prominent among the left-wing, extremist minority of the *Mesame Dasi* was Lado Ketskhoveli, the future friend and mentor of Stalin. Expelled with more than eighty other students from the Tbilisi Theological Seminary in 1894, Ketskhoveli went to Kiev, where he made contact with clandestine groups of Russian socialists and became initiated into the underground revolutionary movement. Arrested in 1896, he was sent back to his birthplace to be kept under police surveillance. He came back to the Caucasus eager to free the revolutionary movement in his homeland out of its provincial swaddling clothes by setting up a secret printing press and embarking on terroristic campaigns. In 1898, another former student from the Tbilisi Theological Seminary joined the militant wing of the group. His name was Joseph Jughashvili—the future Stalin. The nineteen-year-old novice was immediately taken in hand by Ketskhoveli and another thorough-going revolutionary, Alexander Dsulukidze, and set to work on running Marxist study circles for the Tbilisi industrial workers. His task was to lecture on socialism to the tobacco workers, masons, shoemakers, weavers, printers and the conductors of the local horse trams. The workers met in small groups, a dozen or a score in each, in some obscure slum-dwelling, while one member watched outside to make sure that the police had not got wind of what was afoot. In those days, education was the privilege of the few, so that the young student volunteers were treated with respect by the workers, often older men, and accepted as mentors and guides.

It was not long before Ketskhoveli, Dsulukidze and Stalin constituted a well-organized 'action' group within the Tbilisi Social-Democratic organization, parting company more and more with Zhordania and the other moderates. A positive impetus to their movement was provided by a series of well planned strikes which broke out from 1898 onwards in various sectors of Georgian industry. In December 1898, the main Tbilisi railway depot came out on strike in protest against a reduction in wages, the abolition of free railway passes for railwaymen and their families, and other vexatious measures. The strike was directed by both the local Georgian socialists and by workers of revolutionary sympathies who had been deported from Russia; it lasted a week and led to the arrest of forty-one ringleaders. The following year was marked by strikes in a Tbilisi tobacco factory, at the horse tram depot, at the Adelkhanov shoe factory, at the Sharadze printing works, as well as in Batumi at the Rothschild oil refinery. The first of May 1899, was celebrated by the first May Day demonstration to be held in the Caucasus. Between seventy and eighty railway and industrial workers and socialist agitators assembled at a spot called Ghrma-Ghele (Deep Ravine) on the outskirts of Tbilisi. They were addressed by Lado Ketskhoveli and other orators, who stressed the significance of May Day as a symbol of the international solidarity of the toiling masses. The participants took a solemn vow beneath a red flag to close their ranks and fight with all their strength in the death struggle against Tsarism and capitalist exploitation.

'Legal Marxism' and the fighting underground

The only leading member of the *Mesame Dasi* who was equally at home in the militant underground and in the more respectable world of 'legal Marxism' was Sylvester Jibladze. The other legal Marxists, such as Zhordania and Chkheidze, took no direct part in the strikes and other incidents. Their aloofness provoked accusations of 'opportunism' and faint-heartedness on the part of the revolutionary agitators, and signs of an impending breach between the moderate wing, the future Mensheviks, and the militant revolutionary wing, the future Bolsheviks, were already apparent. The Russian authorities, curiously enough, showed an amazing degree of toleration towards Zhordania and his group, who were now in control of the newspaper *Kvali,* in the columns of which they preached the forthcoming collapse of capitalism and the intensification of the class struggle. The Russian Governor-General of the Caucasus, Prince Golitsyn, was more concerned with combating Georgian nationalism and 'separatism' than with preventing the spread of economic doctrines, however potentially explosive. It is known, indeed, that the Tbilisi censors received a special circular from St. Petersburg, directing them to pay exclusive attention to manifestations of local nationalism. They devoted their attention to harassing patriotic citizens like Prince Ilia Chavchavadze, men of substance and respectable liberals, whose demands amounted to little more than home rule for Georgia, education in the national language, civic rights, trial by jury, and so on, within the general pattern of the existing imperial system. The authorities failed to see that the revolutionary ferment spreading all over Russia was a greater danger to the régime than any such symptoms of local pride. 'It was clear that the Censorship Committee was far more afraid of patriotic verses than of discussions on economics.'[70] This situation, with its paradoxical features, was aptly summed up by a contemporary foreign observer who wrote:

'We find in Georgia the same tendency to encourage Socialism as an antidote to middle-class Constitutionalism and Liberalism as in Russia itself, where the famous Zubatoff movement of the

Moscow workmen was actually organized under the auspices of the secret police. Prince Golitsyn and the bureaucrats of the Plehve school were less afraid of Social Democracy than of the Nationalism of the Georgian nobles and intellectuals, whose aims were in the direction of constitutional government, and therefore incompatible with autocracy, of national autonomy which might lead to separatism and the break-up of the Empire, and of an autocephalous Church, which naturally aroused the fears of M. Pobiedonostzeff. . . .[71] Prince Golitsyn hoped to create a breach between the Georgian Nationalist upper classes and the peasantry, and to introduce a mild milk-and-water Socialism, sufficient to weaken the autonomists, but docile and friendly to the authorities.'[72]

This strange and uneasy alliance between the Tsarist gendarmes and the Georgian leaders of the labour movement could not last. Whenever it came to a clash, it was the workers and not the nobles or capitalists whom the Cossacks attacked with their guns and whips. From 1900 onwards, Georgia, like the rest of Russia, was caught up in the backwash of a worldwide economic depression. This had a catastrophic effect on Georgia's budding industrial enterprises. The output of manganese at Chiatura was drastically curtailed. The export of petroleum products from Batumi was reduced and the workers put on to short-time working. Many factories in Tbilisi, Batumi, Kutaisi, Poti and Chiatura had to close down. In the Tbilisi province alone there were over 4,000 unemployed. To make things worse, the harvest in 1901 was bad. Starving peasants invaded the towns in search of work, adding to the chaos and misery.

The manufacturers cut wages and laid off staff, which in turn provoked a wave of strikes and boycotts. In March 1901, the police rounded up and imprisoned the leaders of the militant socialist wing in Tbilisi, including Lenin's disciple Victor Kurnatovsky. Among the few who escaped arrest was young Jughashvili-Stalin, then a clerk at the Tbilisi Observatory, who now went into hiding. From the 'underground', he played a prominent part in organizing opposition to the authorities. Many of his comrades being under arrest, it fell to him to carry through the plans which had been made for a May Day demonstration far more audacious than the inoffensive gatherings of 1899 and 1900.

'The workers of the whole of Russia,' declared a revolutionary broadsheet of the time, 'have decided to celebrate the First of May openly—in the best thoroughfares of the city. They have proudly declared to the authorities that Cossack whips and sabres, torture by the police and the gendarmerie hold no terror for them! Friends, let us too join our Russian comrades! Let us join hands, Georgians, Russians, Armenians; let us gather, raise the scarlet banner and celebrate our only holiday—the First of May!'[73]

The demonstration was fixed for 22 April 1901 (Old Style). At midday, the sounding of the noon cannon shot from the Tbilisi arsenal gave the signal for action. The red flag was unfurled on the Soldatsky Bazaar (the present-day Kolkhoz Square), near the Alexander Garden. The fiery words of revolutionary orators were acclaimed by some 2,000 workers with cries of 'Down with Autocracy! Up the Republic! Long live Liberty!' Before the demonstrators could march on the main boulevards, they were set upon by police and Cossacks. A savage battle ensued. The Governor of Tbilisi hastened to the scene. Reinforcements were called in. At the end, fourteen workers lay dead on the square. Fifty arrests were made. Abortive though it was, this demonstration was of great significance. Lenin commented in his paper *Iskra* (*The Spark*): 'The event which took place on Sunday 22 April, in Tiflis is of historic import for the entire Caucasus: this day marks the beginnings of an open revolutionary movement in the Caucasus.' Following the disturbance, the police rounded up many leading socialist intellectuals whom they had previously treated with tolerance, including Noe Zhordania, who spent several months in the Metekhi fortress jail in Tbilisi.

Despite all repressions, the Georgian revolutionary movement continued to gather momentum. Lado Ketskhoveli proceeded to Baku, the great oil-producing centre in Azerbaijan on the Caspian, and set up an illegal printing press on which he produced the first issues of *Brdzola* (*The Struggle*), the organ of the Tbilisi Social-Democratic organization. Ketskhoveli also made *Brdzola* into a local mouthpiece of the all-Russian Social-Democratic movement, adopting the programme of Lenin's *Iskra*, with its emphasis on the creation of a united all-Russian party to co-ordinate political agitation and work for the dictatorship of the proletariat. Ketskhoveli and his assistants printed broadsheets addressed to the army, inciting the troops to mutiny—'which manifestoes,' according to a gendarmerie report of the time, 'were very widely circulated among the troops'.[74] Ketskhoveli soon afterwards handed over the Baku secret press to another Georgian revolutionary, T. T. Enukidze who passed it on in 1904 to his namesake, Abel Enukidze. This Abel Enukidze later became a close friend of Stalin, who betrayed him and had him shot during the purges of 1936–37.

On 11 November 1901, the first conference of the Georgian branch of the Russian Social-Democratic Workers' Party took place in Tbilisi. The personnel of the branch was virtually identical with that of the Georgian *Mesame Dasi* or *Third Group,* though some members had reservations about joining any organization with an all-Russian label. The committee of nine elected at this conference included Stalin and Sylvester Jibladze, though the latter was soon afterwards arrested and exiled to Siberia. Stalin was sent to Batumi to stir up revolutionary activity among the workers at the important Black Sea port and oil-refinery. It was a promising assignment. The oil pipe-line between Baku and Batumi had recently been completed. Batumi counted over ten large industrial enterprises, including the petroleum container factories of Rothschild, Mantashev, Nobel and others, two tobacco factories, an iron foundry, a nail works, a mineral water bottling depot and several oil loading stations. There were some 11,000 industrial workers, a motley, polyglot mixture of Christians and Muslims, with some of the riffraff always to be found in ports and dockyards. Conditions of life were generally poor. The working day averaged fourteen hours, compulsory overtime bringing it at times up to sixteen hours. Wages were from sixty kopecks to one ruble per day. There was obvious scope for socialist agitation. In fact, a small Russian Social-Democratic committee had functioned in Batumi for a time, until broken up by the police in 1898. The promotion of the workers' interests was then taken over by two founder members of Zhordania's *Mesame Dasi* party, Karlo Chkheidze and Isidore Ramishvili, 'legal Marxists' who abstained from violent measures and engaged for the most part in work of an educational nature and in practical welfare.

When Stalin arrived in Batumi, he was welcomed coldly by

Chkheidze and Ramishvili, who were opposed to clandestine conspiracies and acts of terrorism. Nothing daunted, Stalin convened a meeting of militant elements among the local workers and intellectuals, who assembled on New Year's Eve, 1901. A Batumi Social-Democratic organization was formally constituted on the Leninist model, and eleven workers' circles set up in the principal factories. Stalin set to work writing leaflets and printing them off on a primitive hand press in his lodgings. His efforts soon produced results. In January 1902, a strike at Mantashev's ended in victory for the workers, the management being forced into important concessions.

In the following month, a strike broke out at Rothschild's over the dismissal of nearly four hundred workers suspected of subversive activities. The Military Governor of Kutaisi arrived on the spot and ordered the arrest of thirty-two ringleaders. Stalin and his associates organized a mass demonstration of workers, who paraded through the streets on 8 March 1902, demanding the release of their comrades. Three hundred arrests were made. When it was learnt that all the detainees were to be deported from Batumi, an even larger crowd of demonstrators, including workers from the Rothschild and Mantashev factories, the docks and the railway yards, in all about 6,000, set out for the barracks where the prisoners were held. The military commandant refused to hand over his charges and ordered the workers to disperse. A company of the 7th Caucasian Rifles were called out to clear the square, but were met with jeers and stones. Then the prisoners inside managed to break out and join their comrades outside the barracks. Finally, the troops opened fire, killing fourteen workers and wounding many others. The incident was widely reported in the Russian and foreign press.

The Tsarist secret police or *Okhrana* redoubled its efforts to track down the leaders of the Batumi revolutionary cell. In the end, they succeeded in discovering and raiding a meeting of the Batumi revolutionary committee. Stalin and others were arrested. After spending eighteen months in various Caucasian jails, Stalin was deported for three years to the Irkutsk province in eastern Siberia. However, he promptly made his escape and was back in Tbilisi early in 1904, ready to play his part in the upheavals which shook the Caucasus during the revolution of

1905. In the meantime, his comrade Lado Ketskhoveli, who had been seized and confined in the Metekhi prison at Tbilisi, was shot dead in his cell by the Tsarist police. Another leading Georgian Bolshevik and friend of Stalin, Alexander Dsulukidze, died of consumption in June 1905, at the age of twenty-nine. At the same time, daring and determined young men were continually reinforcing the revolutionary wing of the Social-Democratic party in the Caucasus. Particularly militant were some of the Armenian revolutionaries, who formed several secret societies, some of a nationalist and others of a socialist hue. The animosity of the Armenian community, normally reserved for the Turks, was vented on the Russian government also after 1903, when Prince Golitsyn confiscated the property of the Armenian national Church and perpetrated other discriminatory measures against the Armenians, who were very numerous in Tbilisi itself. The ineptitude of Tsarist policy in Caucasia was strikingly exemplified by this decree of confiscation, which was signed by Tsar Nicholas II at the insistence of Golitsyn and the minister Plehve, but against the vote of a majority of the imperial council of ministers, who justly regarded the proposal as iniquitous and fraught with political danger. The result of this measure was that Stalin's group was reinforced by several daring Armenian terrorists, including the celebrated Ter-Petrossian, known as Kamo. In 1903, Kamo caused a public sensation by scattering socialist leaflets among the audience at the Tbilisi Armenian theatre. He led the hold-up of the Tbilisi State Bank in 1907, and followed this up by a series of escapades which won him an international reputation.[75]

Side by side with the revolutionary movement among the industrial workers, a spontaneous and concerted resistance campaign was gathering momentum among the villagers. Losing hope in a solution from above to the problems of land tenure and the general impoverishment of the countryside, the peasants began to impose their own solution from below. They would make life unbearable for the local squire by various forms of boycott and provocation, until he left of his own accord for the nearest city. In some cases, they would politely escort their former feudal master to the railway station and bundle him on to the next train for Tbilisi. The movement was particularly strong in the south-western province of

Guria, where the small size of the peasant allotments gave rise to an often quoted saying: 'If I tie up a cow on my bit of land, her tail will be in someone else's!' To keep themselves and their families, 80 per cent of the Gurian peasantry were forced to look for permanent or seasonal jobs in the towns, in search of which they travelled as far afield as Odessa and Rostov in southern Russia. Guria was directly affected by the strikes and socialist agitation which were convulsing nearby Batumi. It was not mere coincidence that Guria produced the first Georgian proletarian writer, Egnate Ninoshvili, and the founder of Georgian Marxism, Noe Zhordania.

In 1902, matters came to a head with a direct challenge thrown down by the Gurian peasantry to the Russian authorities and to their own landed proprietors. The Gurian movement began with a series of demands for reduction of rent, and with protests against the usurpation of peasant land by the state. The peasants refused to pay taxes to the government or tithes to the priests. They boycotted unpopular squires as well as all organs and representatives of the Russian administration. The village headmen were powerless to keep order, and were in any case overwhelmingly in sympathy with their stubborn compatriots. The Russians reacted at first with mass arrests and repressions. They sent troops to round up the ringleaders, who included the majority of the local village schoolmasters and a number of socialist agitators who had arrived from the towns. Noe Zhordania, who had just been released from custody and returned to his native Guria, was rearrested; Noe Khomeriki the agronomist, future Minister of Agriculture of independent Georgia, was also taken into custody. The fortresses were filled with captives and many were sent into Siberian exile.

'Down with autocracy!'

The Cossacks and gendarmes could not be everywhere at once. The ferment spread throughout the province and into neighbouring regions as well. Mansions were burnt down. Demonstrations took place, red flags were waved, and the cry of 'Down with autocracy!' was repeatedly to be heard. The priests were forbidden by their flock to repeat in church the prayer for the imperial family, and portraits of Tsar Nicholas II were torn down and burnt. Bodies of murdered policemen and soldiers were refused church burial and had to be discreetly interred by the police themselves. In those centres where the district governor, chief of police, magistrates and other paraphernalia of Muscovite bureaucracy managed to survive at all, they were paralysed and ineffective. The people set up their own popular tribunals, which dealt with all forms of crime and immorality in an effective if rudimentary fashion. They worked in shifts to maintain the roads and bridges. Nobles, priests, peasants and shopkeepers all manfully did their turn of work.

The success of this peasant communism in Guria gave a sudden stimulus to those Georgian revolutionaries who harked back in their outlook to the old Narodniks or Populists, and whose programme was based on agrarian socialism of a utopian variety, with emphasis on peasant ownership of the land. These agrarian revolutionaries formed the Georgian Socialist-Federalist Revolutionary Party, allied to the Russian Social-Revolutionaries or 'S.-R.s'. The leading spirit in this party was Archil Jorjadze, who convened its first conference at Geneva in 1904 and brought out a newspaper *Sakartvelo* or *La Géorgie* which appeared at Paris in Georgian and French. Proscribed in Georgia itself, the fiery pamphlets of the Social-Revolutionaries were smuggled in, and contributed to exacerbate the growing tension in the Georgian countryside.

Plehve and the Black Hundreds

All these local developments in Georgia must, of course, be viewed against the general background of Russia's general political state. Throughout the empire, the situation was deteriorating under the vacillating yet oppressive rule of Nicholas II. A key factor in the situation was the rivalry between the able Minister of Finance, Count Sergius Witte, and the sinister Von Plehve, Minister of the Interior. Plehve's recipe for maintaining authority was compounded of pogroms against the Jews and the forced russification of other national minorities, floggings and shootings of unruly peasants and factory workers, combined with a programme of chauvinistic militarism in the Far East, whereby patriotic zeal would be rallied to the Tsar and attention diverted from troubles at home. In July 1903, a general strike broke out in the southern provinces of Russia, beginning at the great oil city of Baku.

Soon the provinces of Kiev, Ekaterinoslav, Odessa and Nikolaev were largely strike-bound, as well as the Georgian governorates of Tbilisi and Kutaisi. The Tsar sent the Governor-General of the Caucasus, Prince Golitsyn, a personal telegram, demanding 'the most energetic action' to put an end to the disorders. In several Georgian towns, strikers engaged in violent combat with Cossacks and gendarmes, casualties being heavy.

These outbreaks helped to bring about Witte's dismissal from the Ministry of Finance in August 1903. Plehve's influence now became dominant. All criticism of the government was suppressed. Students were forbidden to gather or converse in the streets. Espionage was rampant in universities and schools, and *agents provocateurs* were active in industry and in society. Before any social gathering could be held, permission had to be sought from the police. Witte declared that such policies would one day bring about Plehve's assassination. To this, the all-powerful minister retorted that the country was now on the verge of revolution, and that the one way to avert it was 'a small victorious war'. In the meantime, he kept up the pressure on Russia's minority peoples. By persecuting the Georgian Church and ignoring the warnings and representations of the moderates among the Georgian aristocracy, Plehve and Prince Golitsyn between them effectively rallied all classes of Georgian society against the régime.

When war broke out between Russia and Japan in February 1904, the Georgian Social-Democrats immediately set to work to exploit the new situation. Leaflets were distributed wholesale, denouncing Tsarist militarism and calling on the workers to rally against the chauvinistic and ultra-patriotic Russian movement of the 'Black Hundreds', which the local authorities frequently incited to acts of violence against the minority communities of the empire.

'During the entire month of February,' we read in a document of the time, 'there was evidence of the growth of the revolutionary activity of the Social-Democratic organization, political meetings were held with increasing frequency, broadsheets with various titles in Russian, Georgian and Armenian have been scattered about not only in the streets, in factories, schools, and in the main workshops of the Transcaucasian railways, but even in churchyards and inside the churches themselves. . . . The local Social-Democratic organization has renewed its criminal activity among the workers of the main railway depot, the printing works in the city of Tbilisi, among the salesmen of various shops, in the Adelkhanov tannery and other factories. Propaganda is carried on, as before, at gatherings in which people debate from every angle the burning question of today—Russia's war against Japan; in the same spirit, the Russian government is condemned in all the printed manifestoes. The immediate aim of this propaganda is the desire at all costs to hold an anti-government demonstration on or about 18 April (Old Style: i.e. the First of May), to show that the workers censure the government for pursuing an unnecessary war with Japan, and that they have only one aim: "Down with autocracy!" [76]

By placing the city under martial law, the authorities in Tbilisi nipped in the bud the projected May Day procession there. Numerous incidents and strikes took place in other Georgian centres, leading to clashes with the police and the military in which a number of workers and peasants lost their lives.

In July 1904, Governor-General Golitsyn, who had been wounded in a terrorist attack, left the Caucasus on leave, never to return. On the 28th of that same month, the minister, Plehve, was assassinated in St. Petersburg by the Social-Revolutionary, Sazonov. Russia and Caucasia alike were sliding fast down the slope leading to revolution.

CHAPTER VII

GEORGIA IN THE 1905
REVOLUTION

*Russia and Japan — Bolsheviks and Mensheviks — Bloody Sunday —
The Gurian communes — The Georgian Church Militant — Massacre at Tbilisi Town Hall — Witte and the Duma — The Tsar
regains the upper hand — The Cossacks take over — Blood and fire
in Georgia — The Friends of Georgia Committee*

Russia and Japan

ON 5 FEBRUARY 1904, after months of mounting tension
in the Far East, the Japanese had launched their famous night
attack on the Russian fleet in Port Arthur. The war party at
St. Petersburg, headed by Plehve, cherished high hopes that
Russia's revolutionary fever would be speedily cured by this
timely 'small, victorious war'. But events soon showed that the
despised Japanese were as much a match for Nicholas II as the
British, French and Turks had been for Nicolas I in the Crimean
War fifty years before. Just as the humiliations of the Crimean
War hastened the death of Nicholas I, exposed the weakness of
autocracy, and brought about irresistible demands for the
abolition of serfdom, so did the disasters of the Russo-Japanese
conflict widen the rift between the Tsar, the army and the
aristocracy on the one hand, and the liberal bourgeoisie,
the intelligentsia and the workers on the other, heightening
the already insistent demand for popular participation in the
government of the nation.

During the summer of 1904, bad news from the theatre of
war seriously unsettled Russian public opinion. The Russian
fleet was blockaded in Port Arthur. In Manchuria, the Japanese
land forces forced the Russians to retire on Mukden. After the

assassination of the hated Plehve, the Tsar appointed as his chief minister a moderate man, Prince Svyatopolk-Mirsky. Representatives of the provincial *Zemstvos* or county councils met privately in St. Petersburg in November, and worked out a petition which they submitted to Nicholas, asking for inviolability of the person, freedom of conscience, of speech, of meeting, of the Press, of association, and equal civil rights for every class of society. The majority furthermore went on to request regular popular representation in a separate elective body which should participate in legislation, in drawing up the budget and in exercising control over the administration. Professional associations of professors, lawyers, journalists, engineers and others organized a series of banquets, at which speeches were made and resolutions passed in support of the constitutional movement. This banquet campaign was particularly well supported in Georgia, where natural conviviality reinforced the universal patriotic urge to free Georgia from Russian absolutism.

Bolsheviks and Mensheviks

Further to the left were the Social-Democrats. In July-August 1903, the Russian Social-Democratic Workers' Party had unexpectedly found itself divided into two antagonistic factions —the Mensheviks (literally—Men of the Minority), who aimed at the establishment of a constitutional republic as a step towards socialism, and the Bolsheviks, or Men of the Majority, who stood for the overthrow of the régime by revolutionary methods and the establishment of the dictatorship of the proletariat by a dedicated élite of professional agitators and party men. Both parties acknowledged Marx and Engels as their prophets, the Mensheviks basing their interpretation of the masters' teaching on the revised practice of the Social-Democratic parties of Western Europe, while the Bolsheviks adhered to the uncompromising formulae of the Communist Manifesto of 1848. An ominous feature of the Bolshevik faction was its oligarchical and dictatorial character. Lenin insisted that only those who regularly participated in the underground organization could be enrolled as members of the Party and have the formal right to influence its policy. The members of the clandestine organization were to be the shock troops of revolution, obedient to the orders of the central leadership. The rank and file of the workers would do what they were told and accept the dispensation from on high. Such an ideology imparted great strength and cohesion to the Bolshevik movement, which had no need to pay undue attention to the fluctuating moods of the masses whose name it invoked.

In Georgia, the formal split of the Russian Social-Democratic movement into two camps served to underline temperamental and doctrinal differences which had been agitating the *Mesame Dasi* or Third Group for several years past, and had already given rise to enmity between the pioneer 'legal Marxists' like Zhordania and Chkheidze, and the militant underground headed by Ketskhoveli, Dsulukidze and Stalin. The 'legal Marxists' now became identified with the Menshevik faction, while the militants formed the nucleus of the Caucasian Bolshevik movement and faithfully executed the directives of Lenin and his adherents. In Russia, as in the Caucasus, the Bolsheviks denounced both the moderate, democratic socialists, and the liberal constitutionalists. They saw that if the Tsar granted a truly democratic, parliamentary régime to Russia, with safeguards to the rights of national minorities, then support for terrorism would wither away amid the general rejoicing, and the prospect of a Marxian millennium would recede into the distant future.

Bloody Sunday

The revolutionaries need not have worried on this score. The Tsar and his entourage again and again proved themselves their own worst enemies. In December 1904, Nicholas finally issued a decree, but did not go beyond vague and general promises, no mention being made of a representative assembly. The prospect of reaching a peaceful understanding with the liberals and constitutional reformers was fast vanishing away. The revolution of 1905 was finally rendered inevitable by the tragedy of Bloody Sunday, 9/22 January 1905, when many thousands of working men, women and children, led by the priest, Gapon, marched with icons and singing hymns towards the Winter Palace in St. Petersburg to present a mass petition to their 'little father', the Tsar. Nicholas was away from the capital. The troops fired repeatedly on the defenceless and unarmed crowd, killing about a hundred and fifty people. Prince Svyatopolk-Mirsky resigned in despair, and was succeeded as Minister of the Interior by Court Chamberlain Bulygin. Strikes broke out in Russia's chief cities, and the Social-Revolutionary, Kalyaev, blew up the Grand Duke Sergius in the Kremlin. In the Far East, Port Arthur fell to the Japanese.

These events produced immediate repercussions in Georgia. The railway workers of Tbilisi were already preparing to go on strike in solidarity with their comrades at Baku, the great oil port and revolutionary hotbed on the Caspian. News of the Bloody Sunday massacre precipitated events. The director of the Tbilisi railway department was forced to demand military protection for the city station, and trains had to be convoyed under armed guard. By 20 January, Tbilisi was in the grip of a general strike. Factories were idle and the trams had to be escorted by troops. Four thousand strikers roamed the streets and bazaars. Within a week, the strike movement reached the other main towns of Georgia, including Batumi, Poti, Kutaisi, Chiatura, Tqibuli and Shorapani. Meetings of workers were held and attempts made to send workers' deputations to the Russian authorities with statements of grievances. On 23 January 1905, the official newspaper *Kavkaz* (*The Caucasus*) reported that a crowd some three hundred strong had invaded the railway junction at Samtredia in Western Georgia, whist-ling, shouting and firing off rifles. The rioters dragged the station staff from their posts and forbade them to resume work under pain of death. An attempt was made to sabotage the Batumi-Tbilisi railway, and a military train was derailed. The dock labourers at Poti went on strike, bringing all harbour work to a standstill. Street demonstrations took place in Tbilisi and Kutaisi, red flags were unfurled, the *Marseillaise* was sung, and several policemen were seriously wounded. At Batumi, three workers burst into the house of a senior police officer, murdered him, and made off. On 25 January the Tbilisi chemists and student apothecaries joined the strike, as well as the school-teachers and many of their pupils. Cries of 'Long live unity and freedom! Down with autocracy!' were every-where to be heard.

While many of these incidents bore a spontaneous character, feeling was continually whipped up by fiery proclamations issued by the Tbilisi committee of the Russian Social-Democratic Workers' Party. 'What must we do, Comrades?' the Committee demanded in a broadsheet issued in January 1905.

'We must organize ourselves more and more efficiently, struggle constantly against the government, overthrow autocracy, loudly and insistently call for the ending of this senseless, unnecessary, cruel war, and demand the immediate convocation of a Constituent Assembly, composed of representatives of the entire nation, chosen by universal, equal, direct and secret ballot. Like a fish without water, the proletariat cannot live or breathe without political liberty. Like air or food, we need freedom of the press, of speech, of association, assembly and strike action. Only when this has been won, can we improve our economic condition, and in this struggle we must count on our own efforts alone. Certain other classes of the population, for instance the Liberals, are sick and tired of the Tsar's arbitrary rule, and are not averse to receiving political liberty. But they desire freedom for themselves alone, whereas we, the workers desire it for the entire nation, and we are therefore the only ones to call for the setting up of a democratic republic in Russia. Not the Tsar and his officials, not that band of brigands and robbers, but deputies elected from amidst the whole people without distinction of race, religion or sex—these are the ones to provide the working class with the chance effectively to further its interests. Only when the fetters of slavery fastened by autocracy on every living creature finally fall away will the working class develop its full strength, and win for itself a better life, a socialist system of society.'[77]

The Gurian communes

One of the major achievements of the Georgian Social-Democrats was the speed and success with which their agitators rallied the peasantry to the socialist cause. Within a few days of the outbreak of the strikes, reports were coming in from rural areas of Georgia of disorders and clashes between the gendarmerie and the local inhabitants. On 2 February 1905, the Procurator of the Kutaisi District Tribunal was complaining to his superior in Tbilisi about the position in Guria.

'Over the past fortnight the situation in the Ozurgeti district has begun to deteriorate so rapidly that at present virtually complete anarchy prevails there. The entire territory of the region is now completely in the hands of the *Committee* and its agents, and only where a substantial armed detachment of police guards or cossacks make their appearance is the influence of our government momentarily restored.'

The procurator went on to report that out of eight police officers recently detailed for duty in the Ozurgeti area, one had been killed, another wounded, four had tendered their resignation, and another scarcely dared to emerge from his quarters. Prince Nakashidze, one of the most respected landowners in the province, had been murdered. As the Social-Democrats had placed him under a boycott, not a single gravedigger would dig the prince's grave; not a coachman could be found willing to take his relatives to the funeral; of three priests summoned to conduct the funeral service, only one made his appearance, but was too much frightened of the revolutionaries to consent to officiate. The procurator had abandoned all hope of holding the forthcoming Ozurgeti Quarter Sessions, since 'several cases of political murders were due to be tried at these assizes, but the Ozurgeti police are absolutely unable to afford the Court even the most feeble protection from deeds of violence on the part of the population'. The procurator concluded his report by declaring:

'It is essential to send a strong force of troops into Guria without delay, and to place the area on a war footing for three or four months with field courts-martial, and to take the most decisive measures of a purely military character, for every day and every hour of delay in implementing these measures, inevitable as they are in the long run, only serves to diminish the prestige of the authorities to an even greater extent, and is dyed crimson with the blood of innocent and faithful servants of the government. At this very moment, I have received from Ozurgeti almost simultaneously telegrams relating to two attacks on village constables, resulting in one of them being wounded, and their arms being stolen, also two attacks on village courtrooms, two attempted murders of village headmen, and the assassination of the nobleman Urushadze.'[78]

From Guria, the revolutionary fever spread with lightning rapidity into neighbouring Imereti and Mingrelia. Nor was the insurrection confined merely to the poorer peasantry. Many of the country squires and village priests, either to save their skins or from genuine sympathy with the rising against the Russian overlord, lent support to the insurgents. On 7 February 1905, Lieutenant-General Malama, who had been left in charge of the Caucasian provinces on the transfer of Prince Golitsyn, telegraphed the Minister of the Interior at St. Petersburg:

'The situation in the Ozurgeti district and the surrounding areas is assuming the character of a rebellion, finding expression in open defiance of authority, the murder of government officials, squires, priests and persons not in sympathy with the revolutionary movement. The population is repudiating the oath of allegiance to the crown and pledging fidelity to the revolutionary committee. Officers of the government are fleeing. All measures hitherto taken, including the co-operation of the army, have failed to produce any results.'

General Malama ended by asking for authority to place large areas of Western Georgia on a full-scale military footing. Pending instructions, he detailed Major-General Alikhanov-Avarsky to proceed to Western Georgia with a strong detachment of troops, including artillery, and take over complete control of the affected areas. Alikhanov was given overriding authority to act independently of the civil governors of Kutaisi and Batumi, under whose jurisdiction the districts in question normally came.

In the meantime, however, the Tsar had decided to revive the Viceroyalty of the Caucasus, which had been in abeyance since the retirement of the Grand Duke Michael in 1882. As viceroy he appointed General-Adjutant Count Vorontsov-Dashkov, an elder statesman of an intelligent outlook far removed from that of the chauvinistic Golitsyn, and a kinsman of the distinguished and popular Prince Michael Vorontsov, viceroy from 1845 to 1854, whose memory was much respected throughout the Caucasus. General Alikhanov's punitive expedition was temporarily countermanded. Pending the viceroy's arrival in Tbilisi, a special representative of the viceregal council, Privy Councillor Prince N. A. Sultan Krym-Girey, was sent to Guria to carry out a first-hand enquiry into the underlying causes of the disorders and to assure the population that the viceroy would make every attempt to redress their legitimate grievances.

Sultan Krym-Girey was descended on his father's side from

the former Khans of the Crimea, dispossessed of their dominions by Catherine the Great in 1783; his mother was British. He fully understood the outlook of Russia's national minorities, and made an excellent impression throughout Guria, where he received numerous popular delegations and listened patiently to their tales of woe. The peasant spokesmen for their part were efficiently coached by the local Social-Democratic committee, and put forward a series of demands which included the return to their homes of persons exiled to Siberia without trial; the withdrawal of troops recently sent to intimidate the population; abolition of censorship and establishment of freedom of Press and publication; election of peasant deputies to a Constituent Assembly by free and secret ballot; abolition of the internal passport system, and granting of freedom of movement within the whole Russian Empire; freedom of assembly and association and the right of appeal from arbitrary acts by local officials; enlargement of peasant allotments at the expense of State and Church domains; the abolition of tithes; the regularization of share-cropping and tenantry agreements, with provision for reduction of taxes and dues in the event of bad harvests; provision of schooling for all children; and the reopening of local Georgian libraries and reading rooms, shut down three years previously by the former Governor-General. Sultan Krym-Girey reported favourably on the Gurians' loyalty to Russia, emphasizing that they were in no sense attempting to break away from the Empire, but merely desired to emerge from their colonial status and enjoy the same rights and privileges as the citizens of European Russia. He recommended immediate action to alleviate economic distress, combat the corrupt practices of Russian officialdom, and raise the moral and intellectual standards of the people by improved educational facilities.

Unfortunately, the rising tide of revolution rendered abortive any such overdue attempts at conciliation. Throughout March 1905, the situation grew more and more threatening. The whole of Georgia, from Abkhazia in the north-west to Kakheti in the east was in the throes of insurrection. Peasants were rising against the gendarmes and the landlords, murdering them or turning them out, and seizing property and estates. On 9 March, the whole of Western Georgia was placed on a regular war footing. The Third Congress of the Bolshevik wing of the Russian Social-Democratic Workers' Party, which met in London that April, listened with rapt attention to the report of the Georgian revolutionary Mikha Tskhakaia (1865–1950), and declared: 'That the special conditions of social and political life in the Caucasus have favoured the creation there of the most militant of our party's organizations; that the revolutionary mood of the majority of the population of the Caucasus, both in the towns and in the villages, has already brought about a national uprising against absolutism; that the autocratic régime is already sending an army with artillery into Guria, and preparing the most merciless onslaught on all the chief centres of insurrection; that the victory of absolutism over the popular uprising in the Caucasus, which might be facilitated by the multi-racial composition of the local population, would have the most harmful consequences for the outcome of the revolt throughout Russia as a whole.' The Bolshevik Central Committee and all its branches were directed to make known to workers all over Russia the success of the revolutionary movement in the Caucasus, and prepare if necessary to lend armed support to the insurgents.

The Georgian Church Militant

While the Socialists sought to regenerate Georgia through the application of Marxist principles and the intensification of the class struggle, the Georgian Church, after a century of enforced quiescence, also sought to play an active part in the national movement. It will be recalled that the Georgian Church, whose freedom had been guaranteed by Russia by solemn treaty, had been liquidated in 1811 and absorbed by the St. Petersburg Synod. The Georgian priests and bishops were now emboldened to put forward demands for autocephaly within the Greek Orthodox Communion, as they had enjoyed previously for well over a thousand years, and the election of a Patriarch by the Georgian people. In May 1905, a meeting of Georgian priests and bishops was convened in Tbilisi to discuss this important question. At the instance of the chief Russian bishop in Georgia, troops and police invaded the premises, forcibly broke up the meeting, and beat and maltreated the assembled clergy. This unseemly incident united pious believers with revolutionary unbelievers in a resolve to cast off Muscovite domination at the first opportunity.

Throughout that summer, the revolutionary movement gathered momentum almost everywhere in Russia. The crushing annihilation of the Baltic fleet at Tsushima on 27–28 May provoked fresh demands for an end to the unpopular Russo-Japanese war. At Odessa, mutineers seized the battleship *Potemkin* and defied the Black Sea fleet, while on shore there occurred the notorious massacre of the Odessa Steps.

In Georgia, the agrarian conflict spread from Western Georgia into the district around Tbilisi. In one conflict with army units, forty-eight peasants were killed. The viceroy, Vorontsov-Dashkov, arrived in Tbilisi on 18 May 1905, and found the situation even worse than he had expected. Many officials joined with local Russian residents in supporting the ultra-patriotic, monarchist organization known as the Russian Patriotic League and run by the priests S. Gorodtsev and I. Vostorgov. This society was a branch of the notorious 'Union of the Russian People'. Through its Black-Hundred bands of hooligans and strong-arm gangs it organized pogroms against Jews and other racial minorities both in Russia and in the Caucasus. The Ultras also sought to stir up the fanatical Muslim Turks and Tatars of Transcaucasia against the Christian Armenians, whom many Russian officials suspected of subversive leanings. Massacres of Armenians were in fact connived at by some of the local governors, notably by Prince Nakashidze, a Georgian aristocrat who was Governor of Baku, the oil city on the Caspian. In May, Nakashidze was assassinated by Armenian nationalists. In Tbilisi, the Black-Hundred bands held counter-revolutionary demonstrations in the streets and assaulted Georgian workers and their families.

Heightened tension led to yet another general strike which broke out in Tbilisi on 20 June 1905, and lasted until the end of the month. The strike was again of a largely political nature and was directed by the local Social-Democratic Committee. The city remained without lighting, running water, regular food supplies, and public transport. The strike spread like lightning to the other main Georgian cities. On 27 June, the city and province of Tbilisi were placed under martial law.

From Kutaisi in Western Georgia, the head of the Secret Police reported that the revolutionary movement resembled

'a huge cauldron filled with water and hermetically sealed and suspended above an enormous furnace. Beyond a doubt, when the sides of the cauldron can no longer withstand the pressure of the steam which is formed by the heating of the water and has no other outlet, then they will burst into splinters and fly in all directions as a result of the force of the blast.'

Massacre at Tbilisi Town Hall

The viceroy was inclined to try lowering the political temperature by a few timely concessions to the political and social aspirations of the local peoples. Many of his subordinates, on the other hand, were resolved to do a little blood-letting on their own account. For this, events soon presented them with an excellent opportunity. In August 1905, Tsar Nicholas issued a manifesto drafted by his minister, Court Chamberlain Bulygin, in which he promised to convoke a State Council or *Duma*. This was to be nothing more than a consultative assembly, and the franchise was limited to the middle and upper classes and to the supposedly monarchist peasantry. All parties of the opposition, from the Liberals to the Bolsheviks, condemned the edict as half-hearted and inadequate. On 29 August the Tbilisi Social-Democratic organization arranged a public meeting in the Town Hall to discuss the Bulygin project and other burning questions of the day. The police, who had received advance notice of the assembly, barred the entrances to the building. However, the organizers forced their way in and the meeting began in the presence of an audience of some 2,000, including many ordinary citizens who had come from sheer curiosity. A police officer entered the hall and ordered the meeting to disperse, but was greeted with shouts of derision. Hearing of what was going on, the acting governor of Tbilisi, General Yatskevich, hastened to the scene with several hundred Cossacks and infantry, whom he posted strategically at the exits. Shouts and hoots greeted a renewed order to disperse. Thereupon, Cossacks opened fire on the assembly through the windows, while others invaded the hall and shot down the audience from the platform. One shot killed the orator at his tribune. The mob fled from the building and were shot down indiscriminately or felled with rifle butts and sabres. A woman doctor who happened to be present was wounded, but in spite of her injuries was bandaging other casualties with strips of her own clothing; a Cossack came up and brained her with his rifle butt. Some victims were cornered in the narrow corridors and hacked to death; others were pursued into the streets and shot or cut down on the public highways. About sixty persons were killed and several hundred wounded. The relatives of the dead were refused permission to remove the bodies, which were flung into a common grave.

Journalists and other observers who visited the scene immediately after the massacre have left accounts of the shattered furniture and chandeliers, the huge pool of blood on the floor of the auditorium, and other unmistakable signs of the extreme violence used to break up the gathering. Protest meetings and strikes were held throughout Georgia. Thirty-two members of the Tbilisi Town Council resigned in disgust at the excesses committed by the Cossacks and the desecration of their hall.

'At the present moment,' they wrote, 'when we are witnessing the birth of new forms of government and the working out of fundamental problems, freedom of assembly and of speech, as well as personal security, are elementary and normal conditions without which it is impossible to bring about any measures of reform, or find any way out of the present intolerable situation. Every attempt by the representatives of the people to gather together and discuss the burning questions of the day is met with whips and bullets. All the attempts of the Tbilisi Town Council to protect the local population from every form of arbitrary act have resulted in failure. With increasing frequency, any of our enactments which have exceeded the limits of minor domestic management have been forthwith annulled and prevented from being carried into effect. At present, the public is even excluded from our deliberations; the newspapers have already been long deprived of the possibility of publishing a major part of the councillors' speeches, especially if these speeches touch on any but the most trivial issues. As a crowning outrage, the public, which peacefully and trustfully attended what it understood to be a meeting of the Town Council, has been shot down and hacked to pieces. . . . The walls of the Town Hall are crimsoned with gore and riddled with bullets, on the floor lie pools of blood and traces of the savage and inhuman vengeance meted out to a peaceful crowd. Can we be expected to busy ourselves in docile fashion with the paving and lighting of the city streets when unarmed people are murdered simply because they collected for a peaceful debate? Deprived of the ability to hold our sessions in public and make the population aware of our indignation at the atrocity committed by the government and the cossacks, and considering therefore that our work has been thereby rendered ineffectual, especially within the walls of this building in which so much innocent blood has been shed, we, representatives of the Council, resigning the title of Councillor, renounce all further municipal activity, until the population is granted the elementary conditions of civilized society and until the possibility of a repetition of those bloody events which occurred on 29 August has been eliminated. Among these urgent measures, the most pressing include: the lifting of martial law and the state of emergency, freedom of assembly and the press, security of the person, and the institution of a strict enquiry into, and the committal for trial of the persons responsible for the carnage of 29 August.'

On 1 September, the Chief of Police in the Caucasus, Major-General Shirinkin, telegraphed the Ministry of the Interior in St. Petersburg:

'General strike of Tbilisi workers began this morning as protest against events of 29 August in the Town Hall. All shops closed, tramway ceased functioning. Intensified movement of youths and workers in the streets, some wearing mourning. Anticipate strike of railway workers and clerks, some of whom already out. Two sets of printed proclamations of the "Tbilisi Committee of the Russian Social-Democratic Workers' Party" have appeared; one set urges an organized uprising as a result of the occurrence of 29 August; the other calls for the exposure of Mayor Vermyshev and the entire body of city councillors to public ignominy and boycott, on the ground that the bloodshed on 29 August took place as a result of collusion between the Town Council and the Governor-General. Almost the entire council as well as the Mayor have resigned. The situation is tense. Suitable measures have been taken.'[79]

General Yatskevich, who had directed the killing in person, was transferred to another responsible post. On the fortieth day after the tragedy, when the *Panikhida* or Requiem for the victims was held, nine bombs burst near the Cossack barracks. The Cossacks went berserk and shot down all passers-by, including the Chief Pastor of the German Lutheran colonies in the Caucasus. Criminal elements posing as revolutionaries took advantage of the prevailing chaos to intensify their murderous activities. Prince Amilakhori, a prominent land-owner, was shot dead in a Tbilisi tramcar by unidentified assassins.

On 23 August/5 September 1905, the Russian plenipotentiary Witte signed the Treaty of Portsmouth, whereby peace was concluded with Japan on terms highly unfavourable to Russia. These terms were dictated not only by the rout sustained by Russia's naval and military forces, but also by the Tsar's urgent need to free his hands of foreign commitments and use his standing army to pacify the huge areas of Russia where his writ had ceased to run. As Stalin justly remarked:

'There was a time when the régime refrained from shedding blood inside the country. At that time it was waging war against the "external enemy" and it needed "internal tranquillity". That is why it showed a certain amount of "leniency" towards the "internal enemy" and looked "between its fingers" at the movement which was flaring up. Now times are different. Frightened at the spectre of revolution, the Tsarist government hastened to conclude peace with the "external enemy", with Japan, in order to muster its forces and "thoroughly" settle accounts with the "internal enemy". And thus reaction has set in. . . .'[80]

The force of the first Russian revolution was still far from spent. The feeble concessions granted in the Bulygin project simply whetted the appetite of the nation. Seeing that the Tsar still wavered, the railwaymen went on strike at the beginning of October. Soon factories everywhere had closed down, the postal and telegraph services ceased to function, government and business offices were shut, even the primary school children stayed at home. Communications between St. Petersburg and the provinces were interrupted and the Tsar was isolated at his country palace at Peterhof. On 14/27 October the socialist parties set up a Soviet or Council of workers' delegates in St. Petersburg, which elected Trotsky as its vice-chairman and for a short time wielded effective power in the capital. The Soviets threatened to wreck any factory which did not close down of its own accord. The professional men, liberals and middle-class progressives banded themselves together in a new party called the Constitutional Democrats, commonly abridged into 'Cadets', led by Paul Milyukov.

Witte and the Duma

Count Witte saw that the only means of avoiding the over-throw of the monarchy was to rally the middle classes to the throne by conceding at least the shadow of a modern parliamentary system. On 17/30 October 1905, Nicholas was prevailed upon to issue a new manifesto, guaranteeing 'genuine' inviolability of person, freedom of faith, speech, assembly and association. No law was to be enacted without the consent of the new national assembly or *Duma*. It was noticeable that the word 'constitution' was not mentioned, and that Nicholas reserved to himself the title of Autocrat.

'By providing the bourgeoisie with the semblance of participation in the government of the country, deceiving the people by promises and by liberties of which there was nothing to guarantee the maintenance, the manifesto was designed to split the revolutionary forces, to set a barrier between the liberal opposition and the revolutionary masses of the nation, and to distract the workers and peasants from the only correct outcome of the crisis—namely a revolutionary uprising, towards which the Bolshevik party was urging the people on.'[81]

The Cadets, however, foolishly refused to accept portfolios in Witte's ministry, thus playing into the hands of the extremists of both Right and Left.

Whereas the Bolsheviks denounced the Tsar's manifesto as a sham and declared a boycott of the Duma, the Mensheviks and other moderate socialists were inclined at first to think that their immediate aims were attained. When the proclamation of 17/30 October was read in Tbilisi, Zhordania, Noe Ramishvili and other leaders of the Georgian Mensheviks addressed meetings and triumphantly announced: 'Henceforth there is no autocracy. Autocracy is dead. Russia is entering the ranks of the constitutional monarchies.' The workers, they believed, should renounce terrorism and lay down their arms. The Georgian Bolsheviks, on the other hand, led by Stalin and his associates, declared that the workers should be content with nothing short of the overthrow of the Russian monarchy and the setting up of a popular Constituent Assembly.

'The proletariat will not demand petty concessions from the government, it will not call upon it to rescind martial law and flogging in several towns and villages—the proletariat will not sink to such trifles. . . . It presents only one demand to the Tsarist autocracy: Down with it! Death to it! . . . Only on the bones of the oppressors can the people's freedom be erected, only with the blood of the oppressors can the soil be fertilized for the autocracy of the people! Only when the armed people come out headed by the proletariat and raise the banner of general insurrection can the Tsarist government, which rests on bayonets, be overthrown.'82

Many workers' meetings in Georgia adopted the Bolshevik line, and resolutions were passed calling for an intensification of the death struggle against the régime.

Russia's ruling classes, and such diehard elements as the officials, police, priests, and Cossacks, were furious at what they regarded as the Tsar's weakness in face of the revolutionary menace. With police connivance, Black-Hundred bands of the Society of Patriots run by the priests Gorodtsev and Vostorgov launched a wave of pogroms against Jews all over the country, including Odessa, Rostov and other large towns. In Georgia, the local organization of the league held a monarchist demonstration on the Golovinsky (now Rustaveli) Avenue, after which they invaded the Tbilisi Boys' Secondary School and beat up some of the pupils. On the following day, 22 October 1905, the 'Russian Patriots' gathered in much increased strength. Holding aloft the Tsar's portrait, headed by a detachment of dragoons, and escorted by Cossacks, they once more paraded up the Golovinsky Avenue, and again burst into the Boys' Secondary School, where they tried to bully the pupils into singing Russian patriotic anthems. The students refused and were savagely set upon. The soldiery joined in and the school buildings were soon riddled with bullets. The 'Patriots' also attacked nearby houses, clubs and newspaper offices. Similar incidents occurred all over Tbilisi. About forty people lost their lives, including schoolboys, students and teachers. A day of mourning was declared for the fallen; all shops were closed and tram drivers and even policemen stayed at home.

The following month witnessed further chaos and lawlessness in the capital of Caucasia. Internecine fighting and slaughter had been going on for months in Baku and other parts of Transcaucasia inhabited jointly by Christian Armenians and

Muslim Azerbaijani Turks. Until the autumn, these conflicts had been mainly confined to the present-day Soviet Azerbaijan and Armenia. Towards the end of November, inter-communal strife spread to Tbilisi itself, where large Armenian and Azerbaijani communities also lived side by side. The Caucasian Social-Democratic organizations, which stood by the principle of the international solidarity of the working class and the peasantry, sent 20,000 of their men carrying white flags to pacify the rioters. The Tbilisi police chief, at his wits' end, appealed to local political parties of every shade to co-operate with the Russian authorities in maintaining order. The viceroy, who had completely lost his head, agreed to issue five hundred rifles to a People's Militia directed by the Georgian Social-Democrats, on the understanding that the weapons would be returned at the conclusion of the emergency. Led by Isidore Ramishvili, the Georgian Mensheviks conscientiously fulfilled their part of the bargain, several of their number being killed while trying to restrain the Azerbaijan Turkish mobs. The Russian colonists were furious at what they regarded as a treasonable alliance between Count Vorontsov-Dashkov and these local socialists. The league of 'Russian Patriots' held a protest meeting, called on the Viceroy to withdraw the rifles from the Social-Democrats without delay, and sent Cossacks into the working-class quarters of Tbilisi to retrieve them by force.

No less anarchic was the situation in Western Georgia. In an effort to appease the local population, the viceroy had appointed as Governor of Kutaisi V. A. Staroselsky, an agricultural expert of liberal views. Staroselsky was held in the highest esteem by the Georgians, with whose national aspirations he was in sympathy. When he had occasion to go to Tbilisi on official business, the local revolutionary committee would escort him to the station, put down the red carpet, and see him off with cheers and flag-waving. Staroselsky recommended that martial law should be lifted from Western Georgia, and extensive concessions made to the local population. He was constantly at odds with Russian military commanders like the ferocious General Alikhanov, whose troops were harried by Georgian guerillas and were panting to go into action. As Vorontsov-Dashkov wrote of Staroselsky in a subsequent report:

'He exerted influence only in those cases when it suited the revolutionary organizations, and was so trusting that when the insurgent bands started forcibly removing weapons from members of government units who had been issued with them for their official duties, he failed to perceive that this was in open preparation for an armed uprising in the event of a victory of the proletariat in metropolitan Russia, on which the revolutionaries counted. His entire activity, or rather inactivity, merely succeeded in arousing against him all peace-loving elements of society, who as a result of his attitude even finished by numbering him among the revolutionaries.'[83]

In November 1905, the Cossacks took the law into their own hands. At Kutaisi, Batumi and Akhal-Senaki they broke out of their barracks, terrorized the local inhabitants and massacred a number of them. Fighting was heavy in Batumi, where barricades were erected in the streets and many lives were lost. Staroselsky's life was made so intolerable that he was eventually driven to ask the viceroy for protection not against the Georgian insurgents, but against his own outraged Russian compatriots.

During November and December 1905, the fate of the Russian administration in Transcaucasia hung in the balance. On 10/23 December, General Shirinkin, head of the Caucasian police department, reported to St. Petersburg that the posts and telegraphs had ceased to function; the law courts were paralysed; the newspapers were full of inflammatory appeals to the population. Azerbaijani-Armenian clashes continued around Erivan and Elizavetpol (the modern Kirovabad), though Baku was relatively quiet. The Military Governor of Batumi had threatened to shell the town, which had temporarily quelled the rebels.

'A state of emergency prevails in the Kutaisi province; apart from Governor Staroselsky, no officials are being obeyed. The insurgents have disarmed the gendarmes, seized control of the western sector of the railway line and are themselves selling tickets and maintaining order. On his visit to Tbilisi, the governor, who himself adheres to the revolutionary organization, reported that during the clash between the local people and the cossacks, the Procurator of the local court helped to erect barricades in the streets. I am getting no reports from Kutaisi. The gendarmes have been withdrawn from the firing line and concentrated in Tbilisi. Couriers sent out with reports are searched by revolutionaries and their papers seized; the situation there is quite beyond control. The army units are undoubtedly reliable, but so limited in number that no active operations can be undertaken. . . . The Viceroy has had a nervous breakdown but his condition is not yet hopeless. The Count is attending to reports of major importance but is very weak. I will send details by post or, if that is not possible, by messenger.'[84]

The Tsar regains the upper hand

Throughout Russia the political parties had emerged from the underground. Socialist papers were published and sold openly. While Litvinov and Krassin in St. Petersburg edited *Novaya Zhizn* (*The New Life*), and Trotsky published his brilliant *Nachalo* (*The Start*), down in Tbilisi Stalin and his Armenian fellow-Bolshevik Shaumian brought out a Bolshevik daily with the more prosaic title, *The Caucasian Workers' News-sheet*. These halcyon days were short-lived. Now that the war with Japan was at an end and troops were returning from the Far East in their thousands, the Tsar's government set seriously to work to tame the rebels. At the end of November, the minister Witte ordered the arrest of the chairman of the St. Petersburg Soviet. Martial law was declared in the capital. This touched off a fresh wave of strikes. On 3/16 December, the government arrested the bulk of the Soviet—one hundred and ninety members. Defeated in St. Petersburg, the revolutionaries transferred their headquarters to Moscow. Throughout mid-December, battles raged between the insurgents and government troops, who were finally victorious. Other armed conflicts occurred in Sormovo, Perm, the Donbass, at Novorossiysk, Krasnoyarsk, Kiev, Ekaterinoslav, Samara, Rostov, and in the Baltic provinces. In a desperate move to conciliate public opinion, Witte issued a fresh decree, making the Duma franchise virtually universal. Gradually the government regained the ascendency. People became tired of anarchy and hardship, and hopeful of political evolution towards parliamentary democracy. The general weariness, coinciding with the army's return from Manchuria, enabled the régime to embark very soon on a movement of reprisal and counter-revolutionary terror.

The Cossacks take over

In solidarity with their comrades in Moscow, the Tbilisi Bolsheviks called a general strike for 12/25 December 1905. The strikers seized the railway station and the head offices of the railway administration. The Social-Democratic committee emulated the St. Petersburg Soviet by forming a regular system of municipal administration and taking over the functions of the paralysed Town Council. However, the revolutionaries succeeded only in gaining control of the working-class quarters of Nadzaladevi and Didube, the greater part of Tbilisi remaining in the hands of the Russian authorities. On 14/27 December, the viceroy declared a state of emergency in the Georgian capital. Within less than a week, the forces of counter-revolution gained the upper hand. Cossacks with armed volunteers of the Russian Patriotic League invaded the Nadzaladevi district and overwhelmed the insurgents there. On 23 December 1905/ 5 January 1906, a force of Cossacks and gendarmes advanced on the last revolutionary stronghold of Tbilisi, the Didube suburb. The workers fired on the attackers from roofs, windows and cellars. Home-made bombs were thrown, with deadly though indiscriminate effect. The Cossacks suffered heavy losses. The Viceroy called up regular troops and bombarded the area with field guns, until the entire city was brought under control.

The Bolsheviks saw that the day was lost. At a meeting of workers' representatives in Tbilisi, Stalin, Shaumian and the other local leaders recommended that the Tbilisi Social-Democratic organization should be wound up, its members go underground, and await better days before attempting to renew the death struggle against Tsarism. The workers, they said, should boycott the elections to the bourgeois Duma. The Menshevik delegates present strongly opposed this counsel of despair. They stood for continuance of the Georgian people's campaign against Tsarist absolutism, by every means, fair or foul, legal or illegal, revolutionary or parliamentary. Denouncing the 'opportunism' of the Mensheviks, Stalin and his associates were defeated in the debate and left Georgia in disgust to carry on their revolutionary plotting in the more congenial atmosphere of the Baku oil-wells.

Headed by Zhordania, Chkheidze, Isidore and Noe Ramish-vili and others, the Mensheviks were left in a dominant position in the Georgian political field. They planned to make the most of the forthcoming convention of the Russian Duma, send to St. Petersburg their best orators, and proclaim Georgia's cause from the housetops, to the confusion of their country's oppressors. In this, they were at one with the great Lenin himself. At the Tammerfors conference of the Russian Social-Democratic Party held in 1905, the Master argued against the barren tactics of boycotting the Duma: he saw no reason why revolution should not be furthered from the parliamentary tribune. Revolution, said Lenin, could be preached even from a dungheap or a pigsty. Why not preach it in the 'pigsty' of the Tsarist Duma?[85] On this occasion, Lenin was outvoted by the militant extremists—Stalin among them—who refused to aim for any objective short of the dictatorship of the proletariat, and would have nothing to do with effete middle-class parliamentary democracy.

This does not imply that the Georgian Mensheviks were content from now on with a passive or submissive role. Nor, when occasion demanded, did they renounce the weapon of terrorism. As Zhordania writes in his memoirs: 'We abandoned terrorism as a method of overthrowing autocracy, in the fashion conceived by the Narodniks, but did not reject it as a weapon for self-preservation and for the sowing of panic among the political authorities.' In January 1906, the Tbilisi Social-Democrats decided to eliminate the chief of the Caucasian army's general staff, General Gryaznov, who had taken a leading part in bombarding the workers' suburb. The execution of the plot was entrusted to 'Silva'—the hardened conspirator Sylvester Jibladze—who enlisted the services of an expert bomb-thrower named Arsena Jorjiashvili. Silva stationed Arsena and his assistant in front of General Gryaznov's residence, while himself taking up a position on the Golovinsky Avenue whence he could signal the general's approach to his alert accomplices. At length Gryaznov hove into view, riding home in an open carriage. But Silva remained motionless and gave no signal. Arsena, whose bomb was all ready for hurling, was in a fever of amazement and irritation, until he, like Silva, caught sight of a girl riding by the general's side. In those days, no Georgian gentleman would willingly harm a woman, so the general was spared for that day. But the terrorists, who had made a mental note of his face and appearance, resolved that he would get no second chance. The next day they stationed themselves at the same spot. But no general appeared. In despair, Silva walked into Zhordania's house nearby and threw himself down in a chair. 'We have missed our chance, it was all my fault!' Before he had finished the sentence, a tremendous roar was heard outside. Silva leapt up and rushed into the road shouting: 'I am lost, they have done it without me!' Gryaznov lay dead, and Arsena Jorjiashvili had been seized by the general's escort. Tried and condemned to death, he died like a man, without saying a word that might compromise Silva or his other accomplices.

Blood and fire in Georgia

Such isolated successes were unavailing in face of the military might which Russia was now free to deploy against the Georgian insurgents. Resistance in and around Tbilisi crumpled rapidly. It remained to subdue the more formidable uprising in Western Georgia which, as the authorities admitted, had taken on the aspect not so much of anarchy as of an independent state made up of self-governing communes which recognized no authority but that of the revolutionary committees. 'The events taking place in the Kutaisi province are so amazing when witnessed against the general background of the political structure of the Empire that foreigners are making special trips to the Caucasus with the aim of observing on the spot this new manifestation of Russian political organization.'[86] Recovering at length from his nervous breakdown, Vorontsov-Dashkov pulled himself together sufficiently to dismiss Staroselsky, the over-indulgent Governor of Kutaisi, who was arrested and discharged with ignominy from the imperial service. In January 1906, the ruthless General Alikhanov-Avarsky was appointed Military Governor of Western Georgia, with virtually unlimited power. The insurgents retaliated by blocking a tunnel on the main railway line, so that reinforcements from Tbilisi were held up. Pitched battles between Georgian guerillas and Russian troops and Cossacks occurred in many places. Even where the Cossacks met no resistance, they amused themselves by burning down shops and houses, slaughtering a few inhabitants and raping any women who took their fancy. About 13,000 persons were arrested in various parts of Georgia, many of whom were deported to Siberia. The natives were taught a lesson they would not forget.

The Friends of Georgia Committee

The excesses of the Russian troops and Cossacks in Georgia were extensively reported in Russian and foreign newspapers, and brought considerable odium on the régime. In England, Oliver Wardrop and his sister Marjory, both of them pioneer scholars of Georgian and authors of many contributions to Georgian studies, formed a Georgian Relief Committee, later renamed the Friends of Georgia Committee. The outrages committed against women resulted in the launching of an 'Appeal from the Women of Georgia' directed to public opinion all over the world, and Mrs. N. F. Dryhurst and others constituted a 'Hampstead Committee formed in response to the Georgian Women's Appeal'. The text of this appeal, together with a protest signed by many representatives of the women of England, appeared in The Women's Tribune of 6 July 1906. Vigorous representations were made to the government at St. Petersburg by various British humanitarians, but without any visible result. It seemed that the sacrifices made by the Georgian people during the revolution of 1905 were all in vain. In retrospect, however, it is clear that the débâcle of the Russo-Japanese War and the internal upheavals of that year of crisis caused irreparable damage to the absolutist system. The wounded leviathan, it is true, had plenty of fight left in it. But the events of 1905 showed up the weakness of the régime and made both the Russian masses and the minority peoples of the empire aware of their potential strength. Tsardom had been reprieved. But sooner or later, the struggle would be resumed and autocracy would not be given another chance.

CHAPTER VIII

ON BORROWED TIME: 1906–17

The Georgians in the Duma — The Viborg Declaration — Social-
Democrats and Anarchists — Stolypin and the Second Duma —
Murder of Ilia Chavchavadze — The Georgian Church in crisis —
Plight of the Georgian peasantry — Industrial unrest — War
declared, 1914 — Mussolini and the Georgian Socialists — The
Georgian Legion — Caucasian battlefields — The Turks on the
defensive — Breakdown of Tsarist Russia — Literature, art and
intellectual life up to 1917

The Georgians in the Duma

THE EVENTS of 1905 showed that the absolutist régime of
Nicholas II had lost the confidence of large sections of the
Russian nation and its subject peoples. By agreeing to convoke
the Duma, the Tsar staved off disaster in the nick of time.
Once the emergency was past, the autocrat and his entourage
did their best to annul the concessions which had been wrested
from them. The promised admission of the nation to participation in government was reduced to a farce. The few able men
who might have steered Russia towards modern constitutional
statehood—notably Witte and Stolypin—were betrayed or
undermined by palace intrigue. The course of policy was
influenced disproportionately by grand dukes, second-rate
courtiers and disreputable adventurers like Rasputin. In spite of
undeniable economic progress during the few years which
preceded the outbreak of World War I, the régime was living
on borrowed time.

The year 1906 was marked on the one hand by reprisals
against the demoralized remnants of the revolutionary movement, on the other, by preparations for the convocation of the

First Duma. Count Witte had in a moment of desperation extended the franchise to virtually all classes and conditions of the people. This would normally have been expected to produce increased representation for the extreme left-wing parties. However, the Russian Social-Democrats decided to boycott the Duma. In metropolitan Russia, therefore, the Constitutional Democrats or Cadets under P. N. Milyukov had the upper hand, and only a handful of Russian socialist delegates were returned, under a variety of party tickets.

The one Social-Democratic regional party to ignore the boycott and enter wholeheartedly into the election campaign was that of Georgia, where the native Mensheviks had ousted Lenin's local henchmen from control of the party machine. In spite of intimidation and obstruction by the Russian authorities, the Georgian Social-Democratic candidates were returned almost everywhere with massive majorities. In the city of Tbilisi, 8,078 electoral votes were cast for the Social-Democrats, against 4,173 for all other parties combined. Consequently, 72 out of the 80 members of the Tbilisi electoral college were Social-Democrats, and they in their turn elected Noe Zhordania to represent them in the Duma. In the town of Batumi, the Social-Democrats secured 2,477 votes, against 1,031 for all other parties, while in Kutaisi city, the Social-Democrats got 983 votes against 639 for all others together. All the peasant electors of Kutaisi province turned out to be Social-Democrats, with the result that the provincial assembly returned as its three nominees three Social-Democrats— Isidore Ramishvili, Dr. Gomarteli and the advocate Japaridze.

When the First Duma assembled on 27 April/10 May 1906 at the Tauride Palace in St. Petersburg, the well-organized Georgian Social-Democratic faction under Zhordania's leadership immediately assumed a dominant role in the left-wing opposition. In the Upper House of the Duma, known as the Council of State, a prominent part was played by the famous writer and public figure Prince Ilia Chavchavadze, who had been elected by the Georgian gentry and aristocracy. On his arrival at the Russian capital, Ilia declared that he intended to be not a defender of sectional interests, but a champion of the Georgian national cause. 'The life of our people,' he told the newspaper reporters, 'has been turned into a hell. . . . I shall consistently endeavour while I am here to give a frank, complete and true picture of the misery of our country.' This promise he fulfilled on every possible occasion, denouncing what he called 'the loathsome principles of a narrow-minded, bureaucratic régime, which believes not that officials and government departments exist for the people's sake, but rather that the people exist for the sake of the government departments'. In spite of political differences, Ilia kept in touch with the Georgian deputies in the main Duma, and joined them in giving voice to strong criticism of the Tsarist administration in Georgia.

The Viborg Declaration

The radical temper of the First Duma brought it into constant conflict with the Tsar's government, at the head of which the vigorous Count Witte had been succeeded by the aged Goremykin, a quavering but wily veteran of political manoeuvre. Goremykin declared to the Duma that most of its projected reforms were 'inadmissible', whereupon the Duma passed a unanimous vote of censure on the ministers. In a Western democracy, the government would have fallen. Since the Russian Duma's rights did not extend to ousting the Tsar's ministers, a deadlock ensued, which the Duma tried to solve by an appeal to the country. The Tsar retaliated by dissolving the Duma on 8/21 July 1906.

That night, some two hundred members of the Duma, comprising virtually all the Cadet and Labour members, proceeded over the border into the autonomous Grand-Duchy of Finland and assembled at the town of Viborg. With the active participation of Zhordania, the Georgian leader of the Menshevik faction, the famous Viborg Declaration was drawn up, in which the country was urged to embark on a campaign of passive resistance to the government, and refuse to pay taxes, or send recruits to the army, until the Tsar reconvened the Duma. Nothing had been done to organize any response from the nation as a whole, and the appeal fell flat. The signatories of the Declaration were later proscribed by the régime, forbidden to stand for election to subsequent Dumas, and sentenced when caught to terms of imprisonment. Zhordania and Isidore Ramishvili, who were outstanding among the

Georgian Social-Democrats, had to go into hiding and were debarred from active participation in public life.

Social-Democrats and Anarchists

Another interesting political development of the year 1906 was a determined but short-lived attempt by Kropotkinite Anarchists to win control of the revolutionary movement in Georgia. From 25 March to 2 July 1906, there appeared at Tbilisi a 'legal Anarchist' weekly called *Nobati* (*The Tocsin*), edited and in large part written by M. G. (*Mikhako*) Tsereteli (*b.* 1878), who used the pseudonym Bâton. Among the journal's contributors were Prince Kropotkin himself, Kamando Gogelia, and the veteran Georgian revolutionary Varlam Cherkesov (Cherkezishvili). The Georgian Anarchists launched a vigorous critique of Marxism and the ideological basis of Social-Democracy; they declared their opposition to state socialism and government monopoly of the means of production. 'The State and the People,' they wrote, 'are two perpetual and untiring foes.'[87] They assailed the notion of dictatorship of the proletariat. In fact, they would have nothing to do with dictatorship of any political colour, identifying it with slavery. They preached renunciation of private property, and the ideals of 'voluntary co-operation' in both urban industry and rural life. In one of the last numbers of the paper, Mikhako Tsereteli condemned the Marxists in strong terms, saying:

'For them, the social revolution must be brought about by the agency of the State, within the frontiers of the State and with the aid of the State; but for us, it must be brought about outside the State, in opposition to the State, with the aid of completely new social forces and principles. We shall see which doctrine is the truer and the more effectual.'[88]

The Georgian Anarchists lacked a broadly based popular organization, and could not compete with the dominant Social-Democrats. Before the Kropotkinite movement faded out, however, leading Georgian Marxists spent much energy in combating the Anarchist ideology, which they considered especially pernicious. Stalin himself wrote at the time:

'Marxism and Anarchism are built up on entirely different principles, in spite of the fact that both come into the arena of the struggle under the flag of Socialism. The cornerstone of Anarchism is the *individual,* whose emancipation, according to its tenets, is the principal condition for the emancipation of the masses, the collective body. According to the tenets of Anarchism the emancipation of the masses is impossible until the individual is emancipated. Accordingly its slogan is: "Everything for the individual." The cornerstone of Marxism, however, is the *masses,* whose emancipation, according to the Marxist view, is the principal condition for the emancipation of the individual. That is to say, according to the tenets of Marxism, the emancipation of the individual is impossible until the masses are emancipated. Accordingly, its slogan is: "Everything for the masses." '[89]

Stolypin and the Second Duma

Meanwhile, preparations were going on for the convocation of the Second Duma. The venerable Goremykin was succeeded as Prime Minister by the vigorous and ruthless Peter Stolypin. The new premier set himself on the one hand to crush revolution throughout the Russian Empire, and on the other, to carry through economic reforms which he regarded as overdue. Stolypin's field courts-martial shot or strung up unruly peasants by the score. At the same time, he launched a determined attack on the archaic system of collective ownership of land by village communes, and did everything possible to favour the emergence of a class of yeoman farmer composed of 'the sober and the strong'. Stolypin soon found himself between two fires. The Court considered his ideas too radical, while the Social-Democrats and Social-Revolutionaries belaboured Stolypin for encouraging the loathsome *kulaks* (in Russian, literally 'fists'), as the wealthier peasant farmers were nicknamed.

Stolypin did everything possible to influence the Duma elections. Large categories of voters were arbitrarily struck off the register, while the police held up ballot papers, fixed impossible dates for polling, and did all they could to discourage unreliable elements like Jews and Socialists from voting. The result of this was the opposite from that intended by the régime. The exclusion of the liberals and radicals who had signed the Viborg Declaration simply brought about the election of downright revolutionaries, many of them former political prisoners. The Social-Democrats withdrew their boycott of the Duma, with the result that the Labour group in the Second Duma outnumbered the Constitutional Democrats (Cadets) who had dominated the First. The Social-Democrats alone won fifty-four seats. In Georgia, this party was even more victorious in the elections to the Second Duma than in those for the First. The Tbilisi province returned Archil Japaridze, Katsiashvili, and Jugheli; Kutaisi province elected Irakli Tsereteli, Lomtatidze and Gerasime Makharadze; the Batumi district returned Konstantine Kandelaki, subsequently Minister of Finance in the Georgian Republic; the city of Tbilisi elected Zurabishvili (Zurabov).

The second Duma met in St. Petersburg on 20 February/5 March 1907. The new Georgian deputies worthily filled the places of their proscribed comrades of the First Duma. Irakli Tsereteli proved himself an accomplished orator and parliamentary tactician, and was elected leader of the Duma's Social-Democratic faction, Russian and Georgian deputies alike acknowledging his leadership.

While the Second Duma was in session, the Fifth Congress of the Russian Social-Democratic Party took place in London in May 1907. The Russian delegates were mainly Bolsheviks, but the Georgian representatives, headed by Noe Zhordania (under the pseudonym Castro), were solidly Menshevik. The only exception was Stalin who arrived, as he had done at the previous Congress, with forged credentials from a non-existent Social-Democratic branch in southern Georgia. After some dispute, he was admitted to the Congress as an observer, but without vote. The Menshevik block vote of the Georgian delegation was a sore trial to Lenin and his followers, who had great difficulty in getting their resolutions carried. Zhordania relates in his memoirs that after one meeting, Lenin came up to him in the street and said:

'Look here, Castro—Why don't you Georgians cease meddling in Russia's affairs? You don't understand our people, their psychology, their ways and customs. If only you would leave us alone to sort out our affairs in our own way, we could soon get them straight. Just agree to accept autonomy for yourselves, and do what and how you like in Georgia. We shall not bother you so long as you do not bother us.'

Such a suggestion, coming from the leading champion of

international working-class solidarity, surprised Zhordania greatly. [90] In 1921, when the Russian comrades felt themselves secure, they were to prove less eager to tolerate the independent ideas of their little brothers in Georgia.

Back in St. Petersburg, the Tsar's government was finding the Second Duma as intractable as the First. Unable to silence the tribunes of the people, Stolypin staged a political coup. The Social-Democrats were accused of plotting against the régime, evidence of 'armed conspiracy' being fabricated by *agents provocateurs*. Stolypin demanded the exclusion of the Social-Democrats from the Duma and the surrender of twelve deputies to the police. The Duma refused, whereupon the government dissolved it in the early morning of 16 June 1907. All those Social-Democratic deputies who could be tracked down were arrested. Thirty-one of them were sentenced to four or five years' exile or hard labour in Siberia. Two of the Georgian deputies, Archil Japaridze and Lomtatidze, died in prison, though their comrade Irakli Tsereteli survived to play an outstanding role in the events of 1917. An imperial manifesto was issued, decreeing sweeping changes in the electoral law. The lists of 'electors' whose duty it was to select the actual members of the Duma were so manipulated that the country gentry exercised complete predominance in rural areas. Central Asia was disfranchized entirely. The representation of Poland was reduced from thirty-six to fourteen seats. In other parts of the Empire where a non-Russian population was in the majority, similar measures were taken to secure the return of Cossacks or Russian colonists. The number of deputies allotted to Georgia was reduced to three.

While the First and Second Dumas were in session, General Alikhanov and his punitive expeditions reduced the Georgian countryside to some semblance of obedience, although strikes and sporadic unrest continued throughout 1906 and 1907. The Caucasian revolutionary organizations were forced underground. The Russians resumed their old campaign against Georgian middle-class nationalism and upper-class 'separatism'. This campaign was not without its lighter side. Thus, in February 1907, the poet Akaki Tsereteli was arrested and conducted to the Metekhi Prison in Tbilisi for publishing a lampoon making fun of the governor, Rausch von Traubenberg. Within hours, news of the incident reached every corner of Georgia. A unanimous outcry arose from all classes of society. The next day, the viceroy was compelled to set the poet free.

Murder of Ilia Chavchavadze

Far more serious and tragic was the fate of Georgia's other great man of letters, Ilia Chavchavadze. After his service in the Upper House of the first two Russian Dumas, Ilia returned to Georgia in the summer of 1907. On 28 August, he was way-laid and murdered by a gang of assassins close to his country home at Saguramo, near Mtskheta. His funeral was a national event. Huge crowds followed the cortège from Saguramo to Tbilisi. Akaki Tsereteli, a lifelong friend of Ilia, rose from a bed of sickness to pronounce a sincere and touching funeral oration in which he underlined Ilia's inestimable contribution to the revival of the Georgian nation, and held him up as an example to all future generations. The Tsarist authorities hushed up the affair as much as they could. It was never estab-lished whether the motive for Ilia's murder was robbery, political feud or police provocation. At the time, it was often held that the crime was the work of Georgian revolutionaries, whose methods Ilia had condemned. During World War II, some wretched old man is said to have confessed to being em-ployed by the Russian gendarmerie chiefs to lead the attack on Ilia. A belated official investigation was conducted by the Soviet authorities and the blame laid at the door of the Tsarist administration. A handsome obelisk now marks the spot where Ilia fell.

Whatever the truth concerning Ilia's murder, the summer of 1907 was marked by a revival of Bolshevik terrorism in the Caucasus. Lenin was determined not to let his organization fade away for lack of funds, and found banditry a useful adjunct to revolutionary campaigning. On 23 June 1907, there took place the famous raid on the Tbilisi State Bank, led by the resourceful Armenian Kamo (Ter-Petrossian). The Tbilisi adventure yielded a quarter of a million rubles, which were duly conveyed to Bolshevik headquarters in Western Europe. The notes were in large denominations, and their numbers were circulated to banks all over the world. As a result, several leading Bolsheviks, including Litvinov, the future Soviet

Commissar for Foreign Affairs, were arrested while trying to change the money. A great uproar ensued among the various Social-Democratic factions. Trotsky, then a Menshevik, joined with other rivals of Lenin in accusing the Master of reducing socialism to the level of brigandage and highway robbery. Many of Lenin's critics later became Bolshevik Commissars, and forgot the scruples which they evinced in these early days. The Master's real fault lay in his possessing greater realism and less cant than most of his disciples.

The Georgian Church in crisis

While the Russian police were busy protecting their banks and convoys from Bolshevik bandits, fresh trouble arose from a different quarter. The Georgian Church, which had long been brooding over its wrongs, became more and more vociferous in demanding restoration of its ancient free or 'autocephalous' status, of which it had been arbitrarily deprived by the Russian government in 1811. The Georgian bishops pointed out that under the Russian exarchs sent down from St. Petersburg to run Georgia's ecclesiastical affairs, the Georgian Church had been robbed of some 140 million rubles' worth of property and estates; ancient icons had been stripped of precious gems, sold to line the pockets of Russian governors and army commanders; unique Gospel manuscripts had been ripped from their jewelled bindings and left to decay; Church schools had been closed down, and the use of Georgian in the liturgy discouraged; twenty episcopal sees lay vacant and seven hundred and forty parishes were without pastors. The conference of Georgian clergy which met at Tbilisi in 1905 had been broken up by police and troops. Later, many leading spiritual leaders who protested against the dictates of the St. Petersburg Synod were subjected to disciplinary action and downright persecution. Bishop Kyrion was removed from his diocese, stripped of his episcopal title and deported to Russia, where he was shut up in a cell in Tambov province. Another eminent churchman, Archimandrite Ambrosius, was banned from celebrating the liturgy and confined in the Troitsky Monastery at Ryazan.

Matters reached a head in 1908, when the Russian Exarch of Georgia, Archbishop Nikon, was murdered on 28 May at his residence in Tbilisi by unidentified assassins. Nikon was said to sympathize with the cause of the Georgian Church, and his murderers were alleged to be hooligans from the Russian extremist Black-Hundred gangs who feared that Nikon would intercede for the Georgian Church with the authorities in St. Petersburg. On the other hand, the chauvinists of the Russian Patriotic League, led by the fanatical Fathers I. Vostorgov and S. Gorodtsev, accused Georgian clerics of being behind the crime, and great bitterness was engendered on all sides.

These events aroused world-wide comment among churchmen of all denominations, who were virtually unanimous in championing the Georgians against their Russian persecutors. The British Bishop of Gibraltar intervened with the Russian Synod on behalf of the Georgian Church. The Papacy, which had established a Roman Catholic bishopric at Tbilisi as early as 1329 and counted many Georgian Catholic converts, also lent support to the Georgians. In 1910, Father Michael Tamarati (Tamarashvili), a Georgian Catholic priest, brought out in Rome a detailed and well documented history of the Georgian Church, written in French, in which he showed how this important branch of Christendom, which neither Arabs, Mongols, Turks nor Persians could exterminate, had finally been subjugated and crushed by Russian fellow-Christians of the Holy Orthodox Church. The Russian Embassy in Rome bought up and destroyed as many copies of this important and revealing work as it could. The dispute dragged on indecisively for years, until the outbreak of World War I relegated it temporarily to the background.

The dissolution of the Second Duma in 1907 evoked a general mood of lassitude and gloom in Russian political circles. The elections to the Third Duma were rigged by agents of the government and produced a gratifying swing to the Right. This time, Georgia was permitted to return three deputies only. The nobility elected Prince Sharvashidze, while the popular vote returned Nikolai (Karlo) Chkheidze (*d.* 1926), the future leader of the Petrograd Soviet, and the young lawyer Evgeni Gegechkori (1882–1954), future Foreign Minister of the independent Georgian Republic. The witty and jovial Chkheidze soon became the main spokesman of the twenty Social-Democrats in the Third Duma. The polished but vain

Gegechkori also made his mark, once inviting the Tsar's ministers from the floor of the Duma to change the police spy stationed within the building 'because he had got tired of the man's face'. The Fourth Duma, which sat from 1912 until the Revolution of 1917, was of a similar complexion to the Third. Gegechkori was replaced by Akaki Chkhenkeli, another Menshevik who was head of the Transcaucasian government of 1918 and later Georgian Minister in Paris; Prince Sharvashidze was succeeded by Prince V. Gelovani, a member of the Georgian Federalist party, who perished on the Caucasian Front in 1915.

Plight of the Georgian peasantry

One of the few issues on which the Georgian Social-Democrats and the Russian Viceroy of the Caucasus were agreed was the need to alleviate the agrarian problem and relieve the depressed state of the Georgian peasantry. Particularly unfortunate was the lot of a category of peasant known as *khizani*, originally free migrant peasants who settled on a lord's estates for a period and entered into share-cropping and other contractual relationships with the local squire. The liberation of the peasantry had been effected in 1864 without sufficient regard for the interests of the *khizani*, who were passed over in the general scramble for land. Unable to find enough work in Georgia's nascent industry, the *khizani* together with the former domestic serf class were reduced in course of time to a pitiable condition. The situation of the remainder of the peasantry was, as has previously been noted, far from enviable. Lack of capital and of education prevented any improvement in farming techniques. Too often, the agricultural worker would be seen year after year turning the same shallow furrow in dry and stony ground with a primitive wooden hand-plough. Many were still vainly trying to pay off the redemption dues with which they had been saddled by the Russian government nearly half a century earlier, in consideration for the land which they or their fathers had acquired from their former feudal lords.

In 1912, after agitation by the Georgian deputies in the Duma and much discussion between Count Vorontsov-Dashkov and the government at St. Petersburg, the residual redemption payments were at last written off. The status of 'temporary obligation', or semi-serfdom, in which peasants had remained pending full payment of these instalments, was formally abolished. This long overdue reform could not, however, solve the land hunger of the Georgian peasantry. So long as the Russian Crown, the grand dukes, various foreign concessionnaires, Russian and German colonists, together with the native aristocracy, clung to the lion's share of the land, the grievances of the Georgian peasantry were bound to remain alive. It must be admitted that the estates cultivated by the more enterprising landowners and foreign colonists were precisely those which yielded the best crops and gave the best promise for the country's future prosperity. It was difficult for any responsible government lightly to hand over well-run plantations, vineyards and arable land to an impoverished and backward peasantry whose methods of farming did not rise above bare subsistence level and provided no surplus for export or for the provisioning of urban centres. Such was the unresolved dilemma which faced Georgian society and the Russian administration until 1917, when revolution imposed its own radical solutions.

Industrial unrest

The period under review was also marked by renewed unrest in Georgian industry. A number of strikes and demonstrations took place in Georgia in 1912, in protest at the massacre of workers on the Lena goldfields in Siberia. In Georgian mining centres, justifiable agitation for better working conditions was rife. In 1913, strikes at Chiatura brought the output of manganese to a standstill for weeks at a time, and provoked armed intervention by the Russian authorities. The port workers at Poti and Batumi came out in sympathy. This massive demonstration of working-class solidarity forced the proprietors of the mines to make substantial concessions.

War declared, 1914

On 1 August 1914, Imperial Germany declared war on Russia. The people of the Caucasus, who realized that sooner or later Ottoman Turkey would become embroiled in the struggle, greeted the news with markedly divergent emotions. Russia's

Muslim subjects, exempt as they were from military service, remained passive, though many hoped for Russia's defeat by the Central Powers. The Armenians on the other hand looked forward eagerly to the annihilation of the hated Turk and the establishment of an independent Greater Armenia carved out of the Ottoman Empire and Russian Transcaucasia. The Tsar and his government did everything possible to encourage the Armenians in their wishful thinking. In response to an appeal from the Armenian Catholicos-Patriarch, Nicholas II replied: 'Tell your flock, Holy Father, that a most brilliant future awaits the Armenians.' In the event, as we know, World War I turned out to be catastrophic for the Armenian people, whose fate became a disgrace to the conscience of the world.

The reaction of the Georgians to the outbreak of war was mixed. As Christians, many shared the Armenians' fear and loathing of the Turk and were happy to support the Russian war effort. Others, including extremists both on the nationalist wing and among the revolutionary groups, hoped for a Russian defeat at the hands of Germany and Austria, to be followed eventually by a new order for the peoples of the Tsarist empire.

Mussolini and the Georgian Socialists

The Georgian Menshevik leader Noe Zhordania was in Western Europe at the outbreak of war. Hastening back to Russia, he stopped at Milan where he had an interview with Benito Mussolini, then editor of the socialist newspaper *Avanti* and a militant foe of Austro-German imperialism. The two socialist leaders had a frank exchange of views on the likely outcome of the war and the correct policy for Social-Democrats to adopt towards it. Zhordania told Mussolini that most of his colleagues prayed for a repetition of the military débâcle which had precipitated the Russian revolution of 1905, and doubted whether the Tsarist régime, undermined by revolutionary agitation among the masses, the opposition of liberals in the Duma and the corruption and effeteness of the Court, could stand up to the might of the Kaiser and the Austrian emperor. Mussolini listened for a time and then burst out: 'We shall not permit Germany to crush France!' The Italian socialist made it clear to Zhordania that however much Germany might appear to the Tsar's subjects in the guise of a liberator, many socialists of Western Europe could not reconcile themselves to the prospect of republican France and democratic Belgium and Britain being trampled underfoot by the Prussian jackboot.

Pondering on this paradox, Zhordania returned to Russia. He found the Social-Democrats, Bolsheviks and Mensheviks alike, strongly Germanophile in mood and quite uninterested in the fate of the Western democracies. Some Russian and Georgian socialists genuinely regarded Imperial Germany as more 'progressive' than France, pointing to the superior state of German industry, the excellent organization of the German Trade Union movement and the strength of the German Social-Democratic party, compared with all of which France appeared a stagnant preserve of backward bourgeoisie. Zhordania, who had lived for some years in France and England, parted company on this issue with some of his Menshevik colleagues, notably Noe Ramishvili and Noe Khomeriki, and lively arguments in Georgian socialist circles continued for some time. The Russian Bolshevik party and its Georgian adherents adopted from the first a strongly anti-war line. Under Lenin's direction, the small band of Georgian Bolsheviks carried on an active policy of propaganda and sabotage in the Caucasus. In 1915, a leading Georgian Bolshevik, Prokopi (Alesha) Japaridze (1880–1918), was arrested and exiled to Siberia. However, other Georgian Bolsheviks carried on the struggle, fomenting mutinies among the Russian troops on the Caucasus front and strikes on the railways and in the factories.

The Georgian Legion

Many Georgian émigrés and students in Western Europe also seized the chance to strike a blow against the Tsarist régime. In 1914, a Governing Committee of Independent Georgia was formed under the patronage of the German government, with branches in Austro-Hungary and in Turkey. The chairman of this committee was Petre Surguladze; other members included Prince Giorgi Machabeli, Mikhako Tsereteli (who had given up Kropotkinite Anarchism in favour of extreme Georgian nationalism), Leo and Giorgi Kereselidze, and the Muslim Georgian Kartsivadze (otherwise known as Meliton or Osman Bey). In 1915, a German Caucasus expedition was formed, incorporating a body of Georgian volunteers, some seven hundred strong, known as the Georgian Legion. The Legion's first commander was Lieutenant Horst Schliephack, later succeeded by Count F. W. von der Schulenburg, a former German Vice-Consul at Tbilisi and an expert on Georgian affairs, who also acted as German liaison officer with the Turkish Third Army. In January 1916, a star-shaped badge, the Order of Queen Tamar, was introduced for issue to military men and civilians who distinguished themselves on behalf of the independence of Georgia. During the Russo-Turkish campaign of 1916-17, the Georgian Legion was stationed in the mountains east of Tirebolu, on the banks of the Harshit river not far from the Black Sea. The headquarters of the Georgian Committee at that time were in Samsun, and later in Kerasunt. The legion was officially disbanded in April 1917, after relations between the German-backed Georgian Committee and the Turkish government had become strained. Earlier, Mikhako Tsereteli had been landed in Georgia from a German submarine with instructions to make contact with the leaders of the Georgian Social-Democratic movement and to foment unrest and rebellion within the country. A secret meeting between Mikhako Tsereteli and Noe Zhordania took place in Kutaisi, but Zhordania refused to have anything to do with a movement which he foresaw might have disastrous effects for the Georgian people.

Caucasian battlefields

Though secondary to the main battlefields on Russia's western frontier, the Caucasus front played an important role in World War I, as it had in the earlier Russo-Turkish wars of 1828-29, of 1853-55 and of 1877-78. Far greater bodies of manpower were deployed than on those earlier occasions. Poor communications combined with a severe climate made large-scale operations highly arduous, especially as neither the Russian nor the Turkish Army was up to date in its technical organization. In 1914, railway communications on the Russian side of the frontier ended at Sari-Kamish, some forty miles south-west of Kars and fifteen from the Turkish border. On the Ottoman side, six hundred miles of rough roads and tracks separated the armies operating in the Erzurum area from the nearest railhead at Ankara or the nearest station on the Baghdad railway north-west of Adana. During September and October 1914, the Turkish Third Army, 100,000 strong, assembled in the vicinity of Erzurum. Hostilities began late in October, when Turkey opened the campaign by a naval bombardment of Russian ports on the Black Sea. Liman von Sanders, head of the German military mission in Turkey, proposed landing a Turkish force at Odessa. The Turks, however, preferred to concentrate on regaining the territory lost to Russia in 1877–78, notably the great fortresses of Kars and Ardahan.

The Turkish supreme commander and War Minister was Enver Pasha, who conceived a grand strategy which would, he believed, open the way to the expulsion of Russia from the entire Caucasus. His first objective was the Russian railhead at Sari-Kamish. In spite of the lateness of the season and the remonstrances of his advisers, Enver insisted on launching the attack without delay. The routes by which his army was to advance were snow-covered mountain tracks, and the bulk of the Turkish transport and artillery had to be left behind. Yet such was the endurance and courage of the ill-fed and badly equipped Turkish soldiers that they almost achieved the impossible. While the main Russian force defending Sari-Kamish was engaged with the Turkish 11th Corps, the 10th Corps further to the north made to cut the railway between Sari-Kamish and Kars. At the northern end of the front, a Turkish detachment from Trebizond drove the Russians out of Ardahan.

The Turks on the defensive

The Russian commander, Myshlaevsky, was in a panic and talked wildly of evacuating Transcaucasia altogether and withdrawing the Russian Army north of the Caucasus range. His Chief of Staff, General Yudenich, saved the situation. He mustered his forces for a counter-attack, defeated and virtually destroyed the Turkish 9th and 10th Corps and then repulsed the 11th Corps from its advanced position. The losses of the Turkish Third Army are said to have amounted to 85 per cent of its strength. In spite of Yudenich's brilliant victory, this Turkish incursion into Caucasia caused great alarm in St. Petersburg and led to agitation for Anglo-French intervention against Turkey. This in turn helped to bring about the ill-starred Gallipoli expedition.

During the following year, the Caucasian front reverted to secondary importance in the global strategy of World War I. While the Turks' attention was centred on the Dardanelles, they also built up their shattered Third Army facing the Russian border. On the other side, fresh units were recruited to strengthen the Russian front line. In April 1915, Turkish units supported by Muslim Georgian Laz and Atchar irregulars attempted a raid on the Black Sea port of Batumi, but were repulsed. To the south, the Russians advanced their left into Turkish Armenia and occupied the historic town of Van. The Russians were enthusiastically seconded by detachments of Armenian irregulars, while the Turks wreaked terrible vengeance on the Armenians dwelling within the Ottoman borders. The same year, Vorontsov-Dashkov sent General Lyakhov to slaughter the Muslim Georgian Laz and Atchars as a punishment for their pro-Turkish attitude. Lyakhov ravaged and depopulated the entire Chorokhi valley up to Artvin, in the vicinity of which only 7,000 out of a previous population of 52,000 Georgian Muslims were left alive.

Count Vorontsov-Dashkov, who had reached the age of seventy-eight, was succeeded as viceroy in September 1915 by the former commander-in-chief on Russia's western front, the Grand Duke Nicholas. The arrival of the new viceroy soon brought spectacular results. In February 1916 the Russians captured the great citadel and supply base of Erzurum, from which the Turks retreated in disorder with heavy losses in men and material. Two months later, the Russians occupied the Turkish port of Trebizond (Trabzon) on the Black Sea. The Turkish High Command were just preparing for a counter-offensive when Nicholas launched another massive blow at the remains of their Third Army, which was completely routed. In July 1916 the Russians occupied Erzinjan—about the furthest point within the Turkish dominions in Anatolia ever captured by a Russian army. A new Turkish force, the Second Army, attacked the Russians from the south-west in the Lake Van sector, but was firmly held.

During the winter of 1916–17 no fresh developments of note occurred. The appalling climatic conditions in those windswept and snowbound uplands of Armenia and eastern Anatolia caused terrible suffering to both sides. The transport of troops and supplies was attended by grave difficulties. The Russians strove to extend their railway from Sari-Kamish to Erzurum, but their railhead was still some distance short of that city on the outbreak of the March Revolution. On the southern flank, they hoped to link up with the British in Mesopotamia. Plans were worked out for a Russian thrust on Mosul to coincide with the anticipated British capture of Baghdad, which took place at length in March 1917. All hope of energetic action on the Russian side was by now gone.

Breakdown of Tsarist Russia

It is not necessary to trace here the events which led up to the March Revolution and the ignominious collapse of the titanic structure of Tsarist absolutism. Under the vacillating but obstinate Tsar Nicholas II, Russia had been an autocracy without a real autocrat, while the Rasputin scandal had discredited the imperial court in the eyes of the nation and of the world. In the end, a scramble for bread in the streets of Petrograd was the signal for the downfall of the régime, which fell amid the jubilation of millions who saw its passing as the dawn of a better era.

Even before the news of the fall of the Romanovs reached Georgia, the morale of the local population had sunk to a low ebb. As a result of poor communications with European Russia, and the intolerable strains which World War I imposed on Russia's relatively immature economy, the peoples of Transcaucasia themselves had to bear much of the burden of supplying and provisioning Russia's large forces engaged on the Turkish front. A severe shortage of grain made itself felt by 1916 throughout the country. In January 1917, the town of Kutaisi went without bread for a fortnight owing to the breakdown of the Transcaucasian railway system. Prices of all commodities rose steeply in the bazaars, where the merchants and stall-keepers reverted to the primitive system of trade by barter. Inflation ensued and the value of money depreciated rapidly. Hunger was rife in Tbilisi and other cities, and deaths from famine occurred in country districts. The Caucasian revolutionary societies resumed their clandestine plotting.

To counter the revolutionary menace, the Russian Minister of the Interior sent to Tbilisi a special emissary empowered to deport from Georgia any individual suspected of defeatism or subversive activities, with the sole exception of the viceroy himself. In March 1917, the Russian secret police planned a wholesale round-up of Georgian political leaders of all shades, including the chief of the Georgian Social-Democrats, Noe Zhordania. Before this plan could be carried into effect, the news reached Tbilisi on 15 March 1917 that the imperial régime had ceased to exist.

Literature, art and intellectual life up to 1917

Before finally turning our back on the Tsarist period of Georgian history, it is worth while pausing to survey developments in literature and the arts, where the picture is far less sombre than one might have expected.

A number of outstanding Georgian writers came to maturity in the early years of the twentieth century. Among these may be mentioned Vasil Barnovi (1856–1934), author of historical novels, tales of old Tbilisi, and realistic stories based on contemporary Georgian life, and Shio Aragvispireli (1867–1926), revolutionary agitator, veterinary surgeon and author of powerful short stories in which he exposed the social evils of his time. Even better known was David Kldiashvili (1862–1931), a writer whose forebears belonged to the squirearchy and who served as an officer in the Russian Army before his outspoken sympathy with the Georgian national cause led to his disgrace and dismissal. Endowed with a sharp and observant eye for character and situation, and profound insight into human psychology, Kldiashvili is acclaimed as one of the great masters of Georgian realism, and the authentic chronicler of a vanished era in Georgian society; he also wrote several successful plays. Other important literary figures were the essayist and dramatist Shalva Dadiani (1874–1959), and the novelist Leo Kiacheli, born in 1884, whose novel *Tariel Golua* gives a vivid picture of the impact of the 1905 Revolution on a typical Georgian village.

In poetry, the revolutionary tradition was maintained by Irodion Evdoshvili (1873–1916). From 1910 onwards, however, a reaction against patriotic and civic modes in poetry set in, under the leadership of a group of youthful poets and novelists whose début took place under the fashionable banners of Symbolism and Decadence. They formed a coterie known as the Company of the Blue Drinking Horn (*Tsisperi Qandsebi*), which included such talented young men as Titsian Tabidze, Paolo Iashvili, Valerian Gaprindashvili, S. Kldiashvili, Razhden Gvetadze, Shalva Apkhaidze, Giorgi Leonidze and others. Their early, and now seldom republished works were characterized, according to a Soviet literary manual, by 'mysticism, lack of political content, absence of ideas, extreme individualism, the cult of Bohemian life, the aesthetics of deformity and preciosity'. 'Later on,' the manual tells us, 'thanks to the stimulating influence of the mighty successes of Socialist industrial progress, the best representatives of the Blue Drinking Horn school, liberated from decadence, played a significant role in the evolution of Georgian Soviet literature.'[91] Several of the group, however, perished in the Stalin purges of 1936–37.

From the 1890's onwards, a great revival took place in the Georgian theatrical world. Both in Kutaisi and in Tbilisi, the Georgian stage was in a flourishing condition and often served as a tribune for the symbolical expression of the nation's suppressed political yearnings. Georgian music also revived under the inspiration of Zakaria Paliashvili, whose melodious opera *Abesalom and Eteri* (1913), based on an ancient Georgian poetic legend, is universally beloved and frequently performed throughout Georgia to this day. In painting, a refreshing reaction against the historical realism of the Russian Repin school was launched almost single-handed by the inimitable primitive painter Pirosmani (Niko Pirosmanashvili, 1860–1918). Unappreciated during his lifetime, Pirosmani eked out a life of misery, painting panels for inns and executing chance commissions for any who would employ him. He died in squalor at the height of the Revolution. Only posthumously did fame come his way. His compositions now occupy an honoured place in the Tbilisi Museum of Arts, which is housed in the premises of the old Theological Seminary where Stalin studied; they evoke with their naïve and colourful humour and vivid portrayal of costume and manners a bygone era in Georgian society.

Education and scholarship also made considerable strides during the early years of the twentieth century. Alongside the official Russian network of schools and seminaries, there grew up an unofficial system of independent, purely Georgian scholastic institutions. The Society for the Spreading of Literacy, founded by Ilia Chavchavadze, Gogebashvili and others, continued its useful work. Despite the Russian government's refusal to set up a university in the Caucasus, a number of local pedagogues banded together and organized an unofficial People's University of their own. The tireless archaeologist Ekvtime Taqaishvili (1863–1953) began his regular expeditions throughout Georgia, in which he collected countless ancient inscriptions and registered and described hundreds of ancient buildings and monuments. In 1907, Taqaishvili and others founded the Georgian Historical and Ethnographical Society, whose publications attained a high scholarly standard, and included editions of historical charters, folklore and dialect studies and other valuable material. Not less important was the academic work carried on by Georgians in the universities of Russia, notably at Moscow and St. Petersburg. The most brilliant of these Georgian professors was the late Academician Nicholas Marr (1864–1934). Before embarking on his controversial Japhetic Theory and other speculative linguistic hypotheses, Marr gained a solid and world wide reputation as editor of ancient Georgian texts, and as a brilliant philologist and archaeologist. Among his disciples were Ivane Javakhishvili, the first volumes of whose monumental but unfinished *History of the Georgian People* appeared at Tbilisi in 1913–14, and Akaki Shanidze, the leading grammarian and expert on the history of the Georgian language.

It would be unjust to belittle the support given by the Russian government and by Russian learned societies to the study of Georgian and Caucasian antiquities. During the latter years of the nineteenth century, the Caucasian Museum in Tbilisi (now the State Museum of Georgia) made great strides under its energetic and talented German director, Dr. Radde. Particularly fruitful was the help given to Georgian antiquarian and ethnographical studies by Countess Praskovya Uvarova (1840–1924), who succeeded her husband, Alexey Uvarov, as President of the Imperial Moscow Archaeological Society in

1884. She sponsored a magnificently produced serial publication called *Materials for the Archaeology of the Caucasus*. She financed this and other valuable works both out of her own pocket and by means of subsidies which she obtained from members of the imperial family. The manuscript of Countess Uvarova's own important treatise on the miniatures in mediaeval Georgian Gospel manuscripts was unfortunately destroyed during the 1917 revolution, and she herself died in exile in Serbia.

In spite of the repressive features of the Stolypin era in Russian history, the Tsarist government could not annul all the concessions which had been wrung from it during the revolution of 1905. Among these were freedom of publication, assembly and association. Consequently, the decade before 1917 witnessed a great growth of journals of all shades of opinion and a proliferation of clubs and voluntary philanthropic societies. A new type of journalist and intellectual began to flourish in the cafés and on the boulevards of Tbilisi, Kutaisi and other large towns. This new class was recruited in large part from scions of the old Georgian aristocracy. The latter were no match for the growing class of *kulaks* or wealthy peasant farmers and rural entrepreneurs. These shrewd and hardened individuals usually outclassed in business ability their former feudal lords, who tended to drift into the cities where they felt more at home than in the dilapidated *châteaux* of the remote countryside.

The rise of the Georgian *kulak,* the life of the Georgian aristocratic intellectual and dilettante, and the impact on them both of the revolutionary upheavals of 1917 and 1921 have never been more successfully depicted than in the masterly novel by Mikheil Javakhishvili (1881–1937), *Jaqos khiznebi (Jaqo's Guests)*, first published in 1924–25. With devastating realism and many humorous touches, Javakhishvili contrasts the swashbuckling Jaqo, swindler, seducer and false bon-homme, with his victim, Prince Teimuraz Khevistavi, the amiable and ineffectual philanthropist whom Jaqo robs of his fortune, his wife, and even of his sanity. In the person of Teimuraz Khevistavi we follow the decline and fall of the old nobility. Abandoning his tenants to the good offices of the grasping Jaqo, Teimuraz spends his time in Tbilisi, immersed in the affairs of his journal—a journal, needless to say, published in a very limited edition—of the modest co-operative society with which he concerns himself, in the shaky literary society to which he belongs, in the folk theatre, in free evening classes for working men, and a dozen other good causes. This sprig of the nobility is a radical of advanced social views. His lively pen is always in demand for the drafting of political memoranda, his advice sought on the burning questions of the day.

'Whatever turn the conversation took—the irrigation of the Sudan, British policy in regard to Devil's Island, German colonies in Africa, the disputes concerning the port of Jibuti, the death of the Sultan of Zanzibar, the Chartist movement, the electoral rights of the women of New Zealand, the discovery of a new planet, some fresh scientific invention, the policies of Combes or Lloyd George, or the significance of any oration pronounced by any public figure in any country—then Teimuraz was regularly consulted for his authoritative and final opinion.'

While the worthy Jaqo falsified the estate accounts and plotted the ruin of his trustful lord:

'Teimuraz was writing a treatise in three volumes on the history of Georgian civilization, composing dozens of leading articles, reports, judgements, researches and memoranda; at the same time, he used to attend secret political meetings and, in company with so many of his contemporaries, he went on gnawing and sawing away busily day by day at the mighty branch upon which he nonchalantly dozed and cheerfully fluttered about.'

That mighty branch, of course, was the Tsarist Empire itself. For all its faults, it was a régime towards which a few years hence, under Communist dictatorship, many of its erstwhile opponents would look back with a certain nostalgic affection.

CHAPTER IX

TOWARDS GEORGIAN
INDEPENDENCE: 1917–18

Abdication of Nicholas II — Kerensky and the Georgian Social-Democrats — Economic change and social revolution — Restoration of the Georgian Church — Disintegration of Russia's Caucasian Front — Short rations and Bolshevik broadsheets — The Bolsheviks seize power — The Transcaucasian Commissariat — The Turkish menace — Brest-Litovsk repudiated — An ephemeral federation — Germany takes a hand — Birth of the Georgian Republic

Abdication of Nicholas II

THE STRESSES of World War I precipitated the Russian political débâcle which many observers had long predicted. In March 1917, when the revolution ultimately took place, the fall of Tsardom was comparatively effortless. Bread riots in Petrograd were followed by a mutiny of the garrison there. The Duma refused to obey the Tsar's orders any longer. A provisional government was formed on 14 March, and Nicholas gave in and abdicated without a struggle.

When the news of the revolution reached Georgia, the fabric of authority crumbled and collapsed. In Tbilisi and elsewhere, the police vanished from their posts and administrative offices closed down. Bands of revolutionaries appeared from their hiding places. Mass meetings were held in the principal towns, at which fierce mountaineers and grimy workers fraternized and congratulated one another on the achievement of their longed-for freedom. The once formidable viceroy, Grand Duke Nikolai Nikolaevich, haggard, with bloodshot eyes and trembling hands, declared to the local representative of the British

Press that he recognized the new order in Russia, and regarded it as the sole means of salvation for the fatherland. To the Georgian Social-Democrats Zhordania and Noe Ramishvili, the grand duke expressed the hope that he might himself be granted a seat in the Constituent Assembly which would be called upon to decide the future organization of the Russian state. However, this was not to be. Nikolai Nikolaevich was very soon relieved of his post by the new Petrograd government, and politely escorted to Tbilisi railway station by squads of cheering soldiers waving red banners and singing the *Internationale*.

Aware of the urgency of establishing some form of authority in Transcaucasia, the Provisional Government in Petrograd formed a special committee, consisting in the main of Caucasian members of the Duma, to exercise civil power in Georgia, Armenia and Azerbaijan. The chairman of this committee, the so-called Ozakom, was B. A. Kharlamov. At the outset its only Georgian member was Prince Kita Abashidze.

Kerensky and the Georgian Social-Democrats

Representations by the Tbilisi socialists later brought about the co-option of Akaki Chkhenkeli, the Georgian Social-Democrat, who also acted as the Petrograd Soviet's Commissar for Caucasia and on the Turkish military front. The Ozakom has been described as 'a collective Viceroy, only much weaker and without the prestige which the representatives of the Tsars had enjoyed'.[92] One of the sources of weakness of the Kerensky government in Russia was incessant rivalry between the administration and the Soviets, both of which regarded themselves as the true repositories of revolutionary power. A similar dualism existed in Transcaucasia. Everywhere self-appointed revolutionary bodies sprang up, ready to assume various functions of government. Among these we may mention the executive committees of the cities of Tbilisi and Kutaisi, which represented a wide range of social groups and classes, and normally obeyed the directives of the Ozakom, and the Tbilisi Soviet of Workers' Deputies (Chairman, Noe Zhordania), in which the Georgian Mensheviks had a decisive majority and to which as time went on deputies of the soldiers and peasants also adhered.

Economic change and social revolution

As during the 1905 revolution, the Georgian revolutionary organizations behaved during the trying circumstances of 1917 with moderation and public spirit. They lent their influence to keeping the peace, preventing inter-communal strife, and bringing about social and economic reforms in the midst of the war conditions and general upheaval. The leading Georgian Social-Democrats renounced for the time being the extremist slogans of Bolshevik class war and came out on the side of national unity.

'The present revolution,' Zhordania declared on 18 March 1917, 'is not the affair of some one class; the proletariat and the bourgeoisie are together directing the affairs of the revolution. . . . We must walk together with those forces which participate in the movement of the revolution and organize the Republic with our forces in common.'[93]

The March revolution brought again into the forefront all the old social and economic problems which the Tsarist government had failed to tackle. First and foremost was the agrarian problem. This, obviously, could not be settled overnight. Accordingly, peasants and landowners in many parts of Georgia adopted an interim solution, whereby share-cropping peasants settled on a landowner's estates simply ceased handing over the master's share of the crop, the so-called *gala,* amounting to between one-quarter and one-half of the total. Having no one to cultivate them on their behalf, the nobility found their domains slipping from their grasp, while the peasants were now endowed with both their own former small-holdings and those portions of their former lord's estates which they had formerly cultivated as share-croppers. Access to communal woodlands and pastures, monopolized by the landed proprietors under the terms of the liberation decrees of 1864 onwards, reverted to the peasantry. Plantations, forests and vineyards owned by members of the former Russian imperial family were confiscated and nationalized. Small farms belonging to the lesser squirearchy, a numerous category in Georgian rural society, were relatively little affected.

Restoration of the Georgian Church

Another burning question also swept into the forefront—that of the autocephaly or independent status of the Georgian Orthodox Church. As soon as news of the March revolution reached Tbilisi, the Georgian bishops invaded the headquarters of the Russian exarchate and ejected the Russian chief bishop and his staff. Georgians were appointed to take their places and administer the property and estates of the Georgian Church. The Ozakom was asked to give official sanction to the restoration of the Georgian patriarchate, abolished by Russia in 1811. However, this question was simply shelved until the eventual convention of the all-Russian Constituent Assembly. This did not deter the Georgians from going ahead with the reorganization of their old national Church. Bishop Kyrion was elected Catholicos-Patriarch of All Georgia, taking the title of Kyrion II, and new statutes were worked out at synods held in Tbilisi in 1917 and at the historic monastery of Gelati in 1921. Patriarch Kyrion died in 1918, and was succeeded by Patriarch Leonid, who lived until shortly after the Bolshevik invasion of 1921.

The collapse of the old Tsarist police and gendarmerie inevitably led in some regions of Georgia to anarchy and unrest. During the summer of 1917 criminal elements masquerading as revolutionaries found frequent opportunities for pillage and arson. The Ozakom and the local Executive Committees set up field courts-martial and a number of terrorists were shot. Pending the establishment of a regular People's Guard, Zhordania and his colleagues recruited from Guria a detachment of people's militia commanded by V. and K. Imnadze, which helped to maintain order where needed. Belated steps were taken to introduce into Georgia the Russian Zemstvo or rural district council organization, which had played a leading part in local government affairs as well as in the liberal reform movement since its inception during the 1860's. Ilia Chavchavadze and other leading figures in Georgian public life had for half a century petitioned successive Russian governors to introduce the Zemstvo pattern of local government into Georgia—a demand regularly rejected by St. Petersburg. Only now, when the old order was already in dissolution, could this overdue reform be tried out for a brief season, only to be swept away by the invasion of Communist Russia in 1921.

From March 1917, then, local authority within Georgia resided principally with the Social-Democrats, whose Tbilisi committee, directed by Zhordania and his deputy Noe Ramishvili, formed the backbone of the Petrograd-appointed Ozakom. Between the Georgian Social-Democrats and the Kerensky régime in Petrograd there was little basic divergence of aim. With Nikolai (Karlo) Chkheidze as Chairman of the Petrograd Soviet and Irakli Tsereteli a prominent minister in the Provisional Government, the Georgian Mensheviks were able to make their voices heard insistently in the councils of Russia and the world. In fact, Trotsky and the Bolsheviks were somewhat afraid of what they contemptuously termed the 'Georgian Gironde', and accused Chkheidze, Tsereteli and Zhordania of attempting to dominate and pervert the Russian revolution and foist upon it their own provincial interests and ideology.

Disintegration of Russia's Caucasian Front
Nevertheless, Tbilisi and Petrograd were not always in complete harmony. Divergences often broke out over tactics and priorities. Thus, Zhordania was strongly critical of the 'democratic cretinism' which inspired the Kerensky government to postpone settlement of the many crying social and economic problems left over from Tsardom until these could be referred to a constituent assembly convened with every refinement of electoral procedure from all corners of the far-flung Russian state. Many of the Tbilisi Social-Democrats were also opposed, in private at least, to continuance of the unpopular war with Germany and Turkey which, it was manifest, was beyond Russia's physical resources and presented a serious threat to the future of the revolution. There was indeed much to be said in favour of a ceasefire on the Caucasian front, where the Russian army had conquered vast areas of Turkish Anatolia and Armenia and was holding out deep in Turkish territory against the depleted and demoralized remains of the Ottoman Army. Terms advantageous to Russia could, on this front at least, readily have been obtained. Zhordania later recalled:

'Preoccupied with these matters, we got into direct telephone contact with I. Tsereteli and K. Chkheidze at Petrograd. We had discussions with them and acquainted them with the views of our party and our Soviet. We demanded reforms, decisive steps towards the conclusion of peace, and so forth. No reply could we get, except for vague reassurances and appeals for calm: "We are making preparations, everything will be all right, etc., etc." '[94]

In the meantime, Russia was moving rapidly towards the left. Demands for peace at any price resounded through the land, while Bolshevik agitators urged the peasants to seize the landlords' estates without awaiting the nebulous deliberations of the Constituent Assembly. By failing to come to grips with these two fundamental problems—peace and land reform—the Kerensky government dug its own grave, while Zhordania and his associates impotently fretted and fumed far away in Tbilisi.

In May 1917, the first congress of delegates of the Caucasian army met in Tbilisi. It was dominated by the Mensheviks and the Social-Revolutionaries. There were only a few Bolsheviks among the delegates, notably Korganov, later Commissar of War in the Baku Commune, and the Georgian S. Kavtaradze. The Social-Revolutionaries and Mensheviks professed, in public at least, to believe in the need to continue the war to a victorious end, whereas the Bolshevik minority unsuccessfully demanded peace at any price. Whatever the Georgians might have felt, the need to continue the struggle to the bitter end was irresistibly pressed by the Armenian Dashnaks and other representatives of the Armenian nation. Mortally afraid of the Turks, the Armenians had been encouraged by the American President Wilson to believe that an Allied victory would be followed by the creation of an independent Greater Armenia carved from the debris of the Turkish empire and stretching from the Mediterranean to the Caspian Sea. The Armenians called for complete support of the Petrograd government and the prosecution of war to the death. And so the war on the Caucasian front was allowed to drag on for many months more.

Short rations and Bolshevik broadsheets

As the year 1917 wore on, the situation of Russia's Caucasian Command became increasingly unfavourable. The majority of the half-million troops engaged against Turkey were not Georgians or Armenians, but Russian peasants from the European provinces, whose only concern was to finish fighting as soon as possible and return home to seize their share of the estates of dispossessed landlords. Conditions at the front were extremely harsh. At times, the men of the 4th Caucasian Rifle Division, whose chief of staff was the Georgian General Kvinitadze, received only half a pound of bread per day, and horses only one and a half pounds of barley. There was no meat and no conserves, and the men were boiling soup from the flesh of donkeys, cats and dogs. Bolshevik newspapers and broadsheets began to circulate in the ranks, while democratic changes introduced into army structure by the Provisional Government under pressure from the Workers' and Soldiers' Soviets rapidly affected discipline and morale. In June 1917, the Russian commander in the Caucasus, Yudenich, resigned and was replaced by General Przhevalsky. This change did not improve the military position. The standstill along the front continued, while there was a further increase in incidents and disturbances in the rear echelons. With the October Revolution, demobilization became spontaneous and irresistible, even before Trotsky began the official negotiations that led to the peace of Brest-Litovsk.

In the autumn of 1917, the food shortage in Georgia and Transcaucasia generally became acute. Caucasia had long depended for a large portion of her wheat and other grain supplies on South Russia. With the general anarchy prevailing in Russia, these supplies were largely cut off. On 15 October, a special conference on food supplies was convened in Tbilisi, attended by the Russian commander on the Caucasian front, General Przhevalsky. It was estimated that the requirements of the Caucasian Army amounted to 24 million *poods* (1 *pood* = 36 lb.) of flour and 36 million *poods* of corn, oats and barley annually, while the needs of the civilian population of Transcaucasia amounted to another 51 million *poods* of grain—a total of 111 million *poods*. The procurement of such quantities was out of the question. For the civilian population of Tbilisi, ten wagon-loads of wheat a day were required, whereas only four were currently being delivered. A ship which arrived at Batumi carrying corn from Russia was commandeered by demobilized soldiers, who sailed back to Russia in it without unloading the cargo. The bread ration in Georgia was cut still further, while measures were taken to evacuate town dwellers to country districts. Schools in Tbilisi were shut down and the pupils sent off to rural areas. By such measures as these, the population of the Georgian capital was quickly reduced by some 15,000.

The Bolsheviks seize power

Early in November 1917, news was received in Tbilisi of the successful Bolshevik uprising in Petrograd and the fall of Kerensky's Provisional Government. The reaction of the Georgian, Armenian and Azerbaijani Soviets and executive committees was immediate and hostile. On 8 November 1917, the Regional Centre of Soviets of Workers', Soldiers' and Peasants' Deputies met at Tbilisi together with the executive committees of the Social-Revolutionary and Social-Democratic (Menshevik) parties and resolved that the interests of the revolution demanded the liquidation of the Bolshevik insurrection and the immediate convocation of the all-Russian Constituent Assembly. A few days later, another meeting declared that the war with Germany and Turkey should go on and no separate peace be concluded.

The position of the Georgian Social-Democrats at this juncture was somewhat paradoxical. In their dim, dogmatic way, they were, no doubt, excellent patriots, though rather indifferent nationalists, being wholeheartedly devoted to the fashionable slogans of international brotherhood and working-class solidarity. Since the beginning of the century, they had been stumping the country proclaiming Georgia's destiny to help the workers and peasants of the entire Russian Empire towards economic and political fulfilment, and combating those who thought that Georgia's national salvation lay in independence through separation from Russia. With public speakers of the calibre of Irakli Tsereteli and Nikolai Chkheidze prominent first in the Tsarist Dumas and then under Kerensky, the Georgian Mensheviks exerted an influence in Russian affairs out of all proportion to their numerical strength. The Russian political dog had sometimes been wagged by its Georgian Menshevik tail. With the triumph of Lenin's

Bolsheviks, the Russian dog had cut itself adrift with a vengeance, while the Georgian tail was left wagging furiously in a
void. Far from rejoicing at their new-found freedom, the
Georgian Mensheviks quailed at the prospect before them.
'A misfortune has befallen us,' Noe Zhordania lamented. 'The
connection with Russia has been broken and Transcaucasia
has been left alone. We have to stand on our own feet and either
help ourselves or perish through anarchy.'[95]

Instead of proclaiming Transcaucasia's independence, as
they could readily have done, and coming to terms immediately with Turkey and the Central Powers, the Caucasian
politicians dallied and played for time. On 24 November 1917,
a conference of the Regional Centre of Soviets, the Regional
Soviet of the Caucasian Army, the Tbilisi City Council, the
Ozakom, the trades unions and other representative bodies met
in Tbilisi and decided that since Transcaucasia could not recognize the Bolshevik usurpation in Petrograd, a local régime
would have to be organized. Since this was regarded as merely
a temporary expedient, pending the suppression of the Bolshevik rebels, the Georgians continued to make arrangements
for the forthcoming elections to the all-Russian Constituent
Assembly. This much-heralded body, it was fondly believed,
would soon quell the unspeakable Bolsheviks and bring Russia
back to the paths of reason and order. In the event, the
Constituent Assembly, in which Lenin's followers were a
minority, was forcibly dispersed by Bolshevik troops after one
sitting in January 1918—an event which marked the death-
knell of Russian parliamentary democracy.

The Transcaucasian Commissariat

Meanwhile, the Transcaucasian Soviet and party organizations
had set up on 28 November 1917 a provisional government,
called the Transcaucasian Commissariat. It included three
Georgians, three Azerbaijanis, three Armenians and two
Russians. The Georgian Menshevik Evgeni Gegechkori was
elected chairman, as well as being Commissar of Labour and
External Affairs. The other two Georgian commissars were
Akaki Chkhenkeli (Interior) and Aleksiev-Meskhiev (Education). While predominantly Menshevik in character, the
commissariat also included nominees of the Muslim Musavat

organization, the Armenian Dashnaks, and the Social-Revolutionaries. The Bolsheviks were excluded. On the very next day, a detachment of Georgian Red Guards, recruited from Menshevik workers and led by a former Bolshevik named Valiko Jugheli, seized the Tbilisi arsenal, held hitherto by a detachment of Russian soldiers with strong Bolshevik leanings. Ordered by the Tbilisi Soviet to surrender the place, the baffled soldiers gave in after a token resistance. In this way the Georgian capital was preserved from the marauding hordes of Russian troops returning home pell-mell from the Caucasian front. The capture of the arsenal was a decisive setback to the Georgian Bolsheviks, and Lenin was extremely displeased when the news reached him.

While shrinking still from any formal declaration of independence from Russia, the Transcaucasian Commissariat entered forthwith into negotiations with the Turks for an armistice on the crumbling Caucasian front. A provisional agreement between the Russian General Przhevalsky and the Turkish commander, Vehip Pasha, was concluded at Erzinjan on 18 December 1917. However, Enver Pasha's Young Turk government at Istanbul was well aware of the heaven-sent chance which the Russian revolution offered for Turkey to recover Caucasian territories wrested from her by Russia over the preceding century, so that this move was mainly designed to gain time pending further weakening of Russia's military and political grip on Caucasia. Meanwhile, the Russian Bolsheviks were busily negotiating a separate peace with Germany and Austro-Hungary at Brest-Litovsk, at which conference, however, the Caucasian peoples were not directly represented.

The Turkish menace

During the winter of 1917–18, the situation in the Anatolian border areas around the Russo-Turkish front lines deteriorated still further. Vehip Pasha protested repeatedly to the Russian commander and the Transcaucasian government about alleged massacres of Turks and other Muslims by vengeful Armenian guerilla bands. On 12 February 1918 the Turks broke the truce and advanced against Erzinjan. Before the end of the month, Erzinjan and Trebizond were once more in Turkish hands. The Russian Army had by now virtually melted away. Against Vehip's force of 50,000 men and 160 field guns, the Georgians could muster only about 10,000 men, of indifferent quality and morale, while the small Armenian national army, heroic but hopelessly outnumbered, was spread thinly over a very wide area of difficult and exposed country. The nominal head of these armies was the Russian general, Lebedinsky, but the real confidence of the Transcaucasian government was given to the Georgian commander, General I. Z. Odishelidze, a Knight of the Order of St. George, former Governor of Samarkand, and late chief of staff of one of the Russian armies on the European front. Erzurum was defended by an Armenian garrison under the partisan leader Andronik. The Russo-Caucasian forces were hampered by thousands of panic-stricken refugees, Christian Armenians for the most part, fleeing from the implacable vengeance of the advancing Turks. There was every prospect that hundreds of thousands of the Turks and Tatars living in the Caucasus would rise in support of their triumphant Muslim brethren. Andronik evacuated Erzurum on 12 March 1918, while Batumi, Ispir, Kars and Van were menaced by the Turkish spear-heads.

In the meantime, Trotsky had signed the Treaty of Brest-Litovsk, whereby the Bolsheviks agreed to exclude from Russian territory the districts of Batumi, Ardahan and Kars, where the fate of the population was to be decided by a free plebiscite. In prevailing conditions, this meant abandoning the Armenian and Georgian Christian inhabitants to the mercy of the Turks.

A peace conference between representatives of Turkey and Transcaucasia opened at Trebizond on 14 March 1918. Vehip Pasha immediately demanded the evacuation of all districts abandoned by Russia at Brest-Litovsk. The Transcaucasian delegates, led by the Georgian politician Akaki Chkhenkeli, protested that they did not recognize Brest-Litovsk and were not bound by its conditions. Prolonged parleys took place until the Turks, flushed with victory, delivered an ultimatum demanding the evacuation of the disputed districts not later than 10 April 1918.

Brest-Litovsk repudiated

The Turkish ultimatum was received with the greatest indignation in the Transcaucasian Diet or *Seim*. This new parliamentary body, which assembled at Tbilisi on 23 February 1918, was
a local substitute for the short-lived Russian Constituent
Assembly in Petrograd which had been so unceremoniously
dispersed by Lenin's Bolsheviks. Nikolai Chkheidze and Irakli
Tsereteli, dethroned from their tribunes in the Petrograd Soviet
and Provisional Government, now reappeared in their native
Georgia to raise the clarion call of revolutionary democracy.
A tug-of-war ensued between the Transcaucasian delegation at
the Trebizond peace conference and the government and Diet
in Tbilisi. On 10 April 1918, Chkhenkeli declared himself
willing to accept the Brest-Litovsk treaty and conduct further
negotiations based upon it. Simultaneously, Tbilisi was gripped
by patriotic and warlike frenzy. On 13 April 1918, Irakli
Tsereteli declared in the Diet: 'Turkish imperialism has issued
an ultimatum to Transcaucasian democracy to recognize the
treaty of Brest-Litovsk. We know of no such treaty. We know
that in Brest-Litovsk the death sentence was passed upon
Revolutionary Russia, and that death sentence to our fatherland we will never sign!' Tsereteli's speech was greeted with
thunderous applause. The next day, Evgeni Gegechkori, the
Transcaucasian Premier, telegraphed Chkhenkeli and told him
to break off negotiations with the Turks and leave Trebizond.
That night, despite the manifest reluctance of the Muslim representatives, the Transcaucasian Diet declared war on the Turks.

This bellicose act was a piece of somewhat ridiculous
panache. Divided against itself, Transcaucasia had neither the
means nor, in so far as the Muslim elements were concerned,
the will to resist. On 15 April 1918, it was announced in
Istanbul that the Turkish Army had entered Batumi. Some of
the forts had surrendered without firing a shot and the town
and port had been occupied without resistance. The Muslim
Georgians of Lazistan and of Atchara, of which Batumi is the
main city, were helping the Turks, tearing up railway lines,
wrecking trains and conducting guerilla operations generally.
Having now seized most of the territories they coveted, the
Turks renewed their peace overtures. On 22 April 1918, Vehip

Pasha telegraphed Chkhenkeli and asked whether he was now prepared to resume peace talks. The Transcaucasian Diet had no alternative but to accept the offer.

An ephemeral federation

For the last six months, the Transcaucasian Commissariat had clung to the illusion that Russia would soon quell the Bolshevik usurpers and revert to the paths of true democracy, in which case Transcaucasia would be painlessly restored to the broad bosom of Russian Social-Democracy. While refusing to recognize the surrender at Brest-Litovsk, these half-hearted patriots delayed taking the only step which could preserve their country from complete ruin—namely a declaration of complete independence from Russia, combined with a real effort to enlist the support of interested foreign powers against the Turkish peril. At the end of March 1918 the question of Transcaucasian independence was discussed in the Diet, which voted 'categorically and irrevocably' against independence. On 22 April another lengthy debate on this issue took place, as a result of which the majority of the assembly adopted the motion 'that the Transcaucasian Seim decide to proclaim Transcaucasia an independent Democratic Federative Republic'. The formation of a cabinet was entrusted to the Georgian Chkhenkeli.

On 26 April 1918, Chkhenkeli, who combined the offices of Prime Minister and Foreign Secretary, published the names of the members of his new Transcaucasian Ministry, which contained four Georgians (including Chkhenkeli himself), five Armenians and four Azerbaijani Muslims. The other Georgian ministers were Noe Ramishvili (Minister of the Interior), G. Giorgadze (Minister of War) and Noe Khomeriki (Minister of Agriculture). When presenting his cabinet to the Diet, Chkhenkeli made a speech in which he outlined his government's programme, which featured the writing of a constitution, the delineation of the new state's frontiers, the liquidation of the war with Turkey, the combating of both counter-revolution and anarchy, and finally, the carrying through of land reform. On 28 April 1918, the newly created Democratic Federative Republic of Transcaucasia was recognized by the Ottoman Empire.

The Federative Republic, born under such unfavourable

auspices, lived but one brief month. Three days after its formation, the Turks occupied the great fortress of Kars, from which
thousands of panic-stricken men and women streamed out,
carrying their children and their possessions on their backs.
Those who were too old or too sick to walk were left to the
mercies of the Turk. Food shortages were producing famine in
many regions of Caucasia, notably in Armenia and Azerbaijan.
Another disruptive factor was the situation in the great oil port
of Baku on the Caspian, which was a Bolshevik stronghold
within otherwise Menshevik Transcaucasia. In December 1917,
Lenin had appointed the Armenian Bolshevik Stepan Shaumian
as Commissar Extraordinary of the Caucasus. Shaumian was
chairman of the Baku Soviet, in which he was backed by the
well known Georgian Bolshevik Prokopi (Alesha) Japaridze.
In March 1918, the Baku Soviet was involved in open conflict
with the Azerbaijani nationalist organization, the Musavat.
This led to inter-communal fighting between the Baku
Armenians and Tatars, lasting for several weeks, and resulting
in wholesale massacre of innocent victims. When the streets
had been cleared of thousands of dead bodies and the fires
extinguished, the Bolsheviks emerged as the strongest force in
the city. On 25 April 1918, a local Council of People's Commissars, modelled on the one in Moscow, was formed under
Shaumian's chairmanship. Spurning all allegiance to the
Menshevik régime in Tbilisi, the Baku Bolsheviks nationalized
the vast oilfields around their city and placed them at the disposal of the Moscow government, from which they derived
constant moral support.

The resumed peace talks between Turkey and Transcaucasia
opened at Batumi, now in Turkish hands, on 11 May 1918.
The Transcaucasian delegation, forty-five strong, was headed
by Premier Chkhenkeli, and also included the veteran Georgian
revolutionary and publicist Niko Nikoladze, and the jurist
Zurab Avalishvili. Vehip Pasha stated that the old peace conditions no longer applied, since the Armenians and Georgians
had responded to the earlier Turkish proposals by armed
resistance. Vehip now demanded the cession of the Georgian
regions of Akhaltsikhe and Akhalkalaki and the Armenian
district of Aleksandropol, transfer of the Aleksandropol-
Echmiadzin-Julfa railway to Turkish control and the free use

by the Turks of all Transcaucasian railways so long as the war against Great Britain continued. In view of the impossibility of armed resistance, there seemed nothing to prevent the Turks from establishing complete hegemony over the Caucasian isthmus.

Germany takes a hand

The Turks had reckoned without one very important factor, namely the intervention of their ally Imperial Germany, which at this time dominated the Ukraine and the Crimea and had virtually turned the Black Sea into a German lake. The Germans were in urgent need of the oil of Baku and had no desire to see the entire Middle East, and perhaps Central Asia too, fall into the hands of their ambitious Turkish friends. Thus it was that a strong and alert German delegation also attended the Batumi conference. Headed by the Bavarian general von Lossow, it also included Count von der Schulenburg, a former German Consul in Tbilisi, Arthur Leist, famous as a translator and scholar of Georgian literature, and O. von Wesendonk, later Consul-General in Tbilisi and author of studies on Georgian history and civilization. Von Lossow proffered his services as mediator between the Turks and the Transcaucasians. He also sent to Tbilisi Colonel Kress von Kressenstein, who entered into close touch with the Georgian members of the Transcaucasian government and started collecting together a special German task force from prisoners of war, peasants from the German settlements around Tbilisi, and any other German nationals whom he could assemble. Since the Georgians and Armenians regarded the Germans as among the highest representatives of European culture, science and technology, they were delighted at the sudden prospect of this excellent barrier which would halt Turkey's onward advance. At railway stations and other strategic points German helmets were soon to be seen, which the Christian inhabitants thought vastly preferable to the Turkish fez.

Birth of the Georgian Republic

There was no time to lose, if anything was to be salvaged from the wreck of united Transcaucasia. The Azerbaijani Muslims, who had nothing to lose by a complete Turkish victory, were opposed to further resistance. The Armenians, for all their heroism, were exhausted and incapable of organized action. Each of the Caucasian nations had to look to its own corporate survival. As soon as this became evident, Noe Zhordania, leader of the Georgian Social-Democrats and President of the Georgian National Council in Tbilisi, was summoned to Batumi. There he concerted measures with the Georgian delegation at the peace conference and then returned to Tbilisi with the necessary authority to proclaim Georgia an independent republic and to bring about the final dissolution of the Transcaucasian Diet. On 24 May 1918, von Lossow announced that owing to Turkish intransigence, his efforts at mediation had failed, and that the German delegation would leave Batumi at once on the S.S. *Minna Horn*. Two days later, the Transcaucasian delegation received a Turkish ultimatum, demanding the acceptance of all Turkish proposals within seventy-two hours, including the cession to Turkey of vast tracts of Georgian territory. But the Turks had been outwitted. That same day, 26 May 1918, Irakli Tsereteli in the Diet in Tbilisi had proclaimed Georgia a sovereign country independent of the Transcaucasian Federative Republic, which was now dissolved; Zhordania read a formal Act of Independence; and von Kressenstein and von der Schulenburg appeared in person at the Tbilisi Town Hall, to announce the establishment of a German protectorate over the newly born Georgian republic.

The first Prime Minister of the Georgian Republic was Noe Ramishvili, while Akaki Chkhenkeli received the portfolio of Foreign Affairs. These two new ministers immediately hurried to the Black Sea port of Poti, where von Lossow and his German colleagues were waiting impatiently on board their steamer. A provisional agreement between Imperial Germany and the Georgian Republic was signed at Poti on 28 May 1918. This convention provided among other things for Germany to have free and unrestricted use of Georgia's railway system and all ships found in Georgian ports, for the occupation of strategic points by German troops, the free circulation of German money in Georgia, the establishment of a German-Georgian mining corporation, and the exchange of diplomatic and consular representatives. Von Lossow also sent a secret letter to the Georgian government, pledging his good offices towards securing international recognition for the Georgian republic and safeguarding her territorial integrity. Thereupon, von Lossow and his suite set off across the Black Sea to Constanza, taking with them a Georgian delegation composed of Chkhenkeli, Avalishvili and Nikoladze, who were sent on to Berlin to enter into formal discussions with the Kaiser's government and the officials of the Wilhelmstrasse. Lengthy negotiations between the Georgians and the German Foreign Ministry ensued, only to be rendered abortive by the defeat of Imperial Germany at the hands of the Allies in November 1918.

Back in Batumi, a peace treaty between Turkey and Georgia was signed on 4 June 1918, whereby Turkey regained Batumi, Ardahan and Kars, as well as Akhaltsikhe and Akhalkalaki. However, the main treaty of peace and friendship between Georgia and Turkey was never formally ratified. True to their policy of playing off the Turks and Germans against one another, the Georgian delegation in Berlin declared to the German Foreign Ministry that 'inasmuch as Georgia, under direct pressure from Turkey, was compelled to sign any agreement whatsoever with her alone, the obligations incurred in such conditions must be considered null and void'. An attempt by Turkish troops to take possession of certain border areas of Georgia allegedly ceded to Turkey by the treaty of 4 June was repulsed by Georgian and German troops acting in concert, provoking a regular crisis between the German and Turkish governments. On 20 June 1918, a Georgian delegation headed by Evgeni Gegechkori arrived at Istanbul to take part in a general conference to revise the treaties of Batumi. Before anything had been settled, military defeat brought the Ottoman Empire itself tumbling down in ruin. By the end of 1918, as we shall see, German and Turkish hegemony over Caucasia had melted away, to be replaced for a short season by the rather less popular occupation of the victorious British.

CHAPTER X

INDEPENDENT GEORGIA: 1918–21

Formation of the Georgian cabinet — Trends in Georgian Socialism — The agrarian question — Financial instability — The British replace the Germans — An Armenian invasion — Denikin and the Whites — The British withdrawal — Georgia at the Paris Conference

Formation of the Georgian cabinet

THE GEORGIAN GOVERNMENT formed by Noe Ramishvili on 26 May 1918 included several Menshevik leaders who had already held portfolios in the former Transcaucasian administration. G. Giorgadze was made War Minister, Noe Khomeriki Minister of Agriculture and Sh. Aleksishvili (Aleksiev-Meskhiev) Minister of Justice. Other members of the cabinet were G. Zhuruli (Commerce and Industry), G. Laskhishvili (Education), Ivane Lortkipanidze (Communications, also Vice-Premier) and G. Eradze (Labour and Supplies). During the ensuing weeks, a need was felt to strengthen the formal links between the government and the Menshevik party organization, whose chairman, Noe Zhordania, took over the post of Prime Minister on 24 June 1918, leaving Ramishvili with the Ministry of the Interior. At a later stage, Akaki Chkhenkeli was replaced as Foreign Minister by Evgeni Gegechkori, while Konstantine Kandelaki, leader of the Georgian Co-operative movement, was made Minister of Finance, Commerce and Industry, and R. Arsenidze, Minister of Justice.

With Georgia's declaration of independence, the Transcaucasian Diet automatically ceased to exist. There remained in being only the so-called Georgian National Council, which had never been formally elected by the people. In February 1919, elections were held for a new Georgian Constituent Assembly. Suffrage was universal, equal and secret, and the method of proportional representation was employed. In spite of heavy snow, 60 per cent of the electorate voted. It is a tribute to the broad basis of Georgian democracy that fifteen parties were able to put forward candidates. The Mensheviks were returned to power with an overwhelming majority. Out of 505,477 votes cast, they polled 409,766, giving them 109 out of the 130 seats in the Chamber. The other parties to return delegates to the Constituent Assembly were the National Democrats (30,154 votes, 8 seats), the Social-Federalists (33,721 votes, 8 seats) and the Social-Revolutionaries (21,453 votes, 5 seats). Supplementary elections held some months later in areas of south-western Georgia previously held by the Turks and the Armenians produced broadly similar results.[96] The Constituent Assembly met for the first time on 12 March 1919, and continued in being until the Bolshevik invasion two years later. Cabinet and administration were answerable to the assembly according to the normal conventions of Western parliamentary democracy.

Trends in Georgian Socialism

Few régimes have been more harshly condemned by hostile critics than the Social-Democratic government which ruled Georgia from 1918 to 1921. According to Russian Bolshevik writers, Zhordania and his colleagues were rabid reactionaries, tools of the German and later of the British imperialists, agents of the darkest obscurantism. After Georgia had fallen and her government been forced to flee into exile, the former régime was often criticized from the opposite viewpoint by Georgian patriots who alleged that the Zhordania government placed socialist class warfare before national unity and adopted social and economic policies which played into the hands of the Communists and facilitated the annexation of Georgia by Soviet Russia.

Neither assessment appears altogether just or balanced. The Georgian Mensheviks were indisputably returned to power with an overwhelming majority by popular vote on a platform in which nationalization of industry and natural resources and radical land reform bulked large. Given time and immunity from foreign interference, their economic policy would have turned Georgia into a land of prosperous yeoman farmers and craftsmen and traders. The Mensheviks confiscated the domains of the great landowners and commandeered their city mansions, while the aristocracy often assented to the inevitable with a good grace and served loyally as officers in the republican army. Zhordania believed that, as Marx taught, the transition from a feudal to a socialist society must be accomplished via an intermediate bourgeois order. Accordingly, while declaring its devotion to working-class interests, the Zhordania government refrained from overt persecution of the middle class and former nobility. There was no extermination of bourgeois and aristocratic elements until the Communist annexation in 1921.

It is in fact ironic to observe how the Georgian Social-Democrats, whose leaders were working as late as 1918 for the triumph of democratic socialism in a Russia united and undivided, were at length transformed by the force of circumstances into nationalists of chauvinistic fervour and of an intransigence common in countries where independence has recently been regained after a long spell of alien rule. It was not long before the red banner of the revolution was replaced by an emblem depicting Saint George, the national patron and protector. Georgian was declared the sole permitted medium of official business, the use of Russian being outlawed in the Constituent Assembly, the law courts and the army. Such policies inflicted hardship upon Russian and Armenian officials and professional men, who became estranged from the new régime. They do not, however, support the allegation that the Zhordania régime was backward in fostering Georgia's cultural and linguistic self-consciousness.

It was in the realm of education that the Mensheviks scored their most notable successes. Early in 1918, Georgia's first regular university was opened in Tbilisi, thus realizing a dream cherished by generations of Georgian intellectuals but consistently frustrated by Russian obscurantism. Under such great scholars as the historian Ivane Javakhishvili and the literary historian Korneli Kekelidze, the new-born university rapidly assumed a dominant position in Georgia's educational life. From its walls there soon began to emerge hundreds of keen and well-qualified graduates who rapidly made their mark as teachers, scientific workers and members of the professions.

The agrarian question

The conflict between pure socialist ideals and bourgeois moderation was clearly manifested in the government's approach to the vital agrarian question. In December 1917, before Transcaucasia had proclaimed itself independent of Russia, the Mensheviks had brought the land issue before the Diet, which approved by an overwhelming majority the principle of limiting land holdings and confiscating without compensation all estates above a statutory maximum to be established. The Transcaucasian Commissariat published a decree stating that in order to alleviate the plight of the landless peasants, all estates belonging to the former Russian crown and to the Church would be nationalized, together with lands belonging to private individuals and exceeding certain norms to be subsequently laid down. These norms as eventually promulgated varied according to the type of land and the profitability of the crops normally grown upon it. Where highly remunerative cultures such as grapes and tobacco were produced, the maximum individual holding was fixed at 7 *desyatins*, or about 19 acres. For corn-growing land, the limit was raised to 15 *desyatins*, or about 40 acres. Persons engaged in sheep and cattle raising and other forms of stock-breeding might own up to 40 *desyatins*, or 108 acres. Surplus lands went into a government pool, whence peasants with sub-average holdings could lease extra land.

The reform was carried out with great thoroughness. A special assembly of the Georgian nobility passed a resolution pledging co-operation with the government in its land reform programme. By 1 January 1920 over 4,000 landed estates had been nationalized. The Georgian Social-Democrats were at first undecided as to how to dispose of the vast holdings of land contained in the government pool, estimated at over 5 million acres of forest, a million acres of arable land, and 3 million of pasture land. The Minister of Agriculture, Khomeriki, favoured retention by the state and ultimately, collectivization. However, Georgia was now facing an economic blockade mounted by Bolshevik Russia on the one hand, and Denikin's White Russian forces on the other. There were acute food shortages, while a series of peasant uprisings also helped to force the government's hand. Grumbling at the perverse and reactionary mentality of peasants, the authorities gave in and agreed to sell land from the nationalized estates to peasant small-holders. About a million acres were soon disposed of in this way. The government also embarked on a programme of reclamation of marsh-lands, irrigation of arid steppes and other measures designed to increase fertility. The lot of the Georgian peasantry was materially improved, as is admitted by the Communist writer Elena Drabkina, who states that

'the agrarian reform, incomplete as it was, curtailed the nobility's possession of the land; . . . the entire course adopted by the Social-Democratic government in the villages led to the formation of a strong rural bourgeoisie and the development of capitalism in agriculture, i.e. to the inevitable destruction of all the survivals of feudalism'.[97]

In their labour and industrial policy, the Mensheviks were able to follow socialist principles more faithfully. Hydro-electric power, mineral springs and spas, the Tqibuli coal mines, the Chiatura manganese industry, the ports and railways, were all nationalized. Of the 70,000 full-time workers employed in Georgian industry in 1920, official statistics show that more than half were state employees, while a quarter worked for municipal and co-operative enterprises. Less than 20 per cent were privately employed. A number of labour laws were passed. An eight-hour day was established. Overtime work entitled the worker to double pay. Child labour was proscribed, as well as night work for women and adolescents. Unemployment and sickness insurance was introduced. The right to strike, withheld from the worker under Tsarism and again later under the Communists, was established by law.

Financial instability

Whereas the Georgian government's social and economic policies were basically sound and progressive, their realization was frustrated by financial instability, combined with the prevailing political chaos in Russia and the Near East. The budget was in chronic imbalance. Now that Georgia received no subsidy from the Russian central government, expenditure exceeded income to an alarming extent. For the period from November 1917 to January 1919, the income of the Georgian Treasury amounted to under 100 million rubles, while expenses came to nearly 350 million, leaving a deficit of almost 250 million. Armenian merchants and financiers, as well as their Georgian confrères headed by the millionaire A. M. Khoshtaria, a daring business man who owned concessions in North Persia, plunged into speculation and defrauded the Georgian treasury of vast sums of foreign exchange. Inflation was rife. In 1919, the Georgian government was issuing banknotes of denominations between 50 kopecks and 500 rubles. At the time of the Communist invasion of 1921, common denominations were of 50,000 and 100,000 rubles. Under Bolshevik rule, until the currency reform of 1924, notes of up to 250 million rubles were in current use. Confidence in the currency was fatally undermined.

Such financial instability led to all kinds of hardship and social paradoxes. The salaries of officials and the savings of the middle and upper classes could become valueless in the space of a few weeks. Prince Orbeliani, head of one of Georgia's leading families, had to queue to use one of the lavatories in his requisitioned palace in Tbilisi, and the Georgian Patriarch depended for his daily bread on the private charity of Oliver Wardrop, the British Chief Commissioner. At the same time, the wily financier Khoshtaria safeguarded his own sumptuous mansion by lending it to the British Mission, whose chief could disport himself in a bath adorned with solid silver fittings, squirting water from every conceivable angle.[98] However, there is little doubt that the economic situation would gradually have reverted to normal if the Zhordania government had been left to itself and given time to put its house in order. The vicissitudes of the international situation and the activities of her predatory neighbours cut short the life of the Georgian Republic before she had even emerged from the aftermath of war and revolution.

At first, however, the weather seemed set fair for the new Georgian state. During the summer of 1918, the land was patrolled by German helmets, some actually worn by polite, well-disciplined German soldiers, others lent out to the Georgian National Army and prominently exhibited on sticks at strategic points along the Turkish frontier. The Bolsheviks and the White Russians were not yet strong enough to threaten Georgia's new-found independence. The struggle for power in Caucasia centred now on the neighbouring republic of Azerbaijan. The Baku Soviet, in strange alliance with an anti-Bolshevik Tsarist officer, Colonel Lazar Bicherakov, was locked in a bitter struggle against Muslim Azeri guerillas backed by Turkish troops. By 30 July 1918 the Turks were in sight of the city. The following day, Shaumian attempted to flee the city together with his Georgian lieutenant Alesha Japaridze and his other colleagues on the Baku Soviet, but their ships were intercepted and forced to return to port. Baku was taken over by a coalition government of Social-Revolutionaries and Armenian nationalists, who attempted to defend the city against the Turks with the support of a small British force under General Dunsterville. On 14 September 1918, Dunsterville had to evacuate Baku, which fell to the Turks and Azeris. The twenty-six imprisoned Baku Commissars escaped from Baku in the nick of time, but were landed at Krasnovodsk and shot by the local Russian Social-Revolutionaries. Their execution, which the local British agent failed to prevent, became a *cause célèbre* in the annals of the revolution; responsibility for it has usually been laid at the door of the British 'cannibals', as Stalin termed them in this connexion.

In September 1918, Niko Nikoladze, a member of the Georgian negotiating team in Berlin, returned to Tbilisi and informed Zhordania that Germany's defeat at the hands of the Allies appeared inevitable. Another member of the Berlin delegation, Zurab Avalishvili, was therefore sent to neutral Scandinavia to make contact with British and French diplomats there in an effort to secure recognition of Georgia's neutral status and pave the way for a transfer of allegiance from the German to the Allied side. This *volte-face* had to be accomplished with speed and agility. The armistice of Mudros, concluded on 30 October 1918, obliged Turkey to withdraw to the west of the 1914 Turco-Russian frontier, while the military collapse of Imperial Germany in November 1918 led inevitably to the evacuation of Georgia by the German garrisons there.

The British replace the Germans

The British returned to Baku on 17 November 1918 and soon entered into relations with the Georgian government in Tbilisi, which they regarded with some suspicion, as a former German puppet régime. The British commander, General Thomson, told Zhordania that British objectives included the restoration of the Caucasian viceroyalty in the name of Russian authority. Britain desired to liberate the Caucasus from the Germans and the Bolsheviks; to re-establish order without interfering in the internal affairs of the country; to restore trade with the ports of Persia and other areas not occupied by Bolshevik Russia; and to provide for the movement of Allied military personnel over the Transcaucasian railways. Such a programme, particularly the first item, was naturally unacceptable to the Georgians. In the memoirs which he wrote years later, Zhordania contrasts the 'genuinely noble, profoundly friendly and respectful' manners of the German commander Kress von Kressenstein with the behaviour of the first British representative to arrive in Tbilisi—'like a sergeant-major, coarse, rude, imperious and masterful'.[99] At one point, the Georgians talked wildly of opposing by force the entry of British troops into their country. However, more conciliatory counsels prevailed. By the end of December 1918, Evgeni Gegechkori, who succeeded the pro-German Chkhenkeli as Foreign Minister, was assuring the British Mission in Tbilisi that 'the Georgian government, animated by the desire to work in harmony with the Allies for the realization of the principles of right and justice proclaimed by them, gives its consent to the entry of the troops'.[100]

An Armenian invasion

To some extent, this change of heart was forced on the Georgians by an Armenian invasion of Georgia's southern boundaries. Now free from Turkish occupation, Armenia was basking in the favour of President Wilson and confident of world support in the redressing of her millennial wrongs. When the Turks evacuated Transcaucasia, they deliberately encouraged both the Armenians and the Georgians to move into certain border territories, notably Lori and Borchalo and the town of

Akhalkalaki. They gave the Georgians two days' start, so that when the Armenians moved in, they found the Georgians already in occupation. Sporadic fighting ensued. The Armenians were at first victorious and marched on Tbilisi itself, the large Armenian colony of which was subjected to many outrages at the hands of the incensed Georgians. On 29 December 1918 the Georgians defeated the Armenians at Shulaveri and forced them to retreat. Two days later the British command was able to force peace upon these two uneasy neighbours. The consequences of this Armeno-Georgian conflict have been summed up by Kazemzadeh:

'The Armeno-Georgian war inflicted great injury on the cause of the independence of the Transcaucasian republics. The old hostilities of the Georgians toward the Armenians flared up and reached an intensity unparalleled before, making impossible united Armeno-Georgian action at the Paris Peace Conference. The West was treated to a sad spectacle of two peoples, ruled by parties which were members of the Second International and professed peace to be their chief aim, fighting over a few strips of land in the manner of a Germany or a Russia. Those who were called upon to decide the destinies of mankind at Paris could never again trust Georgia or Armenia. The enemies of Transcaucasia's independence were provided with excellent material, on the basis of which they could, and did, argue that Armenia, Georgia, and Azerbaijan ruled by the Dashnaks, the Mensheviks and the Musavatists, were incapable of preserving order and of guaranteeing a peaceful existence to their peoples. Even in Transcaucasia doubts were raised whether this land could stand on its own feet.'[101]

Denikin and the Whites

If Georgia's relations with her southern neighbour, Armenia, were unsatisfactory, those with the forces now vying to the north for control of Russia were equally so. The main threat from the Russian side appeared at first to derive less from Lenin and Trotsky's Red Army than from the White Russian Volunteer Army of Alekseev and Denikin. General Denikin was a bigoted blockhead of the most reactionary kind, whose myopic policies wrecked all hope of overthrowing the Bolsheviks. Denikin refused to admit any less comprehensive aim than the restoration of Russia's frontiers as they were in 1914 under Tsar Nicholas II.

'Instead, therefore, of making common cause with the other enemies of Bolshevism, with Rumania, Poland, the Baltic and Caucasian States, Makhno, Petlura and the rest, he not only rejected the help but definitely provoked the enmity of these valuable, indeed indispensable, potential allies. Had he possessed the most rudimentary political acumen he would have made friends with Rumania and left the Bessarabian question to be settled after the Bolsheviks were beaten; he would have acted similarly, *mutatis mutandis*, with regard to Poland, the Baltic Republics, the Caucasians, the Transcaucasians and the other Russian 'Succession States' instead of antagonizing them and in some cases actually engaging in hostilities against them.'[102]

In his relations with the Georgian Republic, Denikin's fatuity was matched only by the intransigent volubility of Foreign Minister Gegechkori, who spent months arguing with the White Russians about some insignificant strips of remote territory in the region of Sochi and Gagra along the Black Sea coast. Armed clashes between Denikin and the Georgians had to be quelled by the British military representatives. In November 1919 Denikin launched an economic blockade of independent Georgia and Azerbaijan. He declared: 'I cannot permit the self-styled formations of Georgia and Azerbaijan, which have sprung up to the detriment of Russian state interests and which are clearly hostile to the idea of the Russian State, to receive food supplies at the expense of the areas of Russia which are being liberated from the Bolsheviks.' Denikin further noted with satisfaction that Georgia was specially vulnerable to an economic blockade, since the harvest of 1919 had failed, which aggravated the chronic shortage of grain.[103] Not until February 1920, when the Whites were being rolled back in disorder by the Red Army, did Denikin deign to acknowledge *de facto* the governments of Russia's border areas which were hostile to Bolshevism. By now it was too late to salvage anything from the wreck of the counter-revolution.

The British withdrawal

The British military representatives in Georgia at first tended to identify themselves with Denikin's neo-imperialist fantasies. In 1919, however, the British government took the imaginative step of appointing Oliver Wardrop, the well-known scholar of

Georgian literature and history, to be Chief British Commissioner to the Republics of Georgia, Armenia and Azerbaijan. Wardrop set up his headquarters in Tbilisi and did his best to reconcile the national interests of his beloved Georgia with those of Great Britain and the Entente. British and Indian troops, highly unpopular with the Georgians, were withdrawn to a British military district based on the port of Batumi. The purblind patriots in the Georgian government resented even this last British bridgehead as an affront to their national dignity. Gegechkori and Zhordania continually pestered Wardrop and his successor, Harry Luke, to hand the Batumi military district back to Georgia. In July 1920 when the Bolsheviks were already encircling the Georgian Republic and Mustafa Kemal and his followers sharpening their claws for an onslaught from the Turkish side, the British finally withdrew. The streets of Batumi were bedecked with flags on 7 July 1920 as the British troops marched to the port and the Georgian army under General Kvinitadze entered the city from the opposite direction. Georgia hailed the disappearance of the British imperialists as a major triumph, without giving much thought to the even more formidable foes which now ringed her about.

The Georgians' self-reliance was bolstered by the conviction that their sovereignty was guaranteed beyond all possibility of violation through the Paris Peace Conference and the new international machinery embodied in the League of Nations. Fortified by the idealistic orations of President Wilson, both the Armenians and the Georgians were pathetically certain that the victorious Entente powers meant to establish a just and durable peace in Caucasia. The Armenians for their part sent not one, but two rival delegations to Paris, who put forward the most extravagant territorial demands, including the seven eastern *vilayets* of Turkey, the four Cilician *sanjaks*, as well as large areas of the Georgian Republic itself, including Batumi and parts of Tbilisi province.

When the Paris Conference opened, the Armenians had everybody's wholehearted sympathy, while the Georgians, as former protégés of Germany, were received rather coldly. However, the truculence of the Armenians soon lost them influential friends, while the Georgians' charm and *savoir-faire* made a good impression. The ground had already been ably prepared in London by Zurab Avalishvili, a former member of the Georgian delegation in Berlin, in conjunction with his compatriot David Ghambashidze, a mining engineer who was formerly Secretary of the Anglo-Russian Chamber of Commerce in London. Ghambashidze was a Fellow of the Royal Geographical Society and in 1919 published a useful book, written in English, on the mineral resources of Georgia and Caucasia. Ghambashidze had many friends in British official circles, and was able to enlist the support of Lord Curzon, himself an expert on Near Eastern and Caucasian affairs. On 31 December 1918, Avalishvili and Ghambashidze received from the Foreign Office a note declaring that His Majesty's Government viewed with sympathy the proclamation of independence of the Georgian Republic, and were ready to urge its recognition at the Peace Conference. This good news was communicated to Tbilisi without delay.

Georgia at the Paris Conference

The Georgian delegation in Paris was a high-powered one, headed as it was by the veteran tribunes of the Russian Revolution, Nikolai (Karlo) Chkheidze and Irakli Tsereteli. Most of the year 1919 was occupied in pleading with the Allies to restrain their friends Kolchak and Denikin from attacking the Caucasian republics. It was not until November 1919 that the Allied Supreme Council realised that the Whites were hopelessly defeated, and began to think seriously of encouraging the Transcaucasian Republics as a possible barrier to the expansion of Soviet Russia. Lord Curzon himself took the initiative of proposing to the Supreme Council of the Allies the recognition *de facto* of the republics of Georgia and Azerbaijan. This proposal was adopted unanimously, with the result that France, Great Britain and Italy accorded *de facto* recognition to Georgia on 11 January 1920. The Georgian Republic had already been recognized *de jure* by the Argentine Republic on 13 September 1919. Georgia was recognized *de facto* by Japan and Belgium on 7 February and 26 August 1920 respectively.

In January 1920, conferences took place between the Georgian and Azerbaijani delegates and the British Imperial General Staff to discuss problems of defence in the event of an attack by Soviet Russia. On 19 January the Georgian and Azerbaijani delegates were summoned before a plenary meeting of the Supreme Council at the Quai d'Orsay, where they were confronted by Clemenceau, Lloyd George, Lord Curzon, Winston Churchill, Jules Cambon, Francesco Nitti, Marshal Foch, Admiral Beatty, Sir Henry Wilson and others, who enquired about the ability and determination of the Caucasian peoples to withstand Russian aggression, and their requirements in terms of military aid and supplies. Soon afterwards, however, it was announced that the Allies had no intention of sending any fresh troops to Transcaucasia, though the Transcaucasian republics were promised arms and ammunition. The despatch of these was delayed by the appearance of a fresh bone of contention between Georgia and Armenia—namely the possession of and access to the port of Batumi following its evacuation by the British Army. For weeks a diplomatic battle over this point raged between the Armenian and Georgian delegations. Mr. Robert Vansittart (later Lord Vansittart), the Foreign Office official dealing with Caucasian problems on Curzon's behalf, was driven to despair.

'In the circles of the Supreme Council,' he told a gathering of these rival delegates, 'many are of the opinion that the Transcaucasian Republics have no future at all, as they are unable to achieve any sort of solidarity, and are exhausting themselves in conflicts with each other. . . . Is it not clear to you that the despatch of arms and munitions for you has been delayed precisely because of your divergences, because of the fear that these arms would be used in your conflicts with each other?'[104]

And yet, in spite of such warnings by their well-wishers, these rival sets of politicians stood fast in their pretensions, at the very moment when Azerbaijan was actually falling into the hands of Moscow. An eye-witness has left a graphic description of one of those crucial meetings, in which Karlo Chkheidze, the chief Georgian delegate, 'stood with his head thrown back, his eyes starting from their sockets and his face purple, enraged by the French texts and formulae, the shades of meaning of which he could not quite grasp, all his coolness and self-control gone, in the pose of a minor Polish country squire vetoing an important decision of the Diet'.[105] Small wonder that the patient Vansittart, 'repeating Pilate's gesture, his face expressing perplexity, weariness and boredom', was obliged to wash his hands of the matter and report to Lord Curzon, the British government and the Supreme Council of the Allies that the Transcaucasian republics, unable to agree among themselves, could not be expected to play any useful part in a defence system designed to check the advance of Bolshevik Russia. Curzon's Caucasian policy suffered a major setback, to the ill-concealed glee of Lloyd George, who was himself only too eager to jettison Churchill and Curzon's policy of intervention and come to terms with the Communist régime in Russia.

There were other factors which also helped to render untenable the position of the Allies in Transcaucasia. On 27–28 April 1920, a daring raid by Soviet armoured trains on Baku led to the overthrow of independent Azerbaijan and the proclamation of a Soviet republic. One of the major reasons justifying the British occupation of Batumi was that this port was the Black Sea terminal of the Baku-Batumi pipeline, through which Baku oil was pumped for shipment overseas by the international oil companies. With Baku in Bolshevik hands, no more oil would be flowing to Batumi, the commercial value of which was thereby impaired. On 7 May 1920 the Georgian Menshevik government felt it advisable to sign a treaty of friendship with Soviet Russia, pledging themselves among other things to work for the removal of all foreign troops from Georgian soil. On 11 May, General Sir George Milne, Commander-in-Chief of the British Army of the Black Sea, was accidentally fired upon by Georgian artillery when on an inspection tour of the border area of the Batumi military district. In Batumi itself, Bolshevik agents were active. One of these, Gubeli (real name: S. Medzmariashvili) murdered the White Russian General Lyakhov, notorious for his suppression of the Constitutional movement in Persia and his reign of terror in the northern Caucasus under Denikin. Gubeli was arrested by the British, but such was the popular outcry that Brigadier Cooke-Collis, the British governor, was forced to release him. The special correspondent of Le Temps reported from Batumi: 'This city, as well as the entire province, has become a centre of agitation and corruption, where the Turkish nationalists and the Bolsheviks have already been able to fraternize without danger.' In such circumstances, the British decision to evacuate Batumi early in July 1920 is understandable.

During the nine months which elapsed between the Georgian occupation of Batumi and the final débâcle, the Georgian cause scored more victories and more defeats, but only on paper. On 16 December 1920 Georgia's application for membership of the League of Nations failed to secure the requisite majority, though she was admitted to participation in the League's technical sub-committees. It is interesting to note that among those who spoke most forcibly against Georgia's admission was the British Minister of Education, the historian H. A. L. Fisher. Voting with Great Britain against granting membership of the League to Georgia were Australia, Canada, India, New Zealand and France. However, Georgia had one last diplomatic triumph on 27 January 1921, when France and England accorded her full *de jure* recognition as an independent sovereign state. On 25 February 1921, Akaki Chkhenkeli presented his credentials at the Élysée Palace as Georgia's Minister Plenipotentiary to the French Republic. That same day, the Red Army was marching on Tbilisi, forcing the government of the Georgian Republic to flee for their lives. The events surrounding this closing drama will be unfolded in the next chapter.

CHAPTER XI

GEORGIA AND COMMUNIST RUSSIA
1920–24

Collapse of the White Russians — The Russo-Georgian Treaty — Communist propaganda in Georgia — Upheaval in Ossetia — Rise of Kemalist Turkey — Georgia and the Second International — Krassin and Lloyd George — The Red Army invades Georgia — Death agony of independent Georgia — Lenin versus Stalin on Georgia — Revival of Great Russian chauvinism — The insurrection of 1924

Collapse of the White Russians

FROM THE TIME of the October revolution in 1917 until early in 1920, there was no regular communication between Georgia and Communist Russia. The White Russian forces of Denikin and his associates formed a physical barrier between Moscow and Tbilisi, and political mistrust inhibited any establishment of diplomatic relations between the two centres. Communist Russia, indeed, refused to recognize the existence of independent Georgia, declaring on 24 December 1918 that 'all persons who consider themselves Georgian citizens are recognized as Russian citizens, and as such are subject to all the decrees and the enactments of the Soviet authority of the RSFSR.' All manifestations of Bolshevism in Georgia were suppressed with a firm hand by the unbending Georgian Minister of the Interior, Noe Ramishvili. Two prominent Georgian Bolsheviks, Mamia Orakhelashvili and M. Okujava, sat in Kutaisi jail, while the other members of the Bolshevik Regional Committee left Tbilisi for Vladikavkaz in North Caucasia.

During the winter of 1919–20, the impending collapse of Denikin's army in North Caucasia and the Black Sea region encouraged the Soviet Commissar for Foreign Affairs, Chicherin, to invite Georgia to unite with Russia against the Whites. Zhordania and Gegechkori refused, declaring that they 'preferred the imperialists of the West to the fanatics of the East'.[106] Russia reacted to this rebuff by forming a special committee for the establishment of Soviet authority in the Caucasus. The head of this committee, established by a decree of the Bolshevik Central Committee on 4 February 1920, was the Georgian Communist Sergo Orjonikidze, a friend of Stalin; the deputy chairman was S. M. Kirov, and the other members included the Georgian Bolshevik Budu Mdivani. On 8 April 1920, a North Caucasian bureau of the Central Committee of the All-Russian Communist Party was set up, its members including Orjonikidze, Smilga, Mdivani and Kirov. This bureau later formed the nucleus of an enlarged Caucasian Bureau, which came into being in May. Orjonikidze was also a member of the Revolutionary War Council of the Caucasian front and Kirov a member of that of the Eleventh Red Army.

In spite of his declared hostility to the Kremlin 'fanatics', Zhordania found it prudent to initiate secret negotiations with them in an effort to secure formal Communist recognition of Georgia's independence. Grigol Uratadze, a veteran Menshevik, was sent clandestinely to Moscow to negotiate with Chicherin and the other People's Commissars. While these talks were proceeding, on 27 April 1920, the Red Army launched its lightning attack on Baku. The Azerbaijan government, which had a defensive alliance with Georgia, appealed to Tbilisi for help, but was overwhelmed in a few hours. Confident that the Eleventh Red Army would at once continue its victorious march into Georgia, local Bolsheviks staged an armed uprising in Tbilisi. At one a.m. on 3 May 1920, twenty-five Bolsheviks, mostly Armenians, attempted to seize the Military Academy as a preliminary to a *coup d'état*. It happened that General Kvinitadze, commandant of the Academy prior to his appointment as Georgian Commander-in-Chief two days previously, was still in residence. Kvinitadze and his cadets put up a fight, killing two of the attackers and capturing three others, who were sentenced to death by court martial and shot. At the same time, Georgian frontier troops repulsed Red Army detachments which had penetrated to the Georgian side of the frontier with Azerbaijan.

The Russo-Georgian Treaty

At this juncture, Uratadze reported from Moscow that the Russians were prepared to sign a treaty with Georgia and recognize her *de jure*, provided that the Mensheviks formally undertook not to grant asylum on Georgian territory to troops of powers hostile to the Soviet Union. Gegechkori, the Georgian Foreign Minister, regarded this clause as an infringement of Georgia's national sovereignty, and favoured rejection of the Soviet terms. Zhordania, anxious above all to secure for Georgia *de jure* recognition by all the great powers, overruled his Foreign Minister, and the treaty was signed in Moscow on 7 May 1920. Among other provisions, Georgia undertook to disarm and intern all military and naval units belonging to any organization purporting to constitute the government of Russia, and to surrender such detachments or groups to the Communists. In a secret supplement, not made public for the time being, Georgia made an even greater concession to the Bolsheviks. 'Georgia pledges itself to recognize the right of free existence and activity of the Communist party . . . and in particular its right to free meetings and publications, including organs of the press.' The British Chief Commissioner in Tbilisi noted in his diary on 9 June 1920:

'Text of Georgian Treaty with Soviet Russia published today. Treaty allots town and province of Batum to Georgia. It contains ambiguous clauses which could be read to mean that Georgia is obliged to evict the Allies. The frontier on the Caucasus passes is unfavourable to Georgia and public opinion in Tiflis denounces treaty as veiled subjection of Georgia to Russia. Anti-Bolshevik feeling here strong.'[107]

Both in its provisions and in its consequences, the Russo-Georgian agreement of 1920 indeed contains striking parallels with the treaty concluded in 1783 between Catherine the Great of Russia and King Erekle II of Georgia, which proved to be the prelude to Georgia's complete annexation. That the 1920 agreement would turn out in the same way could, however, scarcely have been foreseen when it was signed.

Communist propaganda in Georgia

Unaware of the secret clause providing for toleration of the Georgian Communist Party, the hard-pressed Georgian Bolsheviks were at first stunned by the news that Moscow had officially recognized the renegade Menshevik government of Zhordania. They were soon reassured. S. M. Kirov, a member of the Caucasian Bureau of the All-Russian Communist Party, was appointed the first Soviet Ambassador to Tbilisi. The British Chief Commissioner there noted on 20 June 1920:

'The Bolshevik Diplomatic Mission to Georgia, which has been dribbling in by instalments, now almost complete with the arrival today of Head of Mission, Kyrov. Staff of Mission, including attendants and a group of seventeen persons ostensibly despatched to settle details regarding Peace Treaty, numbers about seventy. Georgian Government are alarmed at its size and have protested, but Bolsheviks continue to pour in. I understand they propose to make Tiflis headquarters of their eastern propaganda. Kyrov on arrival harangued the crowd which had collected outside his residence. Have protested strongly and, I am thankful to say, effectively against Mission being accommodated, as was desired by the Bolshevik advance guard, in the house immediately facing our Mission.'[108]

The Georgian government were forced to release the local Communist party members and sympathisers from prison. Many of them promptly embarked on an overt campaign to overthrow the Mensheviks by force, with the result that Noe Ramishvili, the Minister of the Interior, clapped them back into jail. This provoked a fiery exchange of notes between Kirov and the Georgian Foreign Ministry.

On 29 June 1920, Kirov threatened that 'if the happenings mentioned by me should not be stopped, my Government would have no other choice but to retaliate against Georgian citizens in the territory of the RSFSR.' Gegechkori retorted that 'members of the Georgian Communist Party in addition to their legal work engage in active propaganda among the troops, in the ranks of the People's Guard, and among the wide masses of the peasantry, using for this purpose huge sums of money received from abroad, and aiming at the overthrow of the order existing in the country'.[109] Given Moscow's determination to use the local Communists to undermine the Zhordania régime, this issue was insoluble; it provided, as the Kremlin intended, a constant irritant and an excuse for Russian propaganda against the existing Georgian government.

Conflict also arose out of Georgia's contacts with Baron Wrangel, who had succeeded the inept Denikin as head of the White Russian movement, and managed to maintain himself from April until November 1920 in the Crimea. The Georgians were in reality as hostile towards Wrangel as they had been towards Denikin. However, they were obliged to negotiate with him concerning the supply of wheat and oats for Georgia, and there were occasions when the Georgians failed to intern and hand over to the Communists certain White Russian units and ships seeking a temporary refuge on Georgian soil or in Georgian ports. Kirov and his successor, Sheinman, seized upon such incidents as a pretext for the accusation that Georgia was abetting the White Russian reactionaries.

Upheaval in Ossetia

Another hotbed of discord was the unsettled situation in South Ossetia, a part of Georgia inhabited by a people of Iranian stock, quite distinct from the Georgians in customs, language and ethnic origin. The territory of the Ossetes straddles the Daryal Pass and extends on the Russian side well into North Caucasia. A peasant uprising had already occurred in South Ossetia in 1918 and been suppressed with great severity by the Menshevik People's Guard commanded by Valiko Jugheli. In 1919, the Tbilisi régime outlawed the so-called National Soviet of South Ossetia, a Bolshevik-dominated body, and refused any grant of national self-determination for the Ossetes. In the spring of the following year, the Caucasian Bureau of the All-Russian Communist Party formed a special South Ossetian Revolutionary Committee to lead an armed revolt against the Georgian government. A Russian-sponsored Ossete force crossed the border from Vladikavkaz in June 1920 and attacked the Georgian Army and People's Guard. The Georgians reacted with vigour and defeated the insurgents and their supporters in a series of hard-fought battles. Five thousand people perished in the fighting and 20,000 Ossetes fled into Soviet Russia. The Georgian People's Guard displayed a frenzy of chauvinistic zeal during the mopping-up operations, many villages being burnt to the ground and large areas of fertile land ravaged and depopulated.

Rise of Kemalist Turkey

Fresh dangers were also beginning to threaten Georgia from another side, namely from the direction of Turkey and Armenia. In the Treaty of Sèvres, signed on 10 August 1920 by plenipotentiaries of the docile Ottoman government in Istanbul, Turkey undertook to recognize Armenia as a free and independent state, within the boundaries of the so-called Wilson Line, as the Allied Powers had already done. The signature of this treaty by the Sultan led the Turkish nationalists under Mustafa Kemal to declare themselves armed opponents of the Allies. Kemal entered into friendly relations with Soviet Russia, whose hostility to the Anglo-French Entente and its protégés coincided with his own. In September 1920, the Kemalists suddenly attacked Armenia, taking Kars and then Aleksandropol. The Russians on their side despatched to the harassed Armenian Dashnaks an ultimatum demanding free passage for Soviet and Kemalist troops through Armenian territory; Armenian renunciation of the Treaty of Sèvres; and the cessation of all relations with the Allied powers. The hollowness of Allied support for Armenia became immediately apparent. Neither President Wilson nor Lloyd George raised a finger in defence of the helpless Armenian Republic which they themselves had created amid such fanfares of democratic idealism. While the Armenians were capitulating to the Kemalists, the Bolsheviks entered their country from Baku. On 2 December 1920, a Soviet Republic was set up in Erivan. In February 1921, during the Russian invasion of Georgia, the Armenian Dashnaks staged a successful revolt against the Communist régime. Armenia's death agony was prolonged until April 1921, when Bolshevik rule was re-established and the country finally parcelled out between Soviet Russia and Kemalist Turkey.

During the summer and autumn of 1920, when Soviet Russia and the Turkish nationalists had once again become dominant factors in Caucasian affairs, while the Western powers, particularly England, had renounced any active policy in that region, the Georgian government chose to ignore Moscow and Ankara and concentrate its efforts on the West. Three ministers—Gegechkori, Kandelaki and P. Gogichaishvili (Minister of State Control), as well as the President of the Constituent Assembly, Karlo Chkheidze, and the special emissary of the republic, Irakli Tsereteli, toured the capitals of the great powers in an attempt to win economic aid, loans and political recognition for the Georgian Republic. The mission fulfilled its task with fair success. It even succeeded in floating a loan in London, and there was talk of leasing the Batumi naval base and oil refineries to Britain. Italian industrialists were granted a concession for exploitation of the Tqvarcheli coal-fields on the Black Sea coast, in the region of Sukhumi. An agreement was concluded with a French commercial syndicate for collaboration in developing silk production in Georgia and exporting silk cocoons to France. On the political front, Gegechkori's efforts finally resulted in the *de jure* recognition of independent Georgia by the Allies on 27 January 1921, a few weeks before the country was overrun by the Red Army.

Georgia and the Second International

Georgia's cause was warmly espoused by the moderate Socialists of the Second International, who viewed her as an outpost of Western democratic socialism on the fringes of the domains of Bolshevist collectivism. In September 1920, a delegation of leading Western socialists visited the Georgian Republic. They included Ramsay MacDonald, Vandervelde, Mrs. E. Snowden, Renaudel, Kautsky, Huysmans and others, who were thrilled by the official honours and gracious hospitality dispensed to them by the Georgian government. In December, a French naval flotilla visited Georgian ports. A French High Commissioner made his appearance in Tbilisi, where he declared with Gallic bravado that any infringement of Georgia's integrity would be resisted to the death by France and her allies.

Krassin and Lloyd George

These comings and goings were viewed by Soviet Russia with deep suspicion. The Kremlin propaganda machine proclaimed that following Wrangel's collapse in the Crimea, Georgia was being turned into a bastion of counter-revolution. Trade talks were proceeding in London at this time between the British government and Krassin, the Soviet special envoy, who exploited Lloyd George's personal opposition to Curzon's policy of propping up the Transcaucasian republics as a bastion against Soviet Russia. Anxious to cut the losses sustained by the Churchillian policy of anti-Bolshevik intervention, Lloyd George was eager to resume normal commercial relations with Russia, from which Britain's strained post-war economy stood to benefit substantially. During Krassin's negotiations in London, he was given to understand that Baku oil—the main commodity he had to offer—lost much of its value without complete Russian control of the Transcaucasian pipe-line leading into Batumi over a section of Georgian territory. The moral of this was that to make his goods more marketable, Krassin had to persuade his masters to gain possession of the land separating Baku from Batumi, namely the Republic of Georgia. No advice could have been more palatable, and the Bolsheviks were not slow to take the hint. In view of Lloyd George's attitude, the Kremlin could discount a telegram of protest from Lord Curzon against Russian mobilization on the Georgian border. Chicherin replied to the British Foreign Secretary that 'Soviet Russia has not committed and will not commit in future any hostile acts against the Republic of Georgia', with which assurance Curzon had to rest content.

On 7 February 1921, a banquet was held in Tbilisi to celebrate the *de jure* recognition of Georgia by the Western Allies. The Soviet Ambassador, Mr. Sheinman, stayed away, but sent as his representative a Georgian Bolshevik, S. Kavtaradze, who made a speech in which he saluted Zhordania as his mentor, a true Socialist leader, whose health he drank 'with complete sincerity', coupled with that of the Georgian toiling people. On the next day, Sheinman declared to the Press that Russia was delighted at Georgia's recognition and desired only to live in peace and amity with her. At that moment, the Eleventh Red Army was poised ready for a full-scale attack.

The Red Army invades Georgia

During the autumn of 1920, Russia had repeatedly protested against the alleged build-up of the Georgian armed forces, which, it was claimed, constituted a threat to the Soviet Union. Soviet agents kept Moscow well informed as to the real strength of the Georgian National Army and People's Guard. Now that the substance of these secret reports has recently been published, it is possible to form an accurate idea of independent Georgia's military might.[110] On 10 September 1920, the Kremlin learnt that the Georgian regular army included 9,700 infantry and 1,000 cavalry, with 52 guns and a number of mortars, a battalion of sappers, one motorized company and one signals company. The People's Guard consisted of 15,000 infantry, 1,600 cavalry, with 76 guns and a machine-gun regiment with 72 machine-guns. The army further possessed 4 or 5 armoured trains, 3 armoured cars, 2 tanks, a motorized machine-gun unit and 18 aircraft. It was estimated that full mobilization could increase the total force in the field to a maximum of 50,000 men within three days.

The Kremlin was apprised during the winter of 1920–21 of certain increases in Georgia's armed strength. On 1 February 1921 the Georgians had concentrated on their frontiers over 32,000 infantry, with 264 horsemen, 521 machine-guns, 56 light and 18 heavy guns. However, the Georgians were scarcely in a position to march on Moscow. The morale of the troops was reported low, the ranks being undermined by revolutionary propaganda; desertion was rife and mutual hostility existed between the regular army and the People's Guard. The Georgian General Staff was far from complacent about the position. General Odishelidze represented to his government in January 1921 that in the event of a Russian attack, his front line forces would be outnumbered two to one. Odishelidze proposed to increase the army to 60,000, buy war materials and munitions abroad, and prepare a careful plan of national defence. At grips with a fiscal crisis, the Zhordania government refused to sanction the outlay. When war actually broke out, Georgia had a small, poorly equipped army with an insignificant cavalry, and a few aeroplanes which remained grounded throughout the campaign through lack of high-grade petrol.[111]

When Baron Wrangel's Crimean force collapsed in November 1920, the Red Army was free to send extra troops to reinforce the Caucasian front. The following month, A. I. Gekker (Hecker), commander of the Eleventh Red Army, sent to Moscow a secret appreciation of the prospects of a military conquest of Georgia. Gekker emphasized that it would first be necessary to secure the benevolent neutrality of Kazim Karabekir Pasha, the Turkish commander in Armenia. Seven infantry divisions and the Second Cavalry Army should then be assembled in Soviet Azerbaijan, while smaller Red Army detachments would operate against the Georgian frontier guards in the Sochi sector on the Black Sea, and the Vladikavkaz-Daryal Pass area in Central Caucasia. Before launching the attack, therefore, Gekker recommended that an understanding be reached with the Kemalists at Ankara, with whom the Kremlin was already friendly, and that reinforcements and stores be massed in Soviet Azerbaijan all ready for a propitious moment to invade the Georgian Republic. 'The above-mentioned points are brought to your attention not in order to demonstrate the impossibility of an attack on Georgia, but because I consider that this attack should be launched only after careful preparation, in order to finish as rapidly as possible with those Tbilisi people'.[112] The Gekker plan soon became known to the Georgian Intelligence; before effective counter-measures could be taken, it had already been carried successfully into effect.

On 11 February 1921, disorders broke out in the Lori district, south of Tbilisi. Simultaneously a revolt began in the nearby town of Shulaveri, near the Armenian and Azerbaijani frontiers. The insurgents were Armenians and Russians, who attacked local Georgian military posts. By 14 February, a regular battle was raging on the Armeno-Georgian border, near a place called Vorontsovka. The Soviet envoy in Tbilisi, Sheinman, received on the next day a secret telegram from Gekker, the Eleventh Red Army commander: 'Resolved to cross the Rubicon. Take action in the light of this decision.' When the Georgian government protested to him about the incidents which were taking place on the frontier, Sheinman played for time, declaring that Russia had no cognizance of military movements in that area; any disturbances which might be taking place must be a spontaneous uprising by the Armenian communists.

A Communist Revolutionary Committee (*Revcom*) had by now been formed in Shulaveri. Its members included such prominent Georgian Bolsheviks as P. Makharadze, Mamia Orakhelashvili and S. Eliava. The Revcom proclaimed a Soviet régime and declared that only the forces of foreign reaction were keeping the Tbilisi Mensheviks in power; an appeal for help was addressed to the toiling masses of Moscow. By a happy coincidence, the Eleventh Red Army was already poised on the frontier between Georgia and Soviet Azerbaijan and crossed the border in force at dawn on 16 February. Retreating westwards, the Georgian National Army blew up railway bridges and demolished roads in an effort to delay the enemy advance. Simultaneously, Red Army units prepared to invade Georgia from the north through the Daryal and Mamison passes and along the Black Sea coast towards Sukhumi. While these events were proceeding, the Soviet Commissar for Foreign Affairs issued a series of statements disclaiming all knowledge of warlike acts between Georgia and the Red Army, and professing willingness to mediate in any internal disputes which might have arisen between Georgia, Armenia and Azerbaijan.

Death agony of independent Georgia

The Georgian Army put up a stubborn fight in defence of the approaches to Tbilisi, which they held for a week in the face of overwhelming odds. The Russian attack on Georgia produced unexpected repercussions in neighbouring Armenia, where the nationalists rose in force, marched on Erivan and overthrew the Bolshevik régime there. Any encouragement which the Georgians might have derived from this was outweighed by the actions of the Turkish commander in Armenia, Kazim Karabekir Pasha. On 23 February 1921, after prolonged consultations with his superiors in Ankara and with the Russian government in Moscow, Kazim issued an ultimatum demanding the evacuation of Ardahan and Artvin by Georgia. Stabbed in the back by the Kemalists, the Georgians were forced to comply and withdrew their forces from the Turkish frontier area. The Georgian commander-in-chief, Kvinitadze, was at length obliged to admit that Tbilisi could hold out no longer. On the night of 24-25 February 1921, President Zhordania left on the last train, hoping to set up his head-quarters at Kutaisi in Western Georgia and continue the struggle from there. Red Army detachments headed by Sergo Orjonikidze entered Tbilisi on 25 February. The city was given over to murder, pillage and rape. Famished and threadbare Russian soldiers swarmed over the town, invading houses, looting furniture, clothes, food and anything they could lay their hands on, including the instruments from doctors' and dentists' surgeries. After a prudent interval for mopping up operations, the Georgian Revcom headed by Orakhelashvili and Eliava ventured into the city and proclaimed the over-throw of the Menshevik régime, the dissolution of the Georgian National Army and People's Guard, and the formation of a Georgian Soviet Republic.

The Mensheviks entertained hopes of aid from a French naval squadron cruising in the Black Sea off the Georgian coast. The French tried to bombard some Bolshevik detachments operating near the shore, but made no attempt to land troops, and sheered off as soon as a Russian aeroplane hove into view. The Georgians' hope of holding out near Kutaisi was further dashed by the bold advance of a Red Army detachment from North Caucasia which traversed the difficult Mamison Pass through deep snow drifts in arctic conditions and advanced down the Rioni valley into Imereti. On 8 March the Revcom invited the Mensheviks to end military resistance, recognize the new Soviet régime in Georgia and form a coalition government with the Bolsheviks. Zhordania at first agreed to negotiate, particularly since both Bolshevik and Menshevik Georgians were united in their desire to prevent the Turks from reoccupying Batumi, which they were on the point of seizing. While the talks were proceeding, Zhordania learnt that the Red Army was at the gates of Batumi. Fearing a trap, he and his government set sail for Istanbul on 17 March 1921. A truce was signed at Kutaisi on the following day, couched in mild terms, and according a general amnesty to the defeated nationalists.

It is interesting to note that during that same week, on 16

March 1921, the British and Soviet governments signed a trade agreement, in which Lloyd George undertook *inter alia* to refrain from anti-Soviet activity in all territories which had formed part of the old Tsarist empire. This effectively precluded any British intervention against the Bolsheviks in Georgia, which Great Britain had recognized as an independent sovereign state less than two months previously. Small wonder that the defeated Georgian patriots were loud in their denunciation of perfidious Albion. Simultaneously, a treaty of friendship was signed in Moscow between Soviet Russia and Kemalist Turkey, whereby the Georgian towns of Akhalkalaki, Akhaltsikhe and Batumi were awarded to the Soviet Union. Broadly speaking, the agreement was extremely favourable to Turkey, the effect being to move the Turco-Soviet frontier virtually to the line existing prior to the war of 1877–78. Although Batumi and the surrounding region of Atchara were retained by the Soviet Union, large areas of territory belonging historically to Georgia were now regained by Turkey.

Lenin versus Stalin on Georgia

The unexpected mildness of the terms offered by the Georgian Communists to their defeated rivals is to be explained in part by divergent reactions to the Georgian affair within the Politbureau in Moscow. Lenin and his colleagues had only given their sanction to the Red Army's advance when they were assured by Stalin, as Commissar of Nationalities, that a massive Bolshevik uprising had occurred in Tbilisi. According to Stalin and his man on the spot, Orjonikidze, the Mensheviks had already been virtually overthrown by the Georgian masses themselves, and the appearance of a few Red Army soldiers would simply consolidate a victory already won. Both Lenin and Trotsky were appalled when they later heard that heavy fighting was taking place and that the Mensheviks had rallied the nation to their side; they were most apprehensive of the impression which would be created among foreign socialists when it was learnt that the Russian Communists were now overthrowing other, independent socialist régimes by force of arms.

The risk taken by Stalin in simultaneously hoodwinking his

own comrades and defying world opinion in this fashion is partly
to be accounted for in terms of his own past career, and his
impatience to settle old personal scores. Twenty years earlier,
in the days of the old *Mesame Dasi* when Social-Democracy
was first taking root in Georgia, young Jughashvili-Stalin
had been the odd man out. Thrust into the background by
Zhordania and the other Mensheviks, Stalin had thrown in
his lot with Lenin and the Russian Communist party. In
October 1917 he had the satisfaction of seeing his compatriots
and rivals Karlo Chkheidze and Irakli Tsereteli, both leading
figures in the Kerensky régime, turned out of Petrograd and
banished to their native Georgia. But it was a standing affront
to Stalin, as Soviet Commissar of Nationalities, to be defied
and held up to scorn in his own native Georgia of all places,
while his sway extended over most of the other territory of the
old Tsarist domains. Georgia must at all costs be brought within the Soviet fold. The Soviet-Georgian treaty of May 1920
was simply a tactical manœuvre; by November, Stalin was
declaring: 'Georgia, which has been transformed into the
principal base of the imperialist operations of England and
France and which therefore has entered into hostile relations
with Soviet Russia, that Georgia is now living out the last days
of her life.' It was Stalin the Georgian who gave independent
Georgia the *coup de grâce*.

In an effort to put a good face on the occupation of Georgia,
Lenin wrote to Orjonikidze after the fall of Tbilisi, urging him
to come to terms with the fallen Menshevik régime. 'I must
remind you that the internal and international position of
Georgia requires of the Georgian Communists not the application of the Russian stereotype, but . . . an original tactic, based
upon greater concessions to the petty bourgeois elements.'
When he learnt that Zhordania and his cabinet declined to
enter into a coalition and had embarked for Europe, with the
full intention of turning the Georgian issue into an international
scandal, Lenin was greatly perturbed. However, the Politbureau was obliged to accept Georgia's annexation as a *fait
accompli*, and Trotsky, though highly critical of Stalin's hand-
ling of the situation, wrote a pamphlet in defence of Russian
policy towards Georgia. In accordance with Lenin's directive,
the Georgian Communist leaders tried at first to win over the

people by fair words. However, they met with nation-wide passive resistance. To make things worse, famine prevailed in the towns and during the summer of 1921 an outbreak of cholera carried off thousands of victims. The desperate shortage of food and the breakdown of medical services resulted in heavy mortality, the Georgian Catholicos-Patriarch Leonid being among the dead.

Even those Tbilisi workers who were most sympathetic towards Communist doctrines remained patriots at heart. A mass meeting of 3,000 representatives of the Tbilisi workers' associations took place on 10 April 1921 at the Opera House on Rustaveli Avenue. It passed resolutions calling upon the Revcom to defend Georgia's rights to self-determination and independence; to hasten the formation of a national Red Army of Georgia; to secure for the working masses of Georgia the right to select their representatives by free elections; to ensure that the new Soviet order was introduced into Georgia in such a way as to respect the customs of the people; and to legalize the existence of all socialist organizations not actually engaging in activities directed against the régime. Though acceptable in the main to the local Georgian Bolsheviks, such resolutions as these were not in accordance with the policies of Stalin and his immediate associates. Far from permitting the formation of a Georgian Red Army, Stalin saw that all military formations were disbanded, and posted Russian garrisons at strategic points. Workers' organizations and trades unions were subordinated to the Bolshevik party committees, which received their instructions from Moscow. Russian agents of the political police or Cheka were sent to Georgia to mop up the local Mensheviks, whom the Georgian Bolsheviks would rather have been left to win over or render harmless in their own way.

Stalin also began to toy with the idea of bringing Georgia into a Transcaucasian Federation of Soviet Republics, into which Armenia and Azerbaijan would also be merged. The local Georgian Bolsheviks, on the other hand, preferred to retain the country as an autonomous Soviet Republic loosely associated with Moscow, and possessing its own political and administrative organs. In July 1921 Stalin came to Tbilisi on a personal visit of inspection and addressed a mass meeting in the working-class quarter of Tbilisi, where he had spent so many months of revolutionary activity. As soon as he appeared on the platform, surrounded by Cheka agents and guards, the crowd began to hiss. Old women in the audience, some of whom had fed and sheltered Stalin when he was hiding from the Tsarist secret police, shouted: 'Accursed one, renegade, traitor!' The crowd reserved its ovation for the veteran revolutionary leader Isidore Ramishvili and another of their leaders, Alexander Dgebuadze, who asked Stalin straight out: 'Why have you destroyed Georgia? What have you to offer by way of atonement?' Surrounded by the angry faces of his old comrades Stalin turned pale and could only stutter a few words of self-justification, after which he left the hall cowering behind his Russian bodyguard. The next day, he stormed into Tbilisi Party Headquarters and made a furious attack on Philip Makharadze, whom he professed to hold personally responsible for his humiliation. Addressing a meeting of Tbilisi Communists on 6 July 1921, he urged them to renounce every vestige of local independence and merge into a single Transcaucasian Federation, in return for which he promised Georgia unlimited free oil from Baku and a loan of several million gold rubles from Moscow. Changing his tone, Stalin went on to attack what he called 'local chauvinism' among the Georgians. The most urgent task of the Georgian Communists was a ruthless struggle against the relics of nationalism. To smash 'the hydra of nationalism', the party must purge its ranks of local patriots and get rid of all who would not subordinate Georgia's interests to those of the entire Soviet Union.

Revival of Great Russian chauvinism

Such language, with its unmistakable overtones of new-born Great Russian imperialism, created a deplorable impression when coming from the lips of a native-born Georgian veteran of the liberation movement. Leading Georgian Bolsheviks like Mdivani, Eliava and Makharadze were dismayed at the abyss which gaped before them and protested vigorously against Stalin's scheme to abolish the autonomy of the non-Russian republics. Stalin was obdurate. Back in Moscow, he ordered the liquidation of all remains of the Georgian Menshevik party and went ahead with his plan for a new, centralistic constitution for the Soviet state. In the Politbureau, the protests of the

Ukrainians and Georgians were upheld by Trotsky, who saw in Stalin's proposals an abuse of power which could not fail to offend the non-Russian peoples and expose as a mere fraud the Communist doctrine of self-determination for all national groups. The grip of the Russian Cheka over Georgia was in the meantime greatly strengthened. The Russian secret police brought with them their well-tried techniques of torture and intimidation, in which some of their local recruits proved very apt pupils. The Metekhi fortress jail, which had served the Tsars as a political prison, was crammed with captives, while the most obstinate cases were 'worked over' in the dreaded Cheka headquarters down in the city, where hundreds of miserable prisoners languished and died in conditions of indescribable squalor. The Georgian Church was the object of special attention on the part of Stalin and his henchmen, who egged on mobs of hooligans to attack priests and loot the sanctuaries, in the course of which many historic relics and works of art were stolen or destroyed.

The moral dilemma confronting the Georgian Communists emerges clearly from a report sent by P. Makharadze, then Chairman of the Georgian Communist Party, to the Central Committee of the Party in Moscow on 6 December 1921.

'The arrival of the Red Army and the establishment of Soviet power in Georgia,' wrote Makharadze, 'had the outward appearance of a foreign occupation because in the country itself there was nobody who was ready to take part in a rebellion or a revolution. And at the time of the proclamation of the Soviet régime there was, in the whole of Georgia, not even a single member of the party capable of organizing action or providing leadership and this task had been accomplished mainly by doubtful or sometimes even criminal elements. . . . We must realize that the Georgian masses had become accustomed to the idea of an independent Georgia. . . . We had to demonstrate that we based our position on the independence of Georgia, but this was simply a form of words; in actual fact we were rejecting this and did not have it as our objective at all. This was an intolerable situation, as it is impossible to deceive the masses in a political question of this nature, and especially the Georgian people, who had gone through ordeals of fire and water in recent years. . . . We were announcing that we were working towards the creation of an independent Georgia . . . while taking systematic steps to nullify our promise.'

When Mdivani and Makharadze refused to agree to Georgia's entry into Stalin's new Transcaucasian Federation, Stalin and Orjonikidze discredited them with trumped-up charges of selfishness and treason to the Bolshevik cause. Unable to credit that Stalin would knowingly offend the national dignity of his fellow-countrymen, Lenin upheld him, with the result that Georgia was obliged to enter the Transcaucasian Federation and Mdivani and Makharadze received a stern rebuke.

The excesses committed by the Cheka and the Russian occupation troops in Georgia led to the formation of a well-organized resistance movement. Guerilla warfare broke out in several regions. In 1922, an underground Independence Committee was formed, consisting of representatives of most Georgian non-Communist parties and organizations. The committee set up a military centre, which was to prepare for a national insurrection. Several members of the former Menshevik government returned clandestinely from exile, including the former Minister of Agriculture, Noe Khomeriki, as well as the commander of the old National Guard, V. Jugheli; both were caught and subsequently shot. A heavy loss was sustained early in 1923 by the Georgian patriots, when fifteen members of the military centre were arrested. Among these were the principal leaders of the resistance movement, Generals Konstantine Abkhazi, Alexander Andronikashvili and Vardan Dsulukidze; they were executed on 20 May 1923. An appeal was addressed by the Georgian Catholicos-Patriarch Ambrosius to the international conference held at Genoa in 1922, in which he described the conditions under which the Georgians were living since the Red Army invasion and begged for the help of the civilized world. Ambrosius was immediately thrown into prison by the Communists and kept there until they imagined that his spirit was broken. The Bolsheviks then staged a public trial, at which the aged and venerated head of the Georgian Church demonstrated such moral fortitude that his ordeal turned into a great victory for his Church and nation. His concluding words were: 'My soul belongs to God, my heart to my country; you, my executioners, do what you will with my body.' The Communists did not dare to execute Ambrosius, who died in captivity in 1927.

Lenin was paralysed during the summer of 1922 by his first

stroke and had to delegate much of his authority to Stalin, now General Secretary of the Party. Following a spate of rumours and complaints coming in from Tbilisi, however, an investigation commission headed by Felix Dzerzhinsky, head of the Soviet secret police, was sent to Georgia to report on the position there. Even the hardened Dzerzhinsky was horrified at the excesses committed by Orjonikidze and his associates under Stalin's orders. Dzerzhinsky's report contributed to Lenin's growing distrust of Stalin and his decision to exclude him from the future leadership of the Party. He resolved also to suspend Orjonikidze from party membership. In his Testament and other documents dictated shortly before his death, Lenin wrote that he 'felt strongly guilty before the workers of Russia for not having intervened vigorously and drastically enough in this notorious affair'. He was disgusted at the 'swamp' in which the Party had landed over the Georgian business. Under Stalin and Dzerzhinsky, the small nations of Russia were exposed to 'the irruption of that truly Russian man, the Great Russian chauvinist, who is essentially a scoundrel and an oppressor, as is the typical Russian bureaucrat'. Stalin had let his personal vindictiveness run away with him, showing himself 'not merely a genuine social chauvinist, but a coarse brutish bully acting on behalf of a Great Power'. The trouble was, Lenin shrewdly diagnosed, that Stalin the Georgian and Dzerzhinsky the Pole had gone out of their way to assume true Russian characteristics. 'It is well known that russified people of foreign birth always overshoot themselves in the matter of the true Russian disposition.' On 5 March 1923, Lenin broke off personal relations with Stalin, and urged Trotsky to defend the Georgian 'deviationists' before the Central Committee of the all-Russian Communist Party. The next day he wired a message to the leaders of the Georgian opposition, promising to take up their case at the forthcoming Party Congress: 'I am with you in this matter with all my heart. I am outraged by the arrogance of Orjonikidze and the connivance of Stalin and Dzerzhinsky.' Lenin also prepared to send Kamenev to Tbilisi on another commission of enquiry. In the middle of these moves, on 9 March 1923, Lenin suffered the third attack of his illness, from which he never recovered; his death took place on 21 January 1924.

The insurrection of 1924

Lenin's illness and death saved Stalin from disgrace. In spite of Lenin's warnings and his own fears, Trotsky came to terms with Stalin and his group. He even helped Stalin, Zinoviev and Kamenev to conceal from the world Lenin's deathbed confession of shame at the intolerant treatment of the non-Russian nationalities, the text of which was not published until 1956. At the 12th Party Congress in April 1923, the Georgian Communists found themselves isolated. With Lenin's notes suppressed, every word uttered from the platform against Georgian or Ukrainian nationalism was greeted with stormy applause, while the mildest allusion to Great Russian chauvinism was received in stony silence. Stalin bided his time before actually striking down his opponents among the Georgian Communist leadership. Budu Mdivani and his associates were not actively molested until 1929, while the real blood bath among the Georgian Old Bolsheviks did not take place until the great purge of 1936–37.

Driven beyond endurance, the Georgian people were now preparing for a last desperate effort to regain their freedom. Plans were laid for a general insurrection, scheduled for 29 August 1924. The plan miscarried. Through some misunderstanding, the mining centre of Chiatura and the surrounding district rose up in arms on August 28 instead of the appointed day. At first the insurgents achieved considerable success. A number of Red Army units were eliminated. But the Russian commander in Georgia, Mogilevsky, reinforced all strategic positions in and around Tbilisi, and repulsed the chief forces of the patriots, led by Colonel Kaikhosro Choloqashvili. Mogilevsky was later killed in a dramatic manner. A young Georgian airman who was piloting his plane crashed deliberately; all the occupants, including the pilot himself, were killed.

The unequal battle raged for three weeks. The rising was crushed and terrible reprisals took place. Conservative estimates place the number of prisoners and hostages killed by the victorious Communists at between 7,000 and 10,000. Many women and children were slain in cold blood. In the village of Ruisi, for instance, every human being carrying the name of

Paniashvili was put to death. About 20,000 persons were sent to Siberia immediately after the insurrection. Many months later, foreign visitors to Tbilisi would receive smuggled notes begging them to intercede for individual prisoners held captive in the dungeons of the Cheka, while lorry-loads of prisoners being driven off into exile were a common sight on the roads.

The death of Lenin, the onset of the Stalin era, and the defeat of the 1924 insurrection mark the final establishment of Soviet rule over Georgia. Not one of the great powers which had accorded the Georgian Republic full recognition only three years previously raised a finger to help the Georgian people in their struggle. At the same time, the abominations committed by Stalin against his own people created a deplorable impression on world opinion. As Lenin rightly foresaw, the Great Russian chauvinism of that vindictive Caucasian exposed the Russian Communist party to world-wide opprobrium, and proved a great obstacle to the Soviet government's attempts to come to an understanding with foreign socialist parties and countries abroad.

CHAPTER XII

THE STALIN ERA: 1924-53

Industrial development — Georgian agriculture collectivized — The war against the kulaks *— 'Dizziness with Success' — The rise of Beria — The Five-Year Plans — Georgia under the purges — Political reorganization and the Stalin Constitution — The Georgian émigrés — Georgia during World War II — The final terror — Death of a dictator*

Industrial development

THE SUPPRESSION of the 1924 uprising was followed by an uneasy calm. Military pacification was soon completed and an appearance of normality returned to the country. The relative prosperity brought to Russia by Lenin's New Economic Policy (NEP), with its tolerance of private enterprise in commerce and agriculture, had a beneficial effect on Georgia. Although the entire land surface had been nationalized following the Bolshevik occupation in 1921, no attempt was made as yet to enforce collectivization, so that the peasants continued for the time being to enjoy the use of the land distributed to them during the period of Georgian independence. The Communist Party of Georgia preferred for a time to use peaceful persuasion rather than armed coercion to extend their hold over the masses. Particular stress was laid on education and the spreading of literacy, while religious teaching was suppressed as far as possible. Far-reaching changes were made in the structure, curriculum and personnel of Tbilisi State University. The Rector, the noted historian Ivane Javakhishvili (1876–1940), was dismissed from his post and replaced by a professor more in tune with Communist aims; as it turned out, this eclipse probably saved Javakhishvili's life, since the then Rector of the University was among the purge victims during the terror of 1936–37.

Substantial progress was made with the industrialization of Georgia even during the NEP period. The impressive Zemo-Avchala hydro-electric scheme was completed during this time. A British trades union delegation which visited the Caucasus towards the end of 1924 saw the scheme under construction and reported:

'Tiflis, like other towns in Russia, is to have a great electricity power station. Plant that will harness 36,000 horse-power from the River Kura is now being erected. . . . The distance of the power station from the city is approximately twelve miles. . . . Already the work has made such progress that the dam is nearing completion. It will form a huge basin, harnessing the surging waters, which will accumulate in prodigious numbers millions of gallons and tons of weight. . . . The machinery is already in position and a perfect plant has been gathered together. The undertaking has another twelve months to run before completion. Three busy shifts are employing approximately a thousand workers in each shift. The men are housed in the best dwelling accommodation obtainable for such under-takings. . . . The wages rise from a rouble a day to 4 roubles; the food is obtained on a co-operative basis and is cheap. Efforts are being made on a practical and effective scale for the entertainment, training, and even the education of the workers employed. The Delegation saw a most industrious and orderly set of men in full and willing co-operation. . . .'[113]

The Zemo-Avchala hydro-electric station named after V. I. Lenin was officially opened by M. I. Kalinin on 26 June 1927.

As was the case in England during the Industrial Revolution of the nineteenth century, the rapid growth of the urban work-ing population of the Soviet Union resulted in a shortage of cheap foodstuffs. The peasants, cherishing their new-found mastery of the land, refused to deliver food to the towns at government-controlled prices. Both in Georgia and in Europ-ean Russia, the breaking up of the old landlords' estates often resulted in loss of efficiency and a fall in production. Small-holdings operated on a primitive subsistence basis proved less productive than the larger, systematically cultivated estates which had existed prior to the 1917 Revolution. This emerges clearly from figures cited in a recent official history of Georgia, which notes that as late as 1925–26, the acreage under grain in Georgia amounted to only 92·8 per cent. of the pre-1914 average, while the harvest as a whole yielded only 94·4 per cent. of the pre-1914 total. It is instructive to note, however, that the return from 'technical cultures', i.e. sub-tropical and specialized crops such as tobacco, tea and citrus fruits, exceeded the pre-1914 figure by 26·7 per cent.[114] This is to be explained by the fact that these crops were grown on lands newly reclaimed from the marshy swamps of Western Georgia, and on plantations exploited as co-operative or state enterprises and equipped with modern tools and machinery.

Georgian agriculture collectivized

The inception of the first Five-Year Plan in 1928, and the great drive towards full-scale collectivization of Soviet agriculture, marked the beginning of a new phase in Georgian as well as in Russian social and economic history. Enterprises like the Chiatura manganese mines, which had for some years been leased on a concessionary basis to the American Harriman interests, were brought under direct state management and expanded at a rapid rate. The Georgian Communist Party resolved to follow the Russian example of large-scale collectivization of agriculture and sent a thousand 'activist' members of the Komsomol or Communist Youth organization to Moscow to study the latest developments in Soviet economic and social theory. When these young enthusiasts returned to Georgia, a propaganda campaign was launched in order to persuade the peasantry of the benefits of the collective farm system. Groups of party workers toured the countryside, urging the people to abandon their antique methods of agriculture and embark voluntarily on the new programme. Special conferences of poor peasants and landless agricultural workers were held, at which their grievances against the more prosperous *kulak* class were vigorously whipped up.

This initial campaign met with scant success. The Georgian peasantry, to whom such characteristically Russian institutions as the peasant *mir* or commune were alien, clung with the courage of desperation to their individual small-holdings. Opposition to the new measures was by no means confined to the rich peasants or *kulaks*, but was met with among the majority of the middling or poorer ones also. This fact was admitted by a number of the leading Georgian Communists, who ventured to express doubt as to whether the elimination of a few so-called *kulaks* would suffice to bring about agricultural reform in a land which was basically one of middling and poor peasants. Holders of such views were denounced as 'rightist opportunists', and extensive purges of lukewarm officials and party workers took place: the Kaspi and Telavi regional committees of the Communist Party, for instance, were drastically overhauled in 1931, all their leading members being dismissed from their posts.

The war against the kulaks

The Secretary of the Central Committee of the Georgian Communist Party, Mikheil Kakhiani, ordered a ruthless, all-out campaign to be launched to achieve full collectivization of Georgian agriculture by February 1931, the tenth anniversary of Soviet rule in Georgia. He declared: 'The *kulaks* as a class must be destroyed.' On 19 January 1930, a decree of the plenum of the Central Committee of the Georgian Communist Party was published, containing the following provisions:

1. All *kulaks* are to be removed from areas scheduled for complete collectivization.

2. Agricultural equipment belonging to *kulaks* is to be turned over to the use of *kolkhozes* (collective farms).

3. When wine-growing areas are subjected to general collectivization, wine cellars belonging to *kulaks* are to be taken from them and handed over to the collectives.

4. Livestock and implements are to be taken from *kulaks*.

5. Lands belonging to *kulaks* are to be confiscated and given to the *kolkhozes*.

6. Economic, administrative and legal sanctions are to be applied against the *kulaks*, and public trials of them staged; all *kulak* property must be confiscated; *kulaks* agitating against collectivization are to be arrested.

7. *Kulaks* are to be forced to engage in public works and compulsory labour.

Five thousand agricultural students and young Communist propagandists were recruited for the campaign. One brigade of Party workers, each with a supporting detachment of OGPU guards or Red Army troops, was assigned to each district of Georgia. They undertook lightning campaigns in selected villages, turning alleged *kulaks* out of their homes and distributing their goods and chattels to the poorer peasants. No objective criterion existed as to what constituted a *kulak*. Those luckless families whom local Communist committees chose to brand as such were driven from their native villages with nothing but the clothes they wore, and drifted homeless and starving about the countryside. Party Secretary Kakhiani reported jubilantly to Moscow: 'Collectivization is going full speed ahead, and the new forms of Soviet economy are meeting with a unanimous and enthusiastic welcome from the peasants.'

In reality, the whole Georgian countryside was in turmoil. In Mingrelia and Abkhazia, groups of women armed with sticks marched through the *kolkhoz* fields, persuading the peasants to abandon work and go home. Oxen were unharnessed and driven into the woods. The women besieged the offices of the local authorities, demanding the release of their husbands from jail, and the abolition of the *kolkhoz* system. Violent and sanguinary clashes took place between NKVD detachments armed with machine-guns and angry peasant women armed with sticks and stones. Armed uprisings took place in southern Georgia in Borchalo and Lori, which had to be put down by entire battalions of Red Army troops. Partisans in mountain Svaneti declared Soviet rule at an end and set up their own administration. On the Georgian military highway, in the Dusheti district, the local militia was disarmed by peasants, who then moved south towards Tbilisi in the hope of joining forces with other insurgent groups. Fierce fighting broke out in Kakheti, where a hundred and fifty soldiers were killed. Over a thousand families were deported to Siberia from Kakheti alone. Different tactics were employed by peasants in the Gori district, who agreed to become *kolkhoz* members and adopted a go-slow policy and sabotaged *kolkhoz* property. If any Communist foreman displayed an excess of zeal, he would disappear in the night and be seen alive no more.

'Dizziness with Success'

Chaotic as was the situation in Georgia, that prevailing in European Russia, especially in the black earth lands of the Ukraine, was far worse. The overwhelming majority of the peasantry confronted the government with desperate opposition. A veritable civil war developed as rebellious villages were surrounded by machine-guns and forced to surrender. Masses of so-called *kulaks* and their families were deported to remote wildernesses in Siberia and left to starve or freeze to death. Those that remained slaughtered cattle, smashed implements and burned crops. Whole regions were cordoned off by troops and NKVD detachments and starved into submission. At last Stalin himself became aware of the consequences of his impetuous drive towards complete collectivization, which threatened the very fabric of Soviet society. On 2 March 1930, he issued a statement entitled 'Dizziness with Success', in which he blamed all the inhuman excesses which had taken place on over-zealous local officials. Stalin admitted that many of the collective farms which had been set up by force were not viable as going concerns, and pretended that his instructions had been misunderstood. Without consulting the Politbureau and the Central Committee of the Soviet Communist Party, that same Stalin who had for months been issuing peremptory directives ordering compulsory collectivization at all costs now declared: 'Collective farms cannot be set up by force', and called for a cessation of violence and a pause for peaceful consolidation.

This *volte-face* caused consternation in Georgian and Transcaucasian Communist circles. A temporary halt in the 'building of socialism' was called while heads of revolutionary committees made a tour of inspection through the villages. An emergency session of the Central Committee of the Georgian Communist Party heard a report by the doyen of Georgian Communists, Philip Makharadze, indicting the local Party organizations for their misplaced zeal. However, the real culprit was the Central Committee itself, whose Second Secretary was forced to admit that local Party committees had been urged to collectivize everything and everybody in a day, 'right down to the last chicken'. The Georgian Communists could not deny that many of those who had been victimized and driven from their homes were not rich *kulaks* at all. Philip Makharadze stated in the newspaper *Komunisti* (*The Communist*):

'It was not only the *kulaks* but also the smallholders and poorer peasants who were affected by the anti-*kulak* campaign. A number of facts are now available which prove that a large part of the 'dekulakized' persons were in fact smallholders. . . . During the campaign, whole families were moved from their homes, including old people of eighty and ninety, invalids, women and children. They were moved from their homes, but where to? No one knew where they were supposed to go. Comrades, the result of these mistakes was that in many areas the peasant smallholders expressed their pity for the *kulaks*. Intimidated by this anti-*kulak* campaign, the peasants joined the *kolkhozes*. We were told here that they were enthusiastic about joining the *kolkhozes*, but this was by no means the case. To crown it all, the cattle taken away from the peasants is being allowed to die off through lack of proper care and their equipment is being allowed to spoil.'

In Moscow, S. Eliava, head of the government of Soviet Georgia, declared at a meeting of the Central Committee of the Communist Party: 'The situation in Georgia and Transcaucasia in general is very grave. Not one corner of the Soviet Union experiences at the moment such difficulties . . . The Georgian peasantry is only waiting for a chance. . . . Thousands of them have gone into the mountains and forests to wage battle against us.'

It was no secret that Stalin himself was personally responsible for all this misery. However, a scapegoat was found in the person of Kakhiani, who was dismissed from the post of Secretary of the Central Committee of the Georgian Communist Party and sent off to a minor post in Turkestan. When the disturbances eventually died down, the net result of Georgia's first collectivization drive was the creation by 1932 of some 3,400 *kolkhozes*, incorporating about 17,000 former peasant holdings, representing 36·4 per cent. of the national total. A score or more of *Sovkhozes* or state farms were also formed. There existed in the whole of Georgia only thirty-one tractor stations, and it was a long time before agricultural production recovered from the chaotic condition into which doctrinaire folly had plunged it.

The rise of Beria

The Georgian Communists could not help resenting the invidious role in which Stalin's bungling had placed them, with the result that mutual antagonisms between him and the local Georgian Party leadership flared up afresh. In 1932, when Stalin's popularity in the Soviet Union had sunk to a low ebb, memoranda on the need to depose him from the post of General Secretary of the Soviet Communist Party began to circulate in the highest quarters. Instrumental in the campaign to oust Stalin were the leading Georgian Bolshevik, Beso Lominadze, who had been secretary of the Communist Party of the Transcaucasian Federation, and Syrtsov, premier of the Russian Federative SSR, both of whom had rendered Stalin loyal aid in defeating his Trotskyist and Bukharinite opponents in the Party. Lominadze and Syrtsov were merely urging the Central Committee to depose Stalin constitutionally by voting him down at a meeting of the Committee; however, they were charged with conspiracy, imprisoned and liquidated. Morbidly sensitive to hostility on the part of his Georgian compatriots, Stalin felt it necessary to place in charge of Caucasian affairs an individual on whose unwavering personal loyalty he could count. His choice fell upon L. P. Beria (1899–1953), a man who was many years later to be unmasked as an enemy of the people and condemned to die as a traitor to the Soviet fatherland.

Lavrenti Beria came of a poor Mingrelian peasant family living in the Sukhumi district of Abkhazia, near the Black Sea. He joined the Bolshevik party in 1917 while studying at a technical college in Baku, and thereafter took part in organizing an illegal underground group of Bolshevik technicians. His skill in this work led to his appointment in 1921 to a post in the Caucasian Cheka. By the time he was thirty-two, he had been Vice-president of the Cheka in Azerbaijan and Georgia, President of the Georgian GPU, and then President of the Caucasian State Police and chief representative of the OGPU in Transcaucasia. His special task was the elimination of all anti-Bolshevik groups in the Caucasus, for success in which task he was decorated with the order of the Red Banner of the Republics of Georgia, Armenia and Azerbaijan. In October 1931, Beria was transferred from his post in the secret police and made Second Secretary of the Central Committee of the Transcaucasian Communist Party, the First Secretary of which, Kartvelishvili by name, strongly disliked Beria's unsavoury personality and methods. Kartvelishvili, a personal friend of the influential Bolshevik leader Sergo Orjonikidze, categorically refused to work with Beria. According to N. S. Khrushchev's historic speech at the 20th Party Congress in 1956,

Beria fabricated a series of untrue charges against Kartvelish-vili, who was soon deported from the Caucasus and put to death. The vacant post of First Secretary of the Transcaucasian Party organization was then occupied by Beria himself.

The Five-Year Plans

From 1932 until 1938, Beria exercised dictatorial powers in Transcaucasia. He played a leading role in implementing the Second Five-Year Plan in Georgia between 1933 and 1937. At the cost of immense effort and sacrifice, Georgian industrial development made great strides forward. The Zestafoni ferro-alloy plant went into production during this period, as did the Tbilisi machine-tool factory named after S. M. Kirov. Further progress was made in harnessing the power potential of Georgia's rivers. The Rioni, Atcharis-dsqali and Sukhumi hydro-electric schemes were completed and a start was made with the hydro-electric station on the River Khrami. Stakhan-ovite labour methods were successfully applied in the Chiatura manganese mines and at the Tbilisi locomotive and railway wagon workshops named after I. V. Stalin. By the end of the Second Five-Year Plan, the Avchala cast-iron factory and the Inguri paper combine were in operation, as well as a new chemical and pharmaceutical laboratory in Tbilisi, new in-dustrial plant at Kutaisi, and tea factories in the Black Sea districts of Western Georgia. Drainage and irrigation schemes were carried out. Private enterprise was eliminated from shop-keeping and commerce. Restaurants, hotels and shops were completely municipalized, though this was far from being an unmixed blessing for the consumer and general public.

Beria kept Stalin supplied with secret denunciations of Georgian Bolshevik leaders, officials, writers and teachers. At the 17th Party Congress in 1934 he was elected to the Central Committee of the Soviet Communist Party; in 1936, he served on the editorial commission for the presentation of the Stalin Constitution. The rise of Beria coincided with the downfall of one of the most distinguished Georgian Bolsheviks, Abel Enukidze, who had begun his career as early as 1904 by running the secret Bolshevik printing press at Baku, and was for years regarded as Stalin's intimate friend. Abel Enukidze was Secretary-General of the Central Executive Committee which was, prior to the promulgation of the Stalin Constitution, the supreme legislative body of the USSR; its decrees bore Enukidze's signature jointly with Kalinin's. Early in 1935, Enukidze was relieved of his post, ostensibly to become Prime Minister of the Transcaucasian Federation. He was shortly afterwards disgraced and suffered death during the purges in 1937.

Beria ingratiated himself further with Stalin by building up the famous 'personality cult'. On 21–22 July 1935, he delivered to a meeting of the Tbilisi Party organization a lecture 'On the history of the Bolshevik organizations in Transcaucasia', in which Stalin is given almost exclusive credit for the success of the Caucasian revolutionary movement from 1900 onwards. Beria himself set out to eliminate any of the Georgian Old Bolsheviks who might have felt inclined to challenge the truth of his assertions. The lecture itself was several times republished in book form, each edition containing more adulatory praise of Stalin, and more vitriolic denunciation of Stalin's rivals, many of whom Beria had himself tortured and shot. In the English edition of 1949, for instance, the dead Abel Enukidze is denounced as a 'mortal enemy of the people', while Budu Mdivani, Vice-Premier of Georgia prior to the great purges, is vilified as a supporter of the 'arch-bandit Judas Trotsky' and a fellow-member, with Mikha Okujava, Mikha Toroshelidze, S. Chikhladze, N. Kiknadze and other liquidated Georgian Bolsheviks, of a Trotskyite spying and wrecking terrorist centre, which Beria claimed credit for unearthing in 1936.

Georgia under the purges

Beria was in his element during the great purges of 1936–37. While the unbalanced and degenerate NKVD chiefs Yezhov and Yagoda were torturing and killing millions of high officials, army officers, intellectuals and ordinary citizens throughout Russia, Beria in the Caucasus eliminated every individual whose adherence to the Party Line could be called in question, or whose survival might conceivably challenge the myth of Stalin's infallibility. The Georgian leaders to whom Stalin had extended effusive and hypocritical congratulations on the occasion of the 15th anniversary of Soviet Georgia in February 1936 were by then already marked down as purge victims. Two separate trials of Georgian Communist leaders for 'terrorism and high treason' were held. The first group included Budu Mdivani and the Georgian planning chief Mikha Toroshelidze. The second group was headed by the Georgian Prime Minister, Mgaloblishvili. Among those tortured to death or shot at this time were Mikha Okujava, Mamia Orakhelashvili, Sergi Kavtaradze, Chairman of the Council of People's Commissars of Georgia, and Lado Dumbadze, Chairman of the first Bolshevik Soviet in Tbilisi. Only Philip Makharadze, then nearing his seventieth birthday, was spared public condemnation. Makharadze was permitted to save himself by confessing his past guilt and pleading for mercy, in return for which he was appointed Deputy Chairman of the Presidium of the Supreme Soviet, an honorific sinecure which he held until his death in 1941.

As in Russia itself, the holocaust in Georgia was carried to diabolical lengths. Denunciations by personal enemies or the receipt of an innocent letter from some friend abroad were sufficient to bring about imprisonment, exile or death. The witch-hunt was carried to great lengths at Tbilisi University, which lost scores of its most brilliant professors and most promising students. Among those who perished was the famous classical scholar and papyrologist Grigol Tsereteli, guilty of having attended international conferences in which scholars from bourgeois countries also participated. The literary historian Vakhtang Kotetishvili vanished without trace, while the outstanding Abkhazian dramatist Samson Chanba (1886–1937) was also put to death. Universal horror was excited by the execution of two of Georgia's greatest national writers, the novelist Mikheil Javakhishvili and the poet Titsian Tabidze, the latter a close friend of Boris Pasternak, who knew him as 'a reserved and complicated soul, wholly attracted to the good and capable of clairvoyance and self-sacrifice'.[115] A close associate of Tabidze was Paolo Iashvili, a remarkable poet of the post-symbolist period, 'brilliant, polished, cultured, an amusing talker, European and good-looking'.[116] So horrified was Iashvili at the news of Tabidze's arrest and execution that he went straight to the headquarters of the Union of Georgian Writers, of which he was secretary, and killed himself there. At a congress of Georgian writers held at Tbilisi in July 1954, the First Secretary of the Georgian Communist Party, V. P. Mzhavanadze, referred to the terrorism exercised by Beria's agents and said:

'Comrades, you all know what injury was done to our people by that gang of murderers and spies who now have been unmasked and done away with by our Party. That gang killed many leading and progressive scientists. . . . The Central Committee of the Georgian Communist Party has found out that the outstanding masters of the Georgian language—Mikheil Javakhishvili, Titsian Tabidze and Paolo Iashvili—became victims of the intrigues and terrorism of that abominable gang of murderers. I have pleasure in declaring in the name of the competent organs that these men have been rehabilitated.'

This statement was greeted with loud acclamation, as were the pronouncements of Stalin and Beria in their time; in reality, the fair name of Georgia's great writers does not depend on Mr. Mzhavanadze and his 'competent organs', but is enshrined in the hearts of the Georgian people and their friends.

The Georgian purges were not confined to the capital, but also enveloped the outlying regions, notably the Autonomous Republics of Abkhazia and Atchara on the Black Sea coast. The Abkhazians had long been subject to colonization both by Russians and Georgians: by 1926, autonomous Abkhazia, covering 3,240 square miles, had a population of 174,000 of which the Abkhazians themselves accounted for less than one-third. Under the Second Five-Year Plan, Abkhazia was directed to step up tobacco production substantially, and more Russians, Georgians, Armenians and Greeks were brought in to work on new plantations and industrial projects. The Abkhazians, who resented these encroachments on their cherished autonomy, protested and in the end fell completely into disgrace with the Kremlin. The leading spokesman of the dissident Abkhaz Bolsheviks, Nestor Lakoba, died a natural death in 1936. In the following year, a purge trial was held at Sukhumi, the Abkhazian capital, at which forty-seven of Lakoba's friends, relatives and associates were charged with complicity in an imaginary plot to murder Stalin. Ten of the defendants were executed. A similar mass trial was staged at Batumi, the capital of Atchara. Eleven persons, headed by Zakaria Lortkipanidze, Chairman of the Central Executive

Committee of Atchara, were accused of belonging to a 'counter-revolutionary and insurgent organization, engaging in espionage, sabotage and diversion', maintaining contacts with émigré *beks, mullahs* and *kulaks*, and destroying crops in plantations and collective farms. The Communist-controlled Georgian Press reported these trials under banner headlines such as: 'Shoot the accused—that is our verdict!' 'Wipe the fascist reptiles off the face of the earth!' 'Death to the despised enemies of the people!' Eight of the accused in the Batumi trial were executed: since Stalin's death, several of them have been posthumously rehabilitated.

Before the Stalin-Beria purges, Tbilisi was famed for 'the high level of culture of the leading section of society—an active intellectual life which, by then, was rarely to be found elsewhere.'[117] The events of 1937 resulted in the elimination or demoralization of the élite among the Georgian intelligentsia. The next fifteen years or more were a period of utter stagnation in Georgian literature, in which writers eked out an existence by composing dithyrambs about life in factories or on collective farms, or sycophantic odes to Stalin the superman. It is only today that a new generation of Georgian authors is emerging unscarred by the experiences of that grim era.

A fitting climax to the Georgian purges was provided by the suicide of the eminent Georgian Bolshevik, Sergo Orjonikidze (1886–1937), long Stalin's right-hand man, a member of the Politbureau and People's Commissar for Heavy Industry for the entire Soviet Union. Vigorous and ruthless when necessary, Orjonikidze had a reputation for decency and tried to thwart Beria's wholesale executions in Georgia. Beria denounced Orjonikidze to Stalin, who sanctioned the liquidation of Orjonikidze's brother. According to the account given by N. S. Khrushchev, Beria and Stalin between them deliberately brought Orjonikidze to such a state of nervous collapse that he killed himself. He was then accorded a grandiose state funeral and admitted to the pantheon of the great dead Bolshevik fathers.

Political reorganization and the Stalin Constitution

Once he had set in motion the necessary machinery to eliminate all potential opposition in the Caucasus, Stalin dissolved the artificial Transcaucasian Federation into its constituent parts, the Georgian, Armenian and Azerbaijan Soviet Socialist Republics. To these was granted, in theory at least, a large measure of political devolution, including the right to secede at will from the Soviet Union. This change took place in 1936, when the Stalin Constitution was promulgated. Two years later, Beria was summoned from Tbilisi to Moscow to take over the NKVD in succession to Yezhov and Yagoda, both of whom, after destroying millions of Soviet citizens, had themselves been declared expendable and put to death. The Caucasus was left in charge of officials who owed their promotion to Stalin and Beria, and whose reliability was beyond doubt.

The Georgian émigrés

After Orjonikidze's death and Makharadze's recantation, there was none of Stalin's old associates among the Georgian Bolsheviks who could question his omniscience or bring up the various unsavoury episodes in his revolutionary past. At the same time, the Georgian Menshevik government in exile in Paris continued to present a certain nuisance value. Karlo Chkheidze had died in 1926, and Noe Ramishvili, the forceful Minister of the Interior in the Zhordania government, was struck down in Paris in 1930 by a Georgian assassin reputedly in the pay of the Soviet government. Most of the émigré ministers, however, were distinguished by their longevity, one or two venerable octogenarians being alive even today. For some years after the fall of independent Georgia, until 1933, the Georgian Mensheviks were able to maintain their legation in Paris; the International Committee for Georgia, the president of which was Monsieur Jean Martin, director of the *Journal de Genève*, kept up a running fight against the admission of the Soviet Union to the League of Nations, which nevertheless took place in 1934. The importance which Stalin attached to the activities of the Georgian émigrés was displayed in 1938, when the Soviet embassy in Paris brought effectual pressure to bear on a pusillanimous French government to ban a celebration of the 750th anniversary of the Georgian national poet Shota Rustaveli, which was to have been held at the Sorbonne. With the rise of Nazi Germany, a number of Georgian exiles joined the Fascist movement. A Georgian Fascist Front was formed, the nucleus of which consisted of a nationalist organization called *Tetri Giorgi* or *White George*, after the patron saint of Georgia. The leaders of *Tetri Giorgi* included General Leo Kereselidze and Professor Mikhako Tsereteli, the former Kropotkinite anarchist, who had in the meantime won a high reputation in the German universities as an expert on the Sumerian and Hittite languages.

Georgia during World War II

After killing Marshal Tukhachevsky and decimating the Red Army high command during the purges, Stalin proceeded in 1939 to make war inevitable by concluding the Molotov-Ribbentrop pact with Nazi Germany. His inordinate self-confidence led him to ignore repeated warnings from foreign governments and from his own agents abroad, with the result that Russia was caught largely unprepared when Hitler launched his lightning attack in June 1941. The Georgians contributed greatly to the defence of the USSR during World War II and played an outstanding part in preventing the Germans from penetrating into Georgia from their advanced bases in North Caucasia. German parachutists were dropped at various points in Georgia, but were promptly mopped up by local military units. There were, however, manifestations of unrest within the country which gave the authorities grounds for disquiet. It is said, for instance, that a meeting was held in 1942 in the Tbilisi Opera House at which leaflets were distributed calling on the people to overthrow Russian Communist rule and proclaim Georgia's independence. On the German side, efforts were made to form a Georgian Legion from émigrés living in Western Europe, combined with Soviet prisoners of war of Georgian extraction. This venture was greatly hampered by the intervention of Rosenberg and other exponents of Nazi racism, who wanted all Georgians sent to extermination camps as non-Aryans, along with the Jews and the Gypsies. The Georgians under Nazi domination were saved only by the intervention of Alexander Nikuradze, a Georgian scientist held in high esteem in the German official world. In 1945, a Georgian sergeant hoisted the flag of victory over the Berlin Reichstag in company with a Russian Red

Army soldier. The inter-allied agreement concluded at the end of the war resulted in the forcible repatriation to Soviet Russia of thousands of Georgians who had sought asylum in the West, many of whom were shot or exiled to Siberia on their return home.

The final terror

The last years of Stalin's life were marked by an intensification of his personal reign of terror. As N. S. Khrushchev declared in 1956, Stalin carried mistrust to the point of mania. 'He could look at a man and say: "Why are your eyes so shifty today?" or "Why are you turning away so much today and avoiding looking me directly in the eyes?" This sickly suspicion created in him a general distrust even towards eminent party workers whom he had known for years. Everywhere and in everything he saw enemies, two-facers and spies.' In metropolitan Russia, Stalin's fantastic delusions manifested themselves in such sinister incidents as the 1949 Leningrad affair, involving the shooting out of hand of the State Planning Chairman Voznesensky, and the bogus 'Doctors' Plot', in which leading Russian physicians narrowly escaped extermination at the hands of the secret police. In the northern Caucasus, Stalin celebrated the retreat of the Germans by ordering the deportation in 1943–44 of the entire Karachay-Balkar and Chechen-Ingush peoples as a punishment for alleged collaboration with the Nazis; the Chechen-Ingush Autonomous SSR was obliterated from the map of the Soviet Union.

After receiving warm commendation for the successful completion of the Fourth Five-Year Plan between 1946 and 1950, Georgia too fell under the dictator's scourge. In 1951, he claimed to have unearthed a nationalist organization centred on Mingrelia, the Western province of Georgia adjoining Lavrenti Beria's homeland. N. S. Khrushchev stated in 1956: 'As is known, resolutions by the Central Committee of the Communist Party of the Soviet Union concerning this case were passed in November 1951 and in March 1952. These resolutions were made without prior discussion with the Politbureau. Stalin had personally dictated them. They made serious accusations against many loyal Communists. On the basis of falsified documents it was proved that there existed in Georgia a supposedly nationalistic organization whose objective was the liquidation of Soviet power in that republic with the help of imperialist powers. In this connexion, a number of responsible Party and Soviet workers were arrested in Georgia. As was later proved, this was a slander directed against the Georgian party organization. . . . There was no nationalistic organization in Georgia. Thousands of innocent people fell victim of wilfulness and lawlessness. All this happened under the "genial" leadership of Stalin, "the great son of the Georgian nation", as the Georgians like to term Stalin.'

Concurrently with the Mingrelian affair, prominent Georgian Communists were accused of embezzling state funds, stealing automobiles and plundering state property. Two Georgian Communist Party secretaries, the Chairman of the Georgian Supreme Court and the Minister of Justice were among those removed from their posts late in 1951. These changes failed to satisfy Stalin. In April 1952, Beria, now Vice-President of the Soviet Council of Ministers, came from Moscow to attend a meeting of the Central Committee of the Georgian Communist Party, at which he subjected the party leadership to severe criticism for failing to instil the Communist creed in Georgian youth and to tear out all traces of local nationalism. A new First Secretary of the Georgian Communist Party, A. I. Mgeladze, was appointed, while the Chairman of the Council of Ministers and the Chairman of the Presidium of the Georgian Supreme Soviet were relieved of their posts. Mgeladze set to work to purge the party and governmental apparatus from top to bottom. In six months he replaced half the members of the Central Committee of the Georgian Communist Party who had been returned in the election of 1949, and brought about a complete upheaval in the administrative hierarchy of the Republic. Many chairmen of collective farms and officials of the Comsomol or Soviet Youth movement lost their jobs. The fact that several high officials removed by Mgeladze, notably Valerian Bakradze, Deputy Chairman of the Georgian Council of Ministers, were personal nominees of Beria was taken at the time as a symptom of Beria's waning prestige in the inner circles of the Kremlin, where rising stars such as Malenkov and Khrushchev were supplanting him in Stalin's favour.

Death of a dictator

At all events, Mgeladze and his deputy, the Georgian Minister of State Security, N. Rukhadze, made use of the extensive files of the Georgian MVD to accuse some of Beria's own agents of nationalist deviation and other crimes. It is probable that these denunciations would in time have touched the person of Beria himself. N. S. Khrushchev has said that at the time of his death in March 1953, Stalin was planning the annihilation of many of the veteran Politbureau members: Marshal Voroshilov was under the extraordinary suspicion of being an English spy; Andreev had been dismissed and relegated to limbo; 'baseless charges' had been brought against Mikoyan and Molotov. 'It is not excluded,' Khrushchev told the 20th Party Congress, 'that had Stalin remained at the helm for another few months, Comrades Molotov and Mikoyan would probably not have delivered any speeches at this Congress.' For many leading Soviet statesmen and officials, Stalin's demise thus came in the nick of time. Whether or not it was due to natural causes is another matter.

Stalin's death removed from the world stage the most formidable Georgian of all time, a man who combined almost superhuman tenacity and force of character with quite subhuman cruelty and criminality. He took over a Russia backward and divided, and pitchforked it forcibly into the twentieth century. By methods which cannot be condoned by any standards of human or divine morality, he fashioned the social and industrial springboard from which the Soviet Union today is leaping irresistibly forward as one of the two dominant world powers of our generation.

CHAPTER XIII

GEORGIA IN OUR TIME

Beria's brief heyday — The Tbilisi riots — Industry and construction — Scientific advances — Growing pains of modernization — The housing crisis — Farming and plantations — Education, medicine and sport — Scholarship and science — The economic potential of Georgia — Russian nationality policy today

Beria's brief heyday

W HEN S TALIN DIED, Beria stepped into place as one of the new Soviet triumvirs, sharing power for a few weeks with Malenkov and Molotov. Beria now moved with speed to repair his political fences in Georgia. A plenary session of the Central Committee of the Georgian Communist Party was held on 14 April 1953, which dismissed the Party Secretariat headed by A. I. Mgeladze and established a new one under an official named Mirtskhulava. Beria's old protégé Valerian Bakradze, whom Mgeladze had dismissed from government office, now became Prime Minister of the Georgian Republic. Several prominent supporters of Beria whom Mgeladze and his faction had imprisoned were released and given portfolios in the Bakradze administration. The ousted First Secretary, Mgeladze, made an abject confession, declaring that charges of nationalist deviationism which he had levelled against high-ranking Georgian Bolsheviks were based on false evidence which he had forged from motives of personal ambition. N. Rukhadze, Georgian Minister of State Security, who had aided and abetted Mgeladze, was imprisoned. Unlike some officials hostile to Beria, Rukhadze was not saved by Beria's fall later in the year; it was announced in November 1955 that he had been executed.

Beria did not long share the sweets of power with Malenkov and Molotov. A struggle for mastery developed at the summit of the Soviet hierarchy. In spite of his powerful position as head of the secret police, Beria fell, dragging down with him many high officials whose careers were linked with his, and whose familiarity with secrets of state made their survival dangerous to the victors. Beria was arrested in July, and his execution for high treason announced late in December 1953. Among other prominent Georgians who fell with him were V. G. Dekanozov, a former Soviet Vice-Minister for Foreign Affairs, and Minister of Internal Affairs in Georgia; B. Z. Kobulov, a former Soviet Deputy Minister of State Security and later Deputy Minister of Internal Affairs; and S. A. Goglidze, a former Commissar of Internal Affairs in Georgia. These persons and others put to death with them were accused of conspiring with Beria to liquidate the Soviet workers' and peasants' régime with the aim of restoring capitalism and the power of the bourgeoisie. While these charges can hardly be taken seriously, little pity need be wasted on Beria and his accomplices, whose hands had for years been dripping with innocent blood.

The elimination of the Beria group in the Georgian government and Party machine brought little joy to the Stalinists whom Beria had ousted. The post of First Secretary of the Georgian Communist Party was filled in September 1953 by the election of a new man, Mr. Vasili P. Mzhavanadze, a former Lieutenant-General in the Red Army. The Second Secretary is a Russian, P. V. Kovanov. On 29 October 1953, a forty-one-year-old engineer and geologist, Mr. Givi D. Javakhishvili, was elected Prime Minister of the Georgian Republic. Under the benign leadership of these gentlemen, Georgia continues to prosper up to the present day. The status of Georgia in the higher counsels of the USSR has been enhanced by V. P. Mzhavanadze's election in June 1957 to candidate membership of the Presidium of the Central Committee of the Soviet Communist Party. The Georgian Communist, Mr. M. P. Georgadze, was in 1958 appointed Secretary of the Supreme Soviet.

The Tbilisi riots

The only major upheaval which has been reported under the present Georgian administration is the serious riot which occurred in Tbilisi on 9 March 1956. This disturbance arose out of perfectly legal demonstrations held to commemorate the third anniversary of Stalin's death. Popular sentiment was apparently inflamed by the violent denunciation of the late Georgian dictator delivered by N. S. Khrushchev at the 20th Party Congress in the preceding month. The sarcastic and bitter manner in which Khrushchev ascribed all the horrors of the purges to the 'genial' leader Stalin, whom, as he ironically put it, the Georgians so much enjoyed calling 'the great son of the Georgian nation', must have rankled with the Georgian masses, who had learnt to be proud of the stupendous role which their Soso Jughashvili had played for long in Soviet and in world affairs. During the disturbances, traffic in Tbilisi came to a halt. Trams were overturned and rioters seized private cars and raced through the streets spreading panic and provoking further incidents. Many university students took part in the disorders during which, according to the Rector of Tbilisi University, Mr. Victor Kupradze, 'illegal and forbidden nationalist slogans' were shouted. Militia and troops soon had the situation under control. During the disorders and subsequent reprisals, one hundred and six persons are said to have been killed, over two hundred wounded, while several hundred more were subsequently deported to labour camps in Siberia.

This isolated incident led foreign observers to draw much exaggerated conclusions as to the present strength of Georgian nationalist sentiment. The Georgians, it is true, are legitimately proud of their past and present achievements in the arts, sciences and letters, and conscious of their national uniqueness among the peoples of the USSR. It is also true that they exhibit at times an unreasonably cantankerous attitude towards neighbouring peoples, including the Russians themselves, from whom they have suffered injury in the past. But this does not mean that the Georgians are forever hatching plots against the Soviet state, as some Western writers would have us believe. N. S. Khrushchev himself ridiculed this idea in 1956, when pouring scorn on Stalin's obsession with a supposed Georgian nationalist movement planning to take Georgia out of the Soviet Union and join her to Turkey.

'This is, of course, nonsense. It is impossible to imagine how such assumptions could enter anyone's mind. Everyone knows how

Georgia has developed economically and culturally under Soviet rule.' 'The industrial production of the Georgian republic,' Mr. Khrushchev continued, 'is twenty-seven times greater than it was before the Revolution. . . . Illiteracy has long since been liquidated, which, in pre-revolutionary Georgia, included 78% of the population. Could the Georgians, comparing the situation in their republic with the hard situation of the working masses in Turkey, be aspiring to join Turkey? . . . According to the available 1950 census, 65% of Turkey's total population are illiterate, and of the women, 80% are illiterate. Georgia has nineteen institutions of higher learning, which have about 39,000 students between them. The prosperity of the working people has grown tremendously in Georgia under Soviet rule. It is clear that as the economy and culture develop, and as the Socialist consciousness of the working masses in Georgia grows, the source from which bourgeois nationalism draws its strength evaporates. . . .'

Industry and construction

The concluding phrase quoted may perhaps contain an element of wishful thinking. None the less, it is undeniable that the Georgians are now reaping the benefit of the industrial and agricultural policies so ruthlessly pursued in the Stalin era. The Soviet government has over the years invested vast sums of money in Georgia, by building factories, dams and hydro-electric stations, draining swamps, constructing airports, schools and other utilities. Between 1913 and 1957, the quantity of electricity generated rose from 20,000,000 to 2,573,000,000 kilowatt-hours. Coal production, which ammounted in 1913 to 70,000 tons, reached 2,967,000 tons in 1957. Iron production rose in the two years between 1955 and 1957 from 436,000 to 640,000 tons, and steel production, totalling only 200 tons in 1940, reached 803,000 in 1957. The total production of rolled metal, of which 20,000 tons were manufactured in 1950, amounted by 1957 to 705,000 tons. Cement production rose between 1932 and 1957 from 133,000 to 1,025,000 tons. Other branches of heavy industry in which production has been appreciably stepped up include machine tools, lorries and electric locomotives.

The reorganization of management in industry and construction works carried out in the USSR in 1957 helped to accelerate the development of the Georgian economy. The country was turned into a single economic region headed by an Economic Council in charge of more than five hundred large industrial establishments. Previously, these enterprises had been under different departments and ministries, many of them based entirely on Moscow, where all decisions had to be made. In the comparatively short period of its working, the Economic Council has demonstrated the advantages of this new form of industrial administration. Management has been brought close to the production floor, while the workers themselves are drawn increasingly into the direction of industry and construction. Workers are encouraged to make suggestions on possible improvements in work methods and techniques, and individuals showing special promise sit on technical committees which exist at the main factories.

Scientific advances

Extensive research has been carried out recently in Georgia into automation, instrument making, electrical engineering and telemechanics. New scientific institutes have arisen such as the Institute of Applied Chemistry and Electrochemistry, the Research Institute of Automation of Production Processes, and a big electronic data-processing centre. Georgian scientists are doing advanced research in nuclear physics, and the physics of low temperatures and cosmic rays. The nuclear reactor recently installed in Tbilisi enables scientists there to carry out investigations into the peaceful uses of atomic energy. The Georgian Academy of Sciences is setting up an Institute of Semi-Conductors which will contribute to the development of computing techniques, telemechanics and automation. Scientific contacts with countries abroad are growing more regular and varied. In 1958, for example, Georgian scientists attended meetings and congresses in Edinburgh, Leyden, Berlin, Leipzig, Geneva, London, Vienna, Bucarest, Rome and Brussels. The observatory at Abastumani is studying variable stars in collaboration with observatories in the United States, Holland and Ireland.

Growing pains of modernization

This modernization is not without its growing pains. Nor has the industrial development of Georgia been achieved without sacrificing something of what we in the West regard as basic facilities and amenities. In spite of its tourist attractions, Georgia suffers from a chronic shortage of hotels and restaurants. This applies to the capital itself: the Tbilisi Intourist hotel on Rustaveli Avenue to which most visitors are directed is as sepulchral in its dusty décor as its management is friendly and civil, and most of the rival establishments which existed prior to the 1917 Revolution have long since been taken over for other uses. While Tbilisi now has its own efficient television studio and transmitter, the production and marketing of television and radio sets, as well as such consumer durables as refrigerators, washing machines and electric cookers, is far from being equal to the potential demand. In December 1959, Mr. V. P. Mzhavanadze told the 20th Congress of the Georgian Communist Party that many industrial and agricultural enterprises in the republic were not operating satisfactorily and that a shortage of consumer goods persisted. Plans for building schools and cultural and medical centres were lagging. 'It is enough to note that during the past two years only 97 schools have been built instead of the planned total of 525; only 77 medical centres instead of 330; only 155 cultural centres instead of 735; and only 77 bath-houses instead of 555.' If Georgia were to pull its weight in the new Seven-Year Plan for 1959–65, then severe sanctions would have to be applied against inferior standards of work and behaviour, Marxist–Leninist ideological campaigns would have to be intensified, and anti-religious propaganda vigorously pursued.

The housing crisis

The housing position in Georgia, though leaving much to be desired, is alleviated somewhat by the fact that the land was not ravaged by the Nazi Germans, as was European Russia, and also by the ease with which simple peasant houses can be run up in this temperate climate from wood, mud and other cheap materials. The rapid growth of Georgia's urban centres since World War II has led to overcrowding and some of the picturesque quarters of old Tbilisi have degenerated into slums. Some 90,000 flats have been built since the war by state and municipal enterprise, and another 40,000 have been put up in

Georgia's towns by factory and office workers on a co-operative basis. During the current Seven-Year Plan, the rate of housing construction is to increase still faster. The state plans to build over 100,000 more dwellings by 1965, and people constructing their own homes will be assisted to erect another 60,000. A personal visit to the suburbs of Tbilisi in August 1960 showed many blocks of modern flats in the course of active construction.

Farming and plantations

Despite the growth of Georgian industry, the country remains to a large extent a land of agriculture, stock-raising and plantations. The most striking progress in recent years has been in the realm of sub-tropical crops and produce. Georgia today has 125,000 acres of flourishing tea gardens, equipped with the latest tea-picking and processing machinery. By 1965, Georgia is to deliver 170,000 tons gross of green tea leaf to the state. The citrus fruit plantations are only now recovering from the disastrous frosts of 1949–50 and 1953–54, and it will be some time before the 1949 harvest of 710 million fruit is equalled or exceeded. Vineyards are to be extended from 170,000 to 300,000 acres and should yield close on half a million tons of grapes. Personal inspection of the Tbilisi brandy factory and the wine cellars at Tsinandali in Kakheti gives a highly favourable impression of the present management and future potential of this industry, which already markets and exports high-quality wine and brandy on an international scale. The areas under tobacco, olives, sugar beet and maize are also to be greatly extended.

By 1958, there were 6,250 tractors and 1,500 combine harvesters at work in the fields of Georgia. However, the extension of tea and citrus fruit plantations has tended to divert attention away from the growing of wheat and other crops needed to feed Georgia's expanding population. Thus, in 1950, Georgia had to import three-quarters of the bread supply from other Soviet republics and hardship was experienced by the masses. The changeover from individual husbandry to collective and state farms, though now virtually universal, is not yet fully accepted by all members of the peasant class, some of whom fail to devote the same loving care to collectivized cows and crops as they do to their own little yards and vegetable plots. It must also be remembered that peasants are drifting away from the countryside into the new urban factories or the prosperous state-run tea or wine combines. Compared with the growth of heavy industry and sub-tropical cultures, the production of basic foodstuffs in Georgia appears rather static. The supply of butcher's meat, for instance, increased between 1950 and 1954 from 51,000 to 84,000 tons; thereafter it rose very slowly, amounting in 1957 to 86,000 tons, a negligible advance. Milk production rose between 1950 and 1956 from 293,000 to 415,000 tons, but sank in the following year to 398,000 tons. Georgia produced in 1950 156 million eggs, a figure which rose to 232 million in 1954, around which quantity annual production has since remained very steady. It is interesting to note that the marketing of eggs remains one of the chief private perquisites of individual peasants, who bring to market over 210 million of them annually, or nine-tenths of the total consumption. Sheep raising in Georgia is clearly on the decline, production of wool having sunk from 4,352 tons in 1950 to 3,894 tons in 1957. However, as the Soviet Union's internal trading and communications system becomes further rationalized, it should be easy to supplement local food production with cheap grain and dairy products from the Ukraine and elsewhere, leaving Georgian growers free to concentrate on the more rewarding sub-tropical and specialized crops for which Georgia's climate is uniquely suited.

Education, medicine and sport

The overall progress in Georgia's economic position is matched by the advances which have been made in education, public hygiene, and sport. The 4,500 schools have a total enrolment of 700,000, which means that one in six of the country's population is attending school. 181 schools have boarding facilities, of which 7,000 children at present take advantage; the boarding system is shortly to be further expanded. There are over ninety technical colleges and similar institutions, with 27,000 students. Eighteen out of every thousand of the population hold a university degree or training college diploma. The number of hospital beds in Georgia amounts to only 27,800, but the proportion of qualified medical practitioners to the general public is high: Georgia has an average of three doctors to every thousand persons, which comfortably exceeds the ratio for Western Europe. Spas and sanatoria at Abastumani, Borzhomi, Sukhumi and other places annually receive thousands of visitors from all parts of the Soviet Union.

Before World War II, sports facilities in Georgia were poor and sparse. Today the republic has 70 stadiums, 1,000 football fields, 4,500 volleyball and basketball courts, 270 gymnasia and 20 swimming pools. Georgia's ten best sportsmen participated as members of Soviet teams in the 16th Olympic Games at Melbourne, eight of them returning home with Olympic medals.

Scholarship and science

Science, scholarship and higher education are in a flourishing condition, as the writer was able to verify when visiting Tbilisi as well as from regular correspondence and personal contacts with Georgian colleagues. The Academy of Sciences of the Georgian SSR now has forty-four specialist branches employing over 2,000 scholars and scientists. There is a separate Academy of Agricultural Sciences. Many of the academicians are also professors at the Tbilisi University and are men of international standing. The physiologist Ivane Beritashvili, for instance, was elected in 1959 an honorary member of the New York Academy of Medical Sciences, on the occasion of his seventy-fifth birthday.

Much attention is given to the study of Georgian language, literature and history. Since 1950, six volumes of a definitive Georgian lexicon have appeared, compiled under the direction of Professor Arnold Chikobava, whose criticism of N. Y. Marr's 'Japhetic' theory led up to Stalin's official repudiation of Marrist linguistic theory and methods. Professor Simon Qaukhchishvili has brought out a new edition of the Georgian Annals (*Kartlis tskhovreba*), based on all the best manuscripts. Professors Akaki Shanidze and Korneli Kekelidze and their disciples continue their outstanding work on the classics of Old Georgian literature, the principal monuments of which are now assembled in a special Institute of Manuscripts under the care of Ilia Abuladze. The Institute of the History of Georgian Literature named after Shota Rustaveli and the Institute of the

History of Georgian Art are only two of many foundations actively studying Georgia's cultural heritage. The teaching of European and Oriental languages is energetically pursued. The principal second language of instruction in Georgian schools and colleges is Russian, but English, French and German are taught in the main institutions. The works of Dickens, Thackeray, Defoe and Sir Walter Scott are among the English classics available in Georgian. Since 1953, one of the main publishing houses has been issuing the works of Shakespeare in Georgian translation, several plays in renderings by Prince Ivane Machabeli (1854–98), the rest translated by Givi Gachechiladze and other modern scholars.

The economic potential of Georgia

It is sometimes objected that the material and cultural advances are outweighed by the loss of Georgia's independence, and the merging of her national destinies into those of the Soviet Union as a whole. There are naturally some Georgians who would like to cast loose the leading strings of Moscow, while retaining the concrete benefits which have accrued in recent years. It is doubtful, however, whether such a development would be either feasible or beneficial, even assuming that Mr. Khrushchev suddenly encouraged Georgia to take advantage of the 'break away' clause in the 1936 Constitution. Economic and political integration with Russia assures Georgia a virtual monopoly of a huge market for tea, wine, citrus fruits, manganese and a score of other valuable commodities, as well as such modern amenities as a twice daily jet plane service to Moscow. There is little or no unemployment, and Georgia is spared the ruinous outlay of maintaining a standing army and other burdens which proved so detrimental both to her kings of old, and to her independent régime of 1918–21.

Russian nationality policy today

Friends of Georgia will naturally hope that further de-Stalinization is in store for her, as well as for the Soviet Union as a whole, and that the monolithic exclusiveness of single-party rule will give way over the generations to a more truly democratic system. There are indeed many signs that the present masters of Russia are alive to the danger which Lenin foresaw when he denounced the oppression of the smaller nations of the Soviet community by the type of person whom he termed 'that truly Russian man, the Great Russian chauvinist, who is essentially a scoundrel and an oppressor', and that Moscow is well aware of the need to avoid flouting the susceptibilities and traditions of the smaller peoples of the USSR.

The Stalin personality cult received a fresh setback at the time of the 22nd Party Congress held at Moscow in October 1961, at which the accusations levelled at the dead Georgian dictator in secret session in 1956 were repeated in public with added vehemence, and his embalmed body removed from the famous mausoleum in Red Square. In Georgia, Stalin's demotion was received with mixed feelings. Relief was mingled with bewilderment, while some people suspected that abuse of Stalin was being used in certain quarters as a pretext for discrediting the Georgians generally. Stalin's name was deleted from the official designation of Tbilisi University, and Stalinir, the capital of South Ossetia, reverted to its old name of Tskhinvali. At the congress of the Georgian Comsomol or Communist Youth organization held in Tbilisi in January 1962, delegates discussed current problems of the day with an outspoken frankness unthinkable a few years ago.

The case of Georgia illustrates the achievements, both good and less good, of the radical and drastic methods of Soviet social engineering when applied to economically backward areas. Not everyone finds the Soviet system of government sympathetic, especially when the interests of the Soviet peoples are represented by a Muscovite Big Brother trying to cow the world by mouthing nuclear menaces. The Georgians have had much to suffer from that same Big Brother in their time. But when one contrasts the dynamic economic and industrial system of Georgia with the chronic instability of some modern countries of the Middle East, or with the deplorable stagnation and effeteness of others, there is no denying the positive side of Russia's work in Georgia. The Soviet formula for a federation of European and Asiatic peoples under the domination of Russian Communists is not a perfect one, especially as it takes absolutely no account of the personal preferences or political aspirations of each national group. But at least it ensures that when at last the day comes for Georgia and other smaller peoples of the Soviet Union to enjoy a larger measure of free speech, genuine democracy and a wider self-determination, they will do so without drifting back into a vicious circle of ignorance, poverty and disease, and be able to stand on their own feet economically and industrially in this competitive modern age.

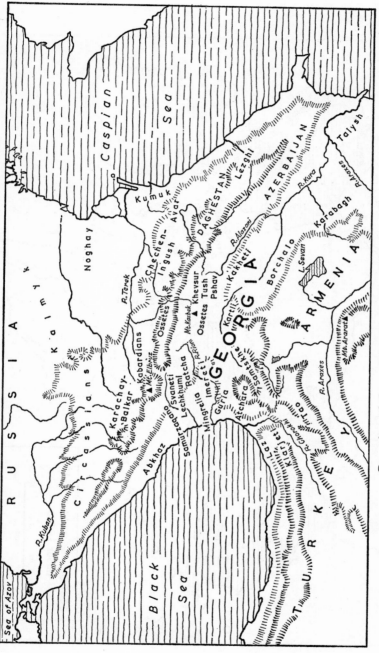

K

Georgia and Caucasia. Regions, Provinces and Tribes

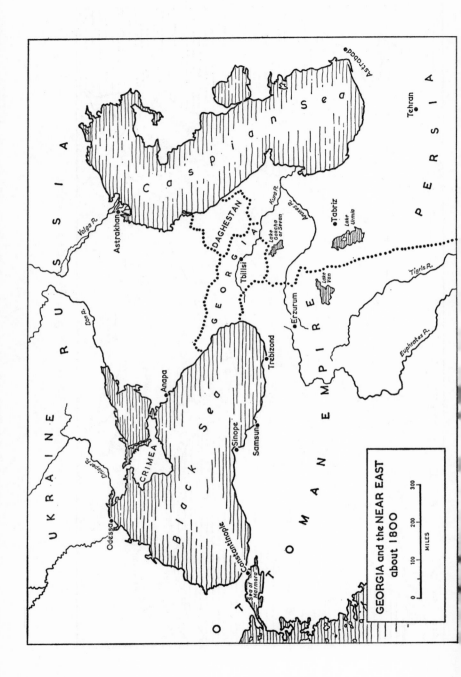

RUSSIA

Volga R.

Astrakhan

Caspian Sea

Astrabad

PERSIA

Tehran

DAGHESTAN

Kura R.

Araxes R.

Lake Gokcha or Sevan

Tabriz

Lake Urmia

GEORGIA

Tbilisi

Tigris R.

Erzurum

Lake Van

Don R.

Euphrates R.

UKRAINE

Anapa

Trebizond

Dnieper R.

CRIMEA

Black Sea

Sinope

Samsun

OTTOMAN EMPIRE

Odessa

Constantinople

Sea of Marmara

GEORGIA and the NEAR EAST
about 1800

0   100   200   300
MILES

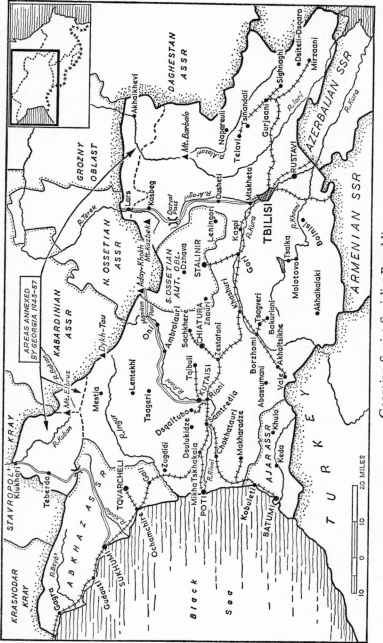

Georgian Soviet Socialist Republic

NOTES

CHAPTER I: THE LAND AND THE PEOPLE

1. Prince Vakhushti Bagration, *Description géographique de la Géorgie*, edit. and trans. by M. -F. Brosset, St. Petersburg 1842, pp. 338-43.
2. Clive Phillipps-Wolley, *Savage Svânetia*, London 1883, Vol. II, pp. 4-5, 94.
3. Max von Thielmann, *Journey in the Caucasus, Persia, and Turkey in Asia*, Vol. I, London 1875, p. 119.
4. See the translation in D. M. Lang, *Lives and Legends of the Georgian Saints*, London: George Allen & Unwin 1956, pp. 13-39.
5. The source here is the Arabic historian Ibn al-Azraq, as cited by V. Minorsky in *Bulletin of the School of Oriental and African Studies*, Vol. XIII, pt. 1, London 1949, pp. 31-34.
6. Sir Harry Luke, *Cities and Men. An Autobiography*, Vol. II, London 1953, p. 129.
7. Odette Keun, *In the Land of the Golden Fleece*. Translated from the French by Helen Jessiman, London 1924, pp. 4-7.
8. Prince Vakhushti Bagration, *Description géographique de la Géorgie*, pp. 62-65.
9. Pitton de Tournefort, *Voyage into the Levant*, Vol. III, London 1741, pp. 137-42.
10. D. M. Lang, 'Georgia in the Reign of Giorgi the Brilliant', in *Bulletin of the School of Oriental and African Studies*, Vol. XVII, pt. 1, 1955, pp. 77-78.
11. The *Evening News*, the *Daily Telegraph*, and *The Times*, 10 November 1959.

CHAPTER II: RISE AND FALL OF THE GEORGIAN KINGS

12. D. M. Lang, *Lives and Legends of the Georgian Saints*, p. 56.
13. A. Christensen, *L'Iran sous les Sassanides*, Copenhagen 1936, pp. 14-17, 98-105, 201-4, 253-54.
14. D. M. Lang, *Lives and Legends of the Georgian Saints*, p. 145.
15. D. M. Lang, *The Last Years of the Georgian Monarchy, 1658-1832*, New York, Columbia University Press 1957, pp. 34-43.
16. Chevalier J. Chardin, *Voyages en Perse*, Vol. II, Amsterdam 1711, p. 149.
17. W. E. D. Allen, *A History of the Georgian People*, London 1932, p. 201.
18. Sir John Malcolm, *History of Persia*, Vol. II, 2nd edition, London 1829, p. 191.
19. D. M. Lang, *The Last Years of the Georgian Monarchy*, p. 239. In this work, the negotiations between the Russian and Georgian governments are traced in much greater detail than is possible here.

CHAPTER III: GEORGIA UNDER THE TSARS: RESISTANCE, REVOLT, PACIFICATION: 1801-32

20. See Russian sources cited in D. M. Lang, *The Last Years of the Georgian Monarchy*, p. 254.
21. We follow the version given by Colonel B. E. A. Rottiers, in his *Itinéraire de Tiflis à Constantinople*, Brussels 1829, pp. 73-83.
22. J. F. Baddeley, *The Russian Conquest of the Caucasus*, London 1908, p. 68.
23. Cited in D. M. Lang, *The Last Years of the Georgian Monarchy*, p. 257.

24. D. M. Lang, *The Last Years of the Georgian Monarchy*, p. 259.

25. Rottiers, *Itinéraire de Tiflis à Constantinople*, pp. 94-95.

26. French diplomatic archives, Quai d'Orsay, Paris, as quoted in D. M. Lang, *The Last Years of the Georgian Monarchy*, pp. 263-65.

27. Sir Robert Ker Porter, *Travels in Georgia, Persia, etc.*, Vol. II, London 1821-22, p. 521.

28. D. M. Lang, *The Last Years of the Georgian Monarchy*, pp. 267-68.

29. Quoted in Baddeley, *The Russian Conquest of the Caucasus*, p. 97.

30. Archives of the French Ministry of Foreign Affairs, Quai d'Orsay, Paris, *Correspondance Commerciale, Tiflis*, Vol. I, pp. 107-8.

31. See Sir Bernard Pares, *A History of Russia*, revised edition, London 1947, p. 365; D. M. Lang, 'The Decembrist Conspiracy through British Eyes', in *American Slavic and East European Review*, Vol. VIII, No. 4, December 1949, pp. 262-74.

32. D. M. Lang, 'Griboedov's Last Years in Persia', in *American Slavic and East European Review*, Vol. VII, No. 4, December 1948, pp. 317-39.

33. W. E. D. Allen and P. Muratoff, *Caucasian Battlefields: A History of the Wars on the Turco-Caucasian Border, 1828-1921*, Cambridge 1953, p. 21.

34. Rottiers, *Itinéraire de Tiflis à Constantinople*, p. 95.

35. Text in D. M. Lang, *The Last Years of the Georgian Monarchy*, pp. 275-76.

36. See the text of the report in the *Akty* or *Collected Documents of the Caucasian Archaeographical Commission* (in Russian), Vol. VIII, Tbilisi 1881, pp. 1-13.

CHAPTER IV: TSAR NICHOLAS AND VICEROY VORONTSOV: 1832-55

37. Lieutenant-General William Monteith, *Kars and Erzeroum*, London 1856, p. 301.

38. On Hamzat Bek, see Lieutenant-General A. A. Neverovsky's short book, *Istreblenie avarskikh khanov v 1834 godu* (*The slaughter of the Avar khans in 1834*), St. Petersburg 1848. A reprint from *Voenny Zhurnal, The Military Journal*, No. 3.

39. Quoted from Baddeley, *The Russian Conquest of the Caucasus*, pp. 310-11.

40. Archives of the French Ministry of Foreign Affairs, Paris, *Correspondance Commerciale, Tiflis*, Vol. II, pp. 84-85.

41. Report of General Golovin to Russian Minister of War, 8 October 1838, in *Akty*, Vol. IX, Tbilisi 1884, pp. 6-10.

42. Archives of the French Ministry of Foreign Affairs, Paris, *Correspondance Commerciale, Tiflis*, Vol. II, p. 109.

43. Akaki Tsereteli, *Perezhitoe* (*Reminiscences*), trans. into Russian by E. Ghoghoberidze, 2nd edition, Moscow 1950, pp. 47-49.

44. *Correspondance Commerciale, Tiflis,* Vol. II, pp. 291-302.

45. Report of the Comte de Ratti-Menton, French Consul in Tbilisi, dated 7/19 February 1834.

46. R. Wilbraham, *Travels in the Trans-Caucasian Provinces of Russia*, London 1839, p. 223.

47. *Correspondance Commerciale, Tiflis,* Vol. II, pp. 517-18.

48. Tsereteli, *Perezhitoe*, pp. 87-88.

49. Tsereteli, *Perezhitoe*, pp. 89, 94.

50. G. K. Bakradze, *Vozniknovenie i razvitie kapitalisticheskoy promyshlennosti v Gruzii v XIX veke* (*The rise and development of capitalist industry in Georgia in the 19th century*), Tbilisi 1958, pp. 25-26.

51. Quoted in the English rendering by Venera Urushadze, from *Anthology of Georgian Poetry*, 2nd edition, Tbilisi 1958, pp. 50-51.

CHAPTER V: SOCIAL CHANGE AND NATIONAL AWAKENING:
1855-94

52. Sir Bernard Pares, *A History of Russia*, revised edition, London 1947, p. 396.
53. Quoted in the translation by Venera Urushadze, in *Anthology of Georgian Poetry*, 2nd edition, Tbilisi 1958, p. 99.
54. S. Yu. Witte, *Vospominaniya (Reminiscences)*, Vol. I, New edition, Moscow 1960, pp. 38-41.
55. S. S. Meskhi, *Nadserebi (Collected essays)*, tom. I, Tbilisi 1903, pp. 211-14.
56. Quoted by V. I. Kotetishvili, *Kartuli literaturis istoria, XIX s. (History of Georgian literature in the 19th century)*, Tbilisi 1959, p. 405.
57. Quoted by V. Gol'tsev, *Stat'i i ocherki (Essays and sketches)*, Moscow 1958, pp. 258-59.
58. Gr. Uratadze, *Sazogadoebrivi modzraoba Sakartveloshi 1821-1921 ds. (The Social Movement in Georgia 1821 to 1921)*, Paris 1939, p. 19.
59. Ia. S. Gogebashvili, *Izbrannye pedagogicheskie sochineniya (Selected pedagogical writings)*, Moscow 1954, pp. 13, 18.
60. J. O. Wardrop, *The Kingdom of Georgia*, London 1888, pp. 162-63.
61. Translated and cited by D. M. Lang, in *Georgian Studies in Oxford, Oxford Slavonic Papers*, Vol. VI, 1955, p. 126.

CHAPTER VI: THE STORM GATHERS: 1894-1904

62. It was fashionable in the nineteenth century to replace the Georgian name endings in *-shvili* and *-dze* (both meaning 'son of') with the Russian termination in *-ov*, e.g. Baratashvili into Baratov, Tsitsishvili into Tsitsianov, and many others.
63. Noe Zhordania, *Chemi dsarsuli. Mogonebani (My Past. Reminiscences)*, Paris 1953.
64 Zhordania, *Reminiscences*, pp. 11-12.
65. Zhordania, *Reminiscences*, p. 26.
66. Quoted by I. Deutscher, *Stalin. A Political Biography*, Oxford 1949, p. 20.
67. Quoted by I. A. Chakhvashvili, *Rabochee dvizhenie v Gruzii, 1870-1904 gg. (The Working-class Movement in Georgia 1870-1904)*, Tbilisi 1958, p. 63.
68. A. Manvelishvili, *Sakutreba; Midsis sakitkhi Sakartveloshi (Property; The Land Question in Georgia)*, Paris 1956, p. 42.
69. Ilia Chavchavadze, *Tkhzulebata sruli krebuli (Complete Works)*, tom. VI, Tbilisi 1956, p. 242.
70. Zhordania, *Reminiscences*, p. 48.
71. K. P. Pobedonostsev (1827-1907), Head Procurator of the Russian Holy Synod; a well-known obscurantist.
72. L. Villari, *Fire and Sword in the Caucasus*, London 1906, pp. 73-74.
73. Quoted by L. P. Beria, *On the history of the Bolshevik organizations in Transcaucasia* (English edition), Moscow 1949, p. 33.
74. Beria, *On the history of the Bolshevik organizations in Transcaucasia*, p. 60.
75. See David Shub, 'Kamo—the Legendary Old Bolshevik of the Caucasus', in *Russian Review*, Vol. XIX, No. 3, July 1960, pp. 227-47.
76. Chakhvashvili, *Rabochee dvizhenie v Gruzii*, p. 303.

CHAPTER VII: GEORGIA IN THE 1905 REVOLUTION

77. S. Maghlakelidze and A. Iovidze, edit. *Revolyutsiya 1905-1907 gg. v Gruzii. Sbornik dokumentov. (The 1905-7 Revolution in Georgia. A Collection of Documents)*, Tbilisi 1956, pp. 88-89.

78. *Revolyutsiya 1905–1907 gg. v Gruzii*, pp. 89–91.
79. Original texts in *Revolyutsiya 1905–1907 gg. v Gruzii*, pp. 278–79, 283.
80. Quoted by Beria, *On the history of the Bolshevik organizations in Transcaucasia*, p. 120.
81. *Bolshaya Sovetskaya Entsiklopediya. Soyuz Sovetskikh Sotsialisticheskikh Respublik (Large Soviet Encyclopedia. Union of Soviet Socialist Republics)*, special volume, Moscow 1947, p. 591.
82. Beria, *On the history of the Bolshevik organizations in Transcaucasia*, pp. 128–29.
83. *Revolyutsiya 1905–1907 gg. v Gruzii*, p. 751.
84. Text taken partly from *Revolyutsiya 1905–1907 gg. v Gruzii*, p. 502, partly from Beria, *On the history of the Bolshevik organizations in Transcaucasia*, p. 137.
85. I. Deutscher, *Stalin: A Political Biography*, Oxford 1949, p. 80.
86. *Revolyutsiya 1905–1907 gg. v Gruzii*, p. 347.

CHAPTER VIII: ON BORROWED TIME: 1906–17

87. *Nobati*, No. 2, 2 April 1906.
88. *Nobati*, No. 12, 18 June 1906.
89. Quoted in Beria, *On the history of the Bolshevik organizations in Transcaucasia*, pp. 166–67.
90. Zhordania, *Reminiscences*, pp. 78–79.
91. A. Baramidze, Sh. Radiani and V. Zhghenti, *Istoriya gruzinskoy literatury (History of Georgian Literature)*, Moscow 1952, p. 234.

CHAPTER IX: TOWARDS GEORGIAN INDEPENDENCE: 1917–18

92. F. Kazemzadeh, *The Struggle for Transcaucasia, 1917–1921*, New York, Oxford 1951, p. 34.
93. Quoted by Kazemzadeh, *The Struggle for Transcaucasia*, p. 37.
94. N. Zhordania, *Reminiscences*, p. 113.
95. Quoted by Kazemzadeh, *The Struggle for Transcaucasia*, p. 55.

CHAPTER X: INDEPENDENT GEORGIA: 1918–21

96. Figures taken from Gr. Uratadze, *Sazogadoebrivi modzraoba Sakartveloshi 1821–1921 ds. (The Social Movement in Georgia 1821–1921)*, Paris 1939, pp. 145–46.
97. E. Drabkina, *Gruzinskaya kontrrevolyutsiya (The Georgian Counter-revolution)*, Leningrad 1928, as cited by Kazemzadeh, *The Struggle for Transcaucasia*, p. 189.
98. Sir Harry Luke, *Cities and Men. An Autobiography*, Vol. II, London 1953, pp. 118–19, 147, 198–9.
99. N. Zhordania, *Reminiscences*, pp. 133–34.
100. F. Kazemzadeh, *The Struggle for Transcaucasia*, p. 171.
101. *The Struggle for Transcaucasia*, pp. 182–3.
102. Luke, *Cities and Men*, Vol. II, p. 88.
103. A. I. Denikin, *Ocherki russkoy smuty (Sketches of Russia in Turmoil)*, Vol. V, Berlin 1926, p. 246.
104. Z. Avalov (Avalishvili), *Nezavisimost' Gruzii v mezhdunarodnoi politike (The Independence of Georgia in International Politics)*, Paris 1924, pp. 265, 268.
105. Avalov, p. 276.

CHAPTER XI: GEORGIA AND COMMUNIST RUSSIA: 1920–24

106. Quoted by Kazemzadeh, *The Struggle for Transcaucasia*, p. 295.
107. Luke, *Cities and Men*, Vol. II, p. 153.

108. Luke, *Cities and Men*, Vol. II, p. 156.
109. See the texts in Kazemzadeh, *The Struggle for Transcaucasia*, p. 308.
110. See A. B. Kadishev, *Interventsiya i grazhdanskaya voyna v Zakavkaz'e* (*The Intervention and Civil War in Transcaucasia*), Moscow 1960, p. 363.
111. Kazemzadeh, *The Struggle for Transcaucasia*, pp. 318–19.
112. *Documents relatifs à la question de la Géorgie devant la Société des Nations*, Paris 1925, p. 67. Professor B. Lewis kindly informs me that the first volume of Kazim Karabekir Pasha's memoirs was published in Turkey in 1960.

CHAPTER XII: THE STALIN ERA: 1924–53

113. *Russia: The Official Report of the British Trades Union Delegation to Russia and Caucasia, Nov. and Dec., 1924*, London 1925, pp. 230–31.
114. N. A. Berdzenishvili, edit., *Istoriya Gruzii. Uchebnik dlya VIII–IX klassov* (*History of Georgia. Manual for the 8th and 9th forms*), Tbilisi 1960, p. 323.
115. Boris Pasternak, *An Essay in Autobiography*, London 1959, p. 114.
116. Pasternak, *An Essay in Autobiography*, p. 110.
117. Pasternak, *An Essay in Autobiography*, p. 111.

BIBLIOGRAPHICAL NOTES AND
SUGGESTIONS FOR FURTHER READING

No connected account of the modern history of Georgia exists in any Western language. This book is based largely on Russian and Georgian original sources, though use has also been made of memoirs, travel literature and special works in English and other European languages which throw light on particular aspects and phases of the period under review.

For the older period prior to the Russian occupation of 1801, reference should be made to the vividly written and finely illustrated work by W. E. D. Allen, *A History of the Georgian People* (London: Kegan Paul, 1932). The events immediately preceding and accompanying the Russian annexation are studied in more detail in my own monograph *The Last Years of the Georgian Monarchy, 1658–1832* (New York: Columbia University Press, 1957). The general history of Russian expansion in Caucasia is dealt with in *The Russian Conquest of the Caucasus* (London: Longmans, Green, 1908) by John F. Baddeley, who also wrote a splendid book of travel and history under the title *The Rugged Flanks of Caucasus* (2 vols. Oxford University Press, 1940). Successive Russian efforts between 1828 and 1921 to use Georgia as a springboard for conquest of the Ottoman Empire are described in detail in *Caucasian Battlefields* by W. E. D. Allen and Paul Muratoff (Cambridge University Press, 1953), which is illustrated with photographs and many excellent sketch maps. Some idea of Georgia's ancient Christian civilization may be gleaned from my little book, *Lives and Legends of the Georgian Saints* (London: George Allen & Unwin, 1956).

For the history of the revolutionary movement in Georgia, reference should be made to Isaac Deutscher's *Stalin: A Political Biography* (Oxford University Press, 1949) as well as to Bertram D. Wolfe, *Three who made a Revolution* (New edition, New York, 1960). The ill-fated Lavrenti Beria's monograph *On the history of the Bolshevik organizations in Transcaucasia* (Moscow: Foreign Languages Publishing House, 1949) contains interesting documents, but can be used only with extreme caution owing to its many distortions and falsifications. The impact of the 1905 Revolution on Georgia is vividly described by an eye-witness in Luigi Villari's *Fire and Sword in the Caucasus* (London: T. Fisher Unwin, 1906).

Georgia's existence as an independent Social-Democratic republic is chronicled with exemplary thoroughness by Firuz Kazemzadeh in his monograph *The Struggle for Transcaucasia, 1917–1921* (New York: Philosophical Library; Oxford: George Ronald, 1951). Sir Harry Luke, British Chief Commissioner in Transcaucasia in 1920, gives in the second volume of his autobiography, *Cities and Men* (London: Geoffrey Bles, 1953) a description of Georgia and his experiences there which is both scholarly and readable. Reference may usefully be made also to *The Independence of Georgia in International Politics, 1918–1921* (London: Headley Bros., 1940) by Zurab Avalish-vili, a leading Georgian politician and man of letters, who disagreed on many issues with the policies pursued by the Menshevik government of Noe Zhordania. A useful book on the economy of Georgia during this period is *Mineral Resources of Georgia and Caucasia* by D. Ghambashidze (London: George Allen & Unwin, 1919).

Most works dealing with Soviet Georgia are to some extent affected by political bias. Walter Kolarz's thorough survey, *Russia and her Colonies* (2nd edition, London: George Philip, 1952) is written from a highly critical viewpoint. More dispassionate is the volume entitled *The Nationalities Problem and Soviet Administration. Selected Readings on the Development of Soviet Nationalities Policies,* selected, edited and introduced by Rudolf Schlesinger, translated by W. W. Gottlieb (London: Routledge and Kegan Paul, 1956). Among works written from a standpoint definitely favourable to the Soviet Union, one may cite *Russia: The Official Report of the British Trades Union Delegation to Russia and Caucasia, Nov. and Dec., 1924* (London: TUC, 1925), as well as a good, up to date little booklet on Georgia written by the present Prime Minister of the Georgian SSR, Mr. Givi Javakhishvili, and published for sixpence in the series *The Fifteen Soviet Socialist Republics Today and Tomorrow* (London: Soviet Booklets, 1960). Sir Fitzroy Maclean's two well known travel books, *Eastern Approaches* and *Back to Bokhara*, give brief but perceptive glimpses of life in Georgia before and after World War II. Among the general economic and geographical surveys of the Soviet Union containing sections on Georgia are *The U.S.S.R. A Geographical Survey* by J. S. Gregory and D. W. Shave (3rd impression, London: Harrap, 1947); Theodore Shabad, *Geography of the U.S.S.R. A Regional Survey* (Oxford University Press, 1951); N. N. Baransky, *Economic Geography of the U.S.S.R.* (Moscow: Foreign Languages Publishing House, 1956), and there are a number of others.

INDEX

INDEX

Chiaureli, Mikheil, Georgian film producer, 22
Chicherin, G. V., Soviet Commissar for Foreign Affairs, 224–5, 231
Chichinadze, Zakaria, Georgian publisher and writer, 122
Chikhladze, S., Georgian Communist, liquidated by Beria, 254
Chikobava, Professor A. S., Georgian philologist, 271
Chkheidze, Nikolai ('Karlo'), Georgian Menshevik leader, 122, 134, 136, 139–40, 148, 166, 178, 196–7, 199, 203, 220–2, 230, 237, 258
Chkhenkeli, Akaki, Georgian Menshevik, Minister in Paris, 179, 200, 202–9, 216, 223
Cholok, river, 6
Choloqashvili, Colonel Kaikhosro, Georgian patriot, 243
Chonkadze, Daniel, Georgian novelist, 100
Chorokhi, river, 6, 28, 185
Christianity, Christians, 4, 5, 11, 20, 25–6, 29, 40, 108, 240–1, 268
Chronicles, Georgian historical, 20, 23, 26–7, 90–1, 271
Chubinov (Chubinashvili), Professor David, Georgian lexicographer, 90–1
Chudetsky, Russian pedagogue, assassinated, 109
Churchill, Sir Winston, 221–2, 231
Cimmerians, 2
Cinema in Georgia, 22
Circassia, Circassians (Cherkess), 4, 5, 18, 37, 58, 62, 71, 73–4, 82–4, 91, 97–8, 103
Clemenceau, Georges, French Premier, 221
Colchis, 2, 6, 23, 25–6, 32, 95
Collectivisation of Georgian agriculture, 246–51
Commerce and trade, 15, 36, 44, 50, 57–9, 74, 85–6, 105–6, 236, 253
Constantine the Great, 11, 26
Constantine, Russian Grand Duke, 59–60
Constantinople (Istanbul), 28, 32
Constanza, 208
Cooke-Collis, Brigadier, British governor of Batumi, 222
Cossacks, 32, 49, 56, 79, 137–8, 142, 144, 156–8, 161–8, 175
Courland, 78
Crimea, 82, 93, 153, 206, 228, 231, 233
Crimean War, 91–5, 97, 104, 146
Crusades, Crusaders, 13, 27–8
Curzon, Lord, British Foreign Secretary, 220–2, 231
Czechs, 108

Dadeshkeliani, Constantine, Svanian prince, murders Prince Gagarin, 96–7
Dadeshkeliani, Michael (Tatarkhan), Svanian prince, 80
Dadeshkeliani, Nicholas (Tsiokh), Svanian prince, 80

Dadiani, Prince Alexander, disgraced by Tsar Nicholas I, 78, 80
Dadiani, Catherine, regent of Mingrelia, 95–6
Dadiani, Prince Nicholas, dispossessed by Russia, 96
Dadiani, Shalva, Georgian dramatist, 187
Dadians of Mingrelia, Dadiani family, 32, 34, 47–8, 80, 87, 95–7
Daghestan, Daghestanis, 4, 17, 32, 36, 38, 48, 55–7, 61, 71–2, 82, 84, 91, 95, 98
Dardanelles, 185
Darejan, Queen Dowager of Georgia, 39–40, 44, 46–7
Dargo, 72, 83
Dargwa people, 4
Darwin, Charles, 111
Daryal Pass, 11, 37, 44, 47, 49, 68, 84, 114, 228, 233–4
Dashnaks, Armenian nationalist party, 197, 201, 217, 229
David, King of Israel, 28
David the Builder, King of Georgia, 13, 28, 41
David Bagration, Prince-Regent of Georgia, 39, 43, 46
David, Saint, mountain and shrine of, at Tbilisi, 14
Decembrist conspiracy of 1825, 59–60, 63, 65
Defoe, Daniel, translated into Georgian, 272
Dekanozov, V. G., Soviet official, 264
Denikin, General Anton, White Russian leader, 213, 217–18, 220, 222, 224, 228
Derbent, 52, 56, 71
Dgebuadze, Alexander, Georgian socialist, 239
Dickens, Charles, translated into Georgian, 272
Didube, suburb of Tbilisi, 165
Dimitri, King of Georgia, 13
Dimitri Bagration, Georgian prince, 68
Diocletian, Roman emperor, 4
Dobrolyubov, N. A., Russian critic, 99
Dodashvili (Dodaev-Magarsky), Solomon, Georgian publicist, 63, 68–9
Don Cossacks, 49
Donbass, 164
Dondukov-Korsakov, Prince A. M., Russian governor-general, 119
Dositheus, Archbishop of Kutaisi, 56
Drabkina, E., Soviet historian, 213
Dryhurst, Mrs N. F., appeals on behalf of Georgian women, 168
Dsibelda, 80
Dsulukidze, Alexander, Georgian revolutionary, 135, 141, 148
Dsulukidze, General Vardan, executed by Communists, 241
Dubrovin, N., Russian historian, 48
Dukhobors, Russian sect, 75
Duma, Russian Imperial, 156, 160, 165–6, 169–76, 178–9, 181, 192–3, 199

289